COACHING FOOTBALL
WITH THE ADOLESCENT BRAIN IN MIND

Dr Perry Walters.

A Theoretical and Practical journey through
the developing adolescent brain.
Providing detail on how football coaches can use
theoretical information to create more understanding,
as well as more in depth coaching practice.

Illustrated by Coco Walters.

THE FOOTBALL COACH

Copyright © 2021 TheFootballCoach.Net

All rights reserved. No part of this publication may be reproduced, distributed, or transmitted in any form or by any means, including photocopying, recording, or other electronic or mechanical methods, without the prior written permission of the publisher, except in the case of brief quotations embodied in critical reviews and certain other noncommercial uses permitted by copyright law. For permission requests, write to the publisher, addressed "Attention: Permissions Coordinator," at the address below.

ISBN: 978-1-716-23023-3 (Paperback)

Any references to historical events, real people, or real places are used fictitiously. Names, characters, and places are products of the author's imagination.

Front cover image by TheFootballCoach.
Book design by TheFootballCoach.
Illustrated by Coco Walters.

Printed by FootballCoaching, Ltd., in the United Kingdom.

First printing edition 2021.

268 Davis Dr,
Morrisville,
NC 27560,
United States

www.Thefootballcoach.net

Coaching Football With The Adolescent Brain In Mind

Delivering theory into practice in football coaching
By Dr Perry Walters

Contents

About the Author
1

Introduction
2

Chapter 1 - Adolescence: A window of opportunity
11

Chapter 2 - Decision-making and the adolescent brain
23

Chapter 3 - Creativity and the adolescent brain
46

Chapter 4 - The emotional spark of adolescence
54

Chapter 5 - The emerging 'social brain' in adolescents
73

Chapter 6 - Coaching with the late adolescent brain in mind
87

Chapter 7 - The learning brain and football
94

Appendix - Integrating neuroscience within coaching sessions - utilising the concepts of 'red-brain' and 'blue-brain'
107

References
118

Practical Sessions
127

"Education changes the brain, and therefore neuroscience is fundamental to teaching and learning"

Professor Sarah-Jayne Blakemore

About the Author

Dr Perry Walters has a Masters in Educational Psychology and a PhD in Education from the University of Bristol. He played football at youth level for Bristol City and Exeter City Football Clubs. Perry has spent much of his career in education both as a secondary school teacher and as a researcher at the University of Bristol, School of Education, where he is currently a Visiting Fellow. Perry has been a UEFA qualified coach for 20 years. He has worked as a coach at Bristol City FC and has lectured at the English Football Association on their elite youth development programmes.

Perry is passionate and knowledgeable about the adolescent brain and young people. His experience in both football and education has helped shape this book into a very practical, yet educational journey that can help improve session design and theoretical understanding.

Introduction

Over the last 20 years scientists have learnt a great deal about how the adolescent brain works. This new knowledge challenges a lot of assumptions on how to motivate and incentivise young people. For football, harnessing this new understanding could help develop better players on the pitch and more fulfilled people off it. This book provides an overview of the recent developments in our understanding of the adolescent brain. It is the first book to integrate emerging knowledge around neural changes in adolescent decision making, judgment, emotional control and social cognition for furthering football understanding and practice.

The authors have sought to transfer neuroscience findings from the laboratory, to the football field through a series of theoretical discussions and practical applications. The first part of the book examines recent theoretical insights into the adolescent brain, applying a football lens where appropriate. The second part of the book offers detailed practical sessions, tailored to what we know about the unique learning potential of the adolescent brain. This is an exciting yet challenging task, however the authors' backgrounds, in both elite football and academia, make them well positioned to undertake such a venture.

The Global Game

The incredible global popularity of football and the abundance of riches at the elite level of the game means that football is beginning to take on insights from diverse fields of knowledge, in an endeavour to maximise technical, physical and psycho-social performance. From advances in sports science to satellite tracking and artificial intelligence, football coaching is integrating new insights and understandings across varied disciplines into its discourse and practice. A field of knowledge that is still to be explored in the context of football however, is that of the brain, and in particular the developing brain. Arsène Wenger, Head of global development at FIFA and former Arsenal manager, recently asserted that neuroscience will be the next 'game changer' for football (Observer; Oct, 2020). In recent years we have seen enormous strides in our understanding of the adolescent brain, in particular, revealing it as a dynamic period of reorganisation, providing unique opportunities for learning, specialising and development. Some of these new findings are potentially important for football coaches, offering a fuller understanding of adolescent players' thoughts, feelings and behaviours with implications for positive interventions that can optimise the potential of the unique adolescent brain.

There appears a consensus within football coaching that psychological and socio-emotional factors contribute significantly to the advancement of elite players (Mills et al, 2014). Despite this, there appears relatively little literature around the psychological development of the adolescent athletes within sport in general and elite football in particular (Pain and Harwood, 2004, Partington and Cushion, 2013). This book seeks to apply a developmental perspective; 'open the bonnet' so to speak, and explore the 'black box' of the adolescent mind and brain and inquire into how this new insight might be useful for football coaches' understanding and practice. It will explore the most up to date science and theory around the developing adolescent brain and translate this new knowledge into practical applications for the coach on the football pitch.

New understandings of the adolescent brain

The last two decades have seen major advancements in our understanding of the developing brain (Blakemore, 2018). New technologies have enabled a fuller appreciation of the dynamic remodelling processes occurring during adolescence and the unique learning opportunities such change affords. The adolescent period, beginning at the onset of puberty and extending well into the third decade of life, is framed as a 'second window of opportunity' because of the dynamic changes in neural connectivity, equally significant as in the first few years of life for learning and development (UNICEF, 2017).

Scientists used to think that the brain was more or less developed by late childhood and that the adolescent brain was simply an adult brain with less 'miles on the clock' and less experience (Jensen, 2015). However, we now know that the brain does not mature by getting bigger, rather it matures by rewiring, making more connections and coordination between brain regions (Giedd, 2015).

In the last twenty years, new brain imaging technology has shown us that networks in the frontal region that underpin judgement and decision-making, abstract and strategic thinking and the control of emotions and behaviour are still developing, beyond the teenage years, and well into the early-twenties. Scientists believe that this delayed maturation may be deliberate and, evolutionary wise, linked to the individual's need to adapt to their environment during the transition process from child to adult. In this regard, connected to the unique 'plasticity' (malleability) of the adolescent brain, the teenage years and early twenties can be understood as an optimal time to develop higher order cognitions, such as decision-making, self-awareness, emotional control, consequential thinking, 'mentalising' (taking others' perspectives) as well as social skills. These abilities and capacities, that are often required of players at the elite level of the game, are being forged and nurtured during this crucial period of growth.

This book will examine recent insights from cognitive neuroscience around the development of the adolescent brain and explore how this new science might be useful and meaningful for those involved with coaching young football players. In doing so, this book will explore a number of key areas:

Key messages about the adolescent brain for coaches

- An increased 'plasticity' (changeability) in the adolescent brain offers unique potential but also vulnerability for adolescent learners
- Extensive neural remodelling from the onset of puberty impacts adolescent processing including changes in; motivation, judgement, decision-making and behavioural and emotional control

Introduction

- Adolescence represents a dynamic period of social re-orientation with strong drives to contribute, connect and belong, especially with peers; alongside a heightened sensitivity toward status and respect
- Adolescence represents a time of intensification in emotion and reward brain circuitry linked to unique motivations, drives and passions. This amplified brain activity provides opportunities for strengthening self-regulation capacities
- The adolescent phase of development is a time of enhanced motivations for novelty seeking, creative exploration, problem solving and risk-taking
- Peaks in the availability of the neurotransmitter 'dopamine', linked with motivation, learning, pleasure and reward make adolescence a unique period of growth and development.

Developmental plasticity (increased changeability)

Developmental science has shown that adolescence represents a unique phase for learning. It is a period of heightened developmental plasticity, where the brain is more malleable and responsive to its environment than at any other stage, particularly in pre-frontal regions associated with decision making, planning, judgement and emotional control. That is, the capacities that are integral to elite footballers are coming on line and ripe for development during adolescence. This period of specialisation, where neural connections are either strengthened or eliminated dependent on their frequency of use, offers unique possibilities for positive interventions which take advantage of the brain's ability to remodel and adapt (Dahl and Suleiman, 2016). This includes instrumental learning where the adolescent brain is especially sensitive to trial and error adjustments to its environment, and is especially responsive to novelty and risk. Neuroscientists suggest that safe and secure environments that support such self-driven exploration and engagement, appear best suited to this unique learning window (Willis, 2010; Immordino-Yang, 2010). This emerging understanding from brain science appears to support current psychological and pedagogical theory on optimal learning environments for young athletes (Light and Harvey, 2017).

Introduction

Decision-making

Adolescents tend, on average, to take more risks and act more impulsively than both children and adults. These behaviours have been linked to the developmental changes in the way the adolescent brain processes risks and rewards. A prime function of adolescence is the transition from child to adulthood and involves the mobilisation of energies that promote engagement with the environment.

The increase in dopamine (a brain chemical linked to learning and pleasure) and hypersensitivity of the brain's reward centres during this period, ensures that adolescents are motivated to try new things; that they will 'get off the sofa' and engage with the environment (Steinberg, 2015). New and different experiences become rewarding and exciting in their own right during adolescence. There appears more of an appetite to lean into uncertainty and explore situations with the promise of reward. Indeed, activity in reward pathways are generally stronger for both the anticipation and receipt of immediate rewards for adolescents, whether they are financial or social. Immediate rewards seem to 'shine brighter' and are likely experienced more intensely for adolescents. This neural and chemical reorganisation is thought to promote risk-taking, novelty seeking and finding pleasure in the quest for experience (Luciana, 2012).

Such emerging knowledge of adolescent-specific motivations offers new understandings for coaches that can underscore how coaching environments might be created; that align with and incentivise these natural instincts and drives. This increase in incentive motivation for new experiences and testing boundaries however, represents both vulnerabilities and opportunities. It is a period associated with the onset of various maladaptive psychological issues, for example, eating disorders, self-harm, substance abuse and depression (Jensen, 2015). However, adolescence has increasingly been seen as an opportunity for positive spirals, initiating healthy patterns of behaviour that can begin productive developmental trajectories both inside and outside of sport (Dahl and Suleiman, 2016). In this way there has been a recent 'paradigm shift' in viewing adolescence as an age of possibility, hope and opportunity rather than a problematic period to survive and endure

(Steinberg, 2015). Indeed recent research has shown that adolescent development has been positively influenced through the construction of potentiating environments which explicitly seek to honour the drive for risk-taking, novelty seeking and exploration as well as positive social interactions (Ward, 2016).

Further, incentive motivations to test boundaries and take risks enable a requisite up-regulation in prefrontal control and judgement capacities. That is, the strong drives and impulses of the adolescent condition require a corresponding improvement in self-regulation abilities; just as a racing driver needs to up-skill their driving abilities to cope with a more powerful engine. In supportive environments this provides opportunity to strengthen neural connectivity between control and emotion brain circuits, helping adolescents strengthen the neural architecture responsible for self-regulation of emotions and behaviours. Armed with this new knowledge, coaches can help scaffold these developmental processes for young people both in sports contexts and in the wider society.

Emotional Intensification

Adolescence is often characterised as a period of impulsivity and emotional intensity. Often, teenagers' response to the world is driven by emotion rather than reason (Jensen, 2015). This is associated with a developmental imbalance in emotional and cognitive circuitry, where sub-cortical systems, buried deep inside the brain, involved in the processing of emotion and reward, are thought to reach maturity by mid-adolescence; whereas circuits tasked with regulating these processes mature later, commonly not until the early to mid-twenties.

There is less activity in frontal control systems compared with deeper emotional systems for adolescents, making it more difficult to control feelings, instincts, drives and impulses. This asymmetrical development has been associated with an emotional bias in decision-making where emotions might 'win out', particularly in aroused contexts involving fear, anger, frustration and excitement, as well as in the presence of peers (Chein, 2011). It is important for adults who spend time with adolescents to be aware of this potential 'emotional hijacking'; to appreciate that your average adolescent might not be processing emotions in the same way as an adult (or child). Indeed this emotional intensification offers opportunities to help develop self control.

The developmental plasticity characterising this period offers potential opportunities to support self-regulation strategies that might strengthen connectivity between frontal (control) and limbic (emotion) circuitry. It is potentially useful for coaches to build environments that are sensitive to this 'emotional overshoot' and provide opportunities for adolescents to reflect upon, manage and direct heightened emotions and impulses, particularly in aroused contexts, thus helping scaffold important self-regulated behaviour patterns.

Social reorientation

UNICEF describe adolescents as having 'an amplified sense of self-conscious emotions including both a strong desire for acceptance, belonging, admiration and respect as well as increased sensitivity to feelings of rejection, disrespect, embarrassment and humiliation'. Developmental neuroscience suggests adolescence as a stage of 'social reorientation' linked to neural remodelling in the circuitry of the 'social brain'.

An area of the inner brain dedicated to understanding other people and to social interaction. There is a developing self-awareness as well as a heightened sensitivity to social evaluation, particularly from peers. Adolescents are primed to notice peers, more sensitive to how they are perceived, with a strong need for belonging and a desire to contribute toward the group. There is an increased motivation to spend time with peers (and less with parents), possibly with evolutionary underpinnings to form attachments away from the immediate environment for reproductive and group safety reasons. Indeed the mere presence of peers primes the reward centres in the adolescent brain and has been linked to increased risk-taking compared to adults. This has been associated with negative outcomes (fast driving, binge drinking) but may also offer opportunities for productive, socially positive risk taking, such as in sports contexts, that also honour adolescents' motivations for status, respect and social acceptance.

The amplified reward centres and increased dopamine (linked to motivation and learning) triggered by peer interaction might offer a potential rich learning resource. Conversely it has been found that the presence of adults can dampen down the reward centres in the adolescent brain. This understanding has potentially significant implications for adolescent learning environments.

Creativity

Research shows that for some domains, such as spatial awareness, adolescents can be more creative than adults (Crone et al, 2017) and further, environments can be developed that better foster creativity than others (Howard-Jones, 2010). Creative exploration is part of the adolescent condition (Siegel, 2014) and coaches can develop environments that help foster creative play, where experimentation and improvisation are welcomed and encouraged. Indeed, informing learners that creativity can be developed has been shown to improve creativity in itself (Crone et al, 2013). Positive emotional environments are essential for creative development. Neuroscience research suggests that a reduction in stress, judgement and establishing a positive emotional environment are important for developing creativity (Hardiman, 2010, Howard-Jones, 2010).

Prolonged adolescence

We now know that adolescence starts earlier and lasts longer than previously thought. Beginning at the onset of puberty, about 12 years of age (slightly younger in girls), and extending well into the third decade of life, adolescence encompasses a wider range than just the 'teenage years'. Scientists have also recently discovered that the 'late adolescent' period (18-22), represents a distinct phase of development with unique learning potential, crucial information for coaches.

Introduction

Recent brain research shows that peaks in learning signals during the late adolescent phase predict that players can learn and remember new information more efficiently than at any other age. However, the environment needs to be conducive for emerging capacities such as planning, decision -making, self-control and inhibition to flourish.
Neurons are still firing at a faster rate in the late adolescent phase of development, however this window of opportunity for learning begins to close depending on the novelty and stimulation provided by the environment (Steinberg, 2014).

When a player reaches adult maturity and or the environment becomes less nurturing, then this heightened period of developmental plasticity decreases, and neural circuits mature (settle down). The rate of firing for dopamine slows when the environment is less challenging or novel, less developmental. This can be a good thing because it consolidates and strengthens existing connections, enabling expertise; however, if the environment is not developmental, empowering or nurturing, then coaches are potentially missing an opportunity for developing capacities during this ripe period for growth.

This book gives an introduction into how these emerging developmental insights are important for coaches working with adolescent players. It attempts to provide an additional layer of understanding for coaches in the psychological corner of development. In doing so, it works toward offering a holistic perspective of the adolescent player which can help inform thinking and practice.

Chapter 1 - Adolescence: A window of opportunity

Main findings:

- Adolescence is a time of specialisation and streamlining, where the brain is becoming more efficient, fine-tuning its neural connectivity in response to the environment. The coaching climate is especially important to take advantage of this ripe period for development.
- Empowering environments, that give autonomy to players and that facilitate self-guided trial and error learning, can help take advantage of the unique potential of the adolescent brain.
- The adolescent brain is more malleable than at any other stage, especially for prefrontal abilities linked to the 'football brain'; including decision making, judgement, emotional control, self-awareness and creativity. Coaches can grasp these opportunities by creating nurturing coaching contexts that help foster these emerging capacities.
- The 'window of opportunity' for learning extends beyond the teenage years up until the mid-twenties where the brain retains its uniquely malleable adolescent qualities. This is especially the case in learning environments that promote autonomy, novelty, security and challenge.

Football - Opportunities of a changing landscape

Are footballers born or made? It's the age old nurture-nature debate. When you think of Messi, Maradona or Ronaldo it seems that they are full of natural born talent. The idea of the 'natural born player' is rife in football folklore. "You can't put in what God left out .. he was born to be a footballer' was a recent quote I heard from a professional football coach. Despite research suggesting that psychological abilities can be cultivated and developed, football can sometimes foreground a binary understanding that a young player either has 'it' or they haven't (Daley et al, 2020). Football has traditionally been characterised as having an insular culture, suspicious of books and academia and slower than other sports at integrating insights from science and pedagogy (Ford and Williams, 2010). This has especially been the case with psychology which, compared to technical, tactical and physical components has struggled to be accepted and integrated into academy programmes (Pain and Harwood, 2004). However, in recent years this picture is starting to change. Ideas that have traditionally sat outside of the football discourse are starting to influence football understanding and practice. Emerging insights from fields including social, humanistic and existential psychology, philosophy, education and coaching pedagogy are starting to inform thinking in new ways (Nelson et al, 2102; Nesti and Sulley, 2015; Gardener et al, 2015; Light and Harvey, 2017).

Research, for example, such as Ericsson's work around the 10,000 hour rule, suggesting that expertise is primarily the product of dedicated, deliberate practice over many years, started to inform understanding in sports, including football (Ericsson, 2006). Social psychology theory has also recently informed football coaching discourse; including Angela Duckworth's GRIT concept, foregrounding the idea of expertise as the culmination of passion and perseverance for long term goals over time (Sigmundsson et al, 2020) and Dweck's 'self-theories' around the malleability of talents, indicative that ability is something that can be acquired, improvable and within the learner's locus of control, linked to practice and dedication (Albert et al, 2019). Much of this research has, at its core, new understandings of how the brain works and changes in response to new experiences (Mangels et al, 2006).

Mind, Brain and Football

Our understanding of learning processes and the malleability of talents has been complemented, in recent years, by emerging knowledge from the field of developmental cognitive neuroscience. This is an interdisciplinary field that explores how the mind changes as children grow up and how that integrates with the developing brain. It can potentially offer a different perspective for coaches that shines a light on the psychological development of the adolescent player, underpinned by the sciences of mind and brain. This new science might help coaches foster a fuller appreciation, a more holistic understanding of the developing mind and brain of the player, something identified as in need of bolstering for professional football coaches (Walters, 2013; Partington and Cushion, 2013; IDYOMS, 2021).

The emerging field of Mind, Brain and Education (MBE) provides a useful overarching framework for exploring how developmental neuroscience, especially around the adolescent brain, can be beneficial for football understanding and practice. Emanating out of Harvard University approximately twenty years ago, this field of inquiry looks to blend insights from different disciplines to generate new understanding for the benefit of learning. This collaborative approach seeks to generate discussion and research between scientists and practitioners on specific issues related to education. It works under the premise that 'good learning environments require the inputs of various disciplines' (Hille, 2011). In this way it is informed by a transdisciplinary approach, that is, where differing disciplinary perspectives are integrated with the aim to produce new knowledge that sits beyond what is already known in each individual field. A way to understand the concept of transdisciplinarity might be to think of different disciplinary experts entering a new space and leaving their respective 'hats at the door'. Here they can generate, through dialogue and integration of differing perspectives, new insights that reach further than what is already known in any one particular field.

It has been suggested that the complex issues in education today (including football education) require such complex and sophisticated approaches, requiring the application of multiple lenses. Transdisciplinarity has been advocated as an approach 'to examining and solving complex problems through the collaborative efforts of multiple diverse partners' (Samuels, 2009). In relation to Mind Brain and Education it is suggested that the inter-relation of the 'core disciplines' of neuroscience, psychology and education has the potential to offer a different perspective 'that changes the lens' on pedagogical processes

(Tokuhama, 2011).

The authors believe that this framework also has the potential to be useful for football. Issues important to the game, such as developing 'creative' and 'independent' decision-makers ('Future Game'), exploring optimal learning environments or developing 'motivated', 'resilient' players with self awareness and control might be productively illuminated using a transdisciplinary framework. One that generates new understanding from blending the insights from, but not limited to, neuroscience, psychology, education and coaching pedagogy. This book will focus specifically on how insights from the adolescent brain can be usefully blended with existing understanding to inform football pedagogy.

New Science of adolescence

Adolescence can be understood as that transitionary period between the onset of puberty and assuming an adult role in society. A journey from dependence on parents and care givers toward one of increasing independence and autonomy, leaving the nest and pushing out to explore, discover and make new connections in the wider world. In this developmental process the brain begins to remodel, kickstarted by the release of sex hormones, sparking changes which include faster processing and interconnectivity between brain regions. These changes enable increasing capabilities such as improvements in planning, decision-making, mentalising, and consequential awareness as well as the ability for more abstract thought and conceptual understanding. A qualitative shift that allows adolescents to contemplate their own identity and place in the world and a sense of their own person distinct from that of their family unit.

These increased capacities facilitate an improved ability and desire to take on responsibility and make independent decisions of consequence. These neural shifts mean that the adolescents are increasingly able think in different ways than their younger selves and primes them to gain new experiences in creative and novel ways. To experiment and figure out for themselves new ways of doing things. Research shows that the actual experience of exploration and discovery feels more exciting and thrilling for adolescents than at any other stage of life, prompting behaviours that push boundaries and test limits. Strong emotions seem to propel adolescents through uncertainty, to hang in there and grapple with new experiences despite potentially negative outcomes in an energised way that lessens into adulthood.

Scientists used to think that the brain was more our less fixed after childhood but in the last two decades, with the advent of new imaging technologies, we now know that the brain is actually plastic, that is, it changes in response to experience. It's a process whereby the outside world gets inside us and changes us; where our interaction with the environment changes the architecture of our brain. We know that the brain is malleable throughout the lifespan but has been found to be particularly modifiable and open to change during the adolescent years. This period of maturation has been identified as representing a distinct phase of 'developmental plasticity' (Steinberg, 2015), during which the adolescent brain is more sensitive and finds it easier to adapt to environmental stimuli, that is, it is better at learning. It is a time when the brain is more efficient at rewiring in response to experience.

We intuitively know that younger people are quicker at learning new things, think of the child at school learning a language compared to an adult. However, it is only in recent years, with new technologies, that we are understanding why young people, adolescents in particular, are more efficient at learning. Much of this relates to the way the adolescent brain is motivated toward and processes new information. The reward centres in the brain, linked to an uptick in the neurotransmitter dopamine, are amplified and particularly sensitive to new and novel stimuli during adolescence. Processing appears more efficient for remembering positive outcomes linked to increases in both dopamine and stronger links between reward and memory systems (hippocampus and striatum). The adolescent brain seems primed to try new things. The learning signals are stronger, particularly to trial and error engagements with the environment. This suggests that the brain is more 'learning sensitive' and can pick up new information quicker and easier than at other stages of development (Dahl et al, 2018). For coaches this might mean creating conditions that empower adolescents toward independent decision making, where they can explore and test boundaries, push limits in a culture of challenge yet support. This exciting potential for learning and growth is important information for not only coaches but for parents and adolescents themselves, and will be examined in more detail in subsequent chapters.

A time to sculpt 'the football brain'

Recent neuroscience findings might be interpreted to suggest that the period of adolescence is an optimal time to forge the 'football brain'. It is a unique phase of growth that suggests a 'window of opportunity' to strengthen capacities that are needed to become an elite player. During the adolescent years, the brain is at its most malleable, an opportune time for moulding to the needs of the environment. This is particularly the case in frontal brain regions associated with planning, decision-making, self-regulation and abstract thought. A neuroscientific process called Graph Theory has shown that during this period of dynamic change, the pre-frontal cortex (PFC) is the last to connect and coordinate with other parts of the brain, enabling not only increasing control of emotions and behaviour, but also supporting the development of reasoning networks and increased conceptual understanding (Giedd, 2015).

This means that adolescents can begin to grapple with more complex issues and develop interest in purposes beyond the self and immediate environments. The recent youth initiatives around climate change, led by adolescents, is a case in point. It is also an optimal time to strengthen connectivity in systems linked to character traits and learning dispositions such as agency, empathy, resilience, perseverance and discipline (Heckman, 2001). This suggests that adolescence is an ideal time to 'stamp in' good 'habits of mind' (Costa and Kallick, 2000). As such, this period presents an ideal opportunity for coaches to help foster positive learning dispositions and instil desired values and ethics in young players.

Adolescence: A window of opportunity

The most recent neuroscience research suggests that cognitive functions associated with the prefrontal cortex (that sits just behind the eyes) such as planning, decision making, anticipation, consequential thinking and understanding others are starting to come 'on-line' and be forged in the adolescent years (Shulman et al, 2016). A question for football coaches might be, can we develop and improve the quality of these capacities for young elite football players? What environments can coaches provide that facilitate the development of essential skills and capabilities that are needed both on and off the pitch? Can coaches create opportunities where adolescent players are encouraged to make decisions, where they can experiment and practice taking on different roles and responsibilities? This might include, for example, having a role in planning session designs or pre-match warm ups; contributing to half-time team talks or co-creating goals for the team. Much of this is undertaken by coaches already but if we know that facilitating the refinement of these capacities in young players is actually helping shape the architecture of their developing brains - then this helps provide a rationale of why it is beneficial to do so.

Further, this might suggest a slightly different role for the coach, a power shift that starts to give relatively more autonomy and responsibility to the player and suggests less of a command style of coaching. We know that this is the direction of travel in terms of coach education (FA Advanced Youth Award) and for some of Europe's top football academies (Nest and Sulley, 2015). Arguably, the recent science around the adolescent brain suggests that this is an ideal time to help nurture these developing capacities. Possibly the last significant stage, suggests psychologist Lawrence Steinberg, to strongly influence brain development (Steinberg, 2015). The authors believe that this new knowledge and understanding from developmental science can improve football educators understanding and practice, which in turn can positively impact adolescent players learning and performance.

When we talk about the elite football player who has a great 'football brain' we might think of Hazard, Messi, Aguerro or De Bruyne. These players have vision, 'read' the game well, anticipate play, are innovative, good decision makers, can stay calm and focussed when it matters. Their thinking seems to be quicker and often more creative; more 'outside the box'. We now know that the networks that are associated with such abilities are some of the last brain networks to mature. Scientists used to think that the brain was more or less developed by the start of puberty, this was perhaps because the brain is 95% adult size by late childhood. However, we now know that the brain matures, not by getting larger, but through rewiring, refining existing connections and coordination across more distant brain regions (Blakemore, 2018).

In the last two decades brain imaging technology has shown us that the networks in the frontal region, that underpin higher order thinking and the control of emotions and behaviour are still developing well into the mid-20s. In contrast, networks associated with motor and sensory control, located toward the back of the brain, develop first and are mature by the end of childhood. Crucially, abilities linked to strategic, abstract thinking and sound judgment show delayed development and are located in the frontal regions of the brain. Scientists believe that this delayed maturation serves an evolutionary purpose and relates to the individual's need to adapt to their surroundings during the transition process from child to adult. In this regard, linked to the unique 'plasticity' (changeability) of the adolescence brain, the teenage years through to the early twenties are an optimal time to forge 'higher order' cognitions. In the authors' opinion, this is a ripe time for moulding the kind of mental strengths and capabilities that elite players need to thrive in football environments and beyond.

The research is strongly suggesting that the adolescent brain is impressionable, open to influence, and provides a great inflection point to reinforce positive learning dispositions and desirable character traits. A time to enhance emerging capacities such as appreciating others' needs and perspectives, controlling thoughts and behaviours, being mindful of the consequences of one's action, making reasoned choices and becoming more self aware. We now know that these important qualities needed for youth to thrive, both in elite football and the wider world, are open to change and ripe for development during the adolescent period. Can coaches create the conditions where adolescents can practice developing these core capabilities in supportive contexts?

A work in progress

Neuroscience is starting shine a lens on why adolescence offers such unique potential for learning and growth. The adolescent brain is a 'work in progress'; a time where higher order capacities are being sculpted and refined in response to the individual's environment and individual circumstances. The frontal networks in the adolescent brain are going through a process of simultaneously pruning excess connections and strengthening those that are regularly used.

In this way there is a 'streamlining process', a sharpening and perfecting of those skills and capacities needed for the adolescent's surroundings. At the onset of puberty there is an explosion, an overproduction of new synapses (grey matter), designed to enable the acquisition of a wide range of different skills. In a 'use or lose it' fashion, grey matter that is redundant, not used, is cut away like excess growth in a garden, allowing for a stronger, more efficient functioning of the connectivity that remains. This process is associated with streamlining and specialisation. At the same time, connections between neurons that are used regularly are strengthened and part of this process is through myelination; the coating of connections between neurons with a fatty substance called myelin (see Figure 1).

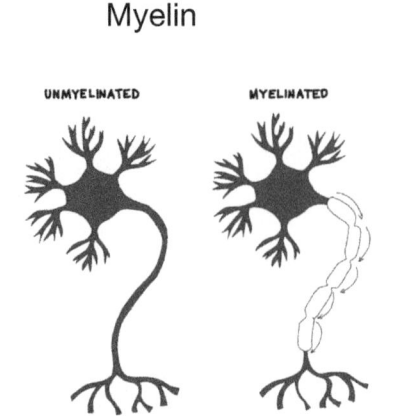

Myelin

Figure 1 - An illustration of myelinated and unmyelinated axons. Myelin increases processing efficiency, coordination and connection between neurons across the brain

This process is associated with a massive increase in both processing efficiency (up to 3,000 times faster processing speed) and the coordination and connection across wider brain areas, enabling increasingly fine tuned and integrated brain function (changes linked with improved capacities to think in more complex and abstract ways). By the adolescent years this maturation process has already taken place in sensory motor areas (toward the back of the brain) but is still being refined in the frontal regions. For frontal capacities, 'the cement is still wet'; the 'plasticine at its most pliable' and thus with an understanding of the developments of the adolescent brain, this period might be used to help cultivate still-developing prefrontal functions such as judgement, decision making and self-control.

Exploiting the developmental window

Former Manchester United coach Dave Sexton said that teams were made up of 'soldiers' and 'artists' and many coaches have tried to develop the artistic, inventive player who exudes imagination and originality. The English Football Association, for example, aspires to develop creative, independent decision makers who are innovative and can think 'outside the box' (Future Game, 2010). Many of these qualities are seen as 'natural gifts', something people after born with rather than something that can be cultivated. This has especially been the case in football (Daley, 2020). Emerging scientific understanding, however, is suggesting that the adolescent years are an opportune time to strengthen pre-frontal capacities necessary for elite football that we might previously have thought were beyond the influence of the coach.

Capacities needed for the elite player that are ripe for development during adolescence might include; decision-making, emotional control, creativity, mentalising (seeing things from others' point of view), consequential awareness and autonomy. Development of the frontal cortex is deliberately slow. It matures slowly for a reason, for evolutionary advantage. Coaches need to be mindful that this protracted period of growth has a slower developmental trajectory for adaptive purposes. It matures slower in order to be able to modify and adjust to the changing environment and offers unique possibilities for positive interventions (Suleiman and Dahl, 2017). This includes instrumental learning where the adolescent brain is especially sensitive to trial and error, real-time adjustments to its environment.

For coaches this new understanding can inform practice design and coaching methods. This might include adopting more of a patient approach with players, understanding that dynamic brain changes mean that decision making and other frontal capacities are still refining - a 'growth spurt' of the mind if you like - where tyheoughts and behaviours may not be consistent. It might also suggest encouraging risk-taking, experimentation and autonomy supportive behaviours, that take advantage of natural motivations at this developmental stage. Safe and secure environments that support such self-driven exploration and engagement might exploit this potential learning window (Willis, 2010). It is an optimal time to initiate positive spirals both on the pitch but also off of it, such as strengthening capacities like empathy, respect for others, as well as moral and ethical dispositions.

The adolescent period is especially evolved to be more sensitive to the changing environment. From a football perspective, it might be an optimal time to help forge those mental attributes that might be associated with a good 'football brain'.

'Green Bananas'

Football educators need to be mindful that the footballer at sixteen or seventeen is not the finished product. If a player is not the best decision maker; finds it difficult to control emotions or not the best reader of the game, then there is still time to develop those higher cognitive skills. Belgian coach educator Kris van Der Haegen, in his experience working with elite Belgian youth players, talks of the 'Green Bananas'; the likes of Kevin De Bruyne and Dries Mertens who were late developers, who needed the nurturing environment that would develop and help ripen their undoubted talents. He suggests emphasising a 'developmental' perspective that foregrounds process and longer term goals for player development which intuitively understands the protracted development of the adolescent brain. Indeed, late adolescence might be an opportune time to strengthen certain learning capacities (see chapter on the 'late adolescent brain'). The science shows us that there is a potential mismatch between physical and psychological maturity, with players in their late teens and early twenties bearing all the hallmarks of physical maturity, yet not possessing adult psychological functioning.

The environment, and that includes coaching instruction, can still influence brain development well into the mid twenties. The best coaches can interpret and adapt this information. Much of it is nuanced with no specific mapping onto particular practice, but rather enables the progressive coach to utilise these new understandings to help build a more holistic understanding of player development. It might be that coaches show a more patient approach with certain players, mindful that these 'higher cognitive' capacities are still rewiring and developing; not discard players who, with guidance, might attain a higher level of cognitive functioning than they would if left to develop without external support.

Perhaps traditional coaching thought that by late teens these mental capacities, including decision-making, creativity, 'mentalising' (perspective taking) and self-control were either rigid or 'cemented in', beyond external influence. The latest neuroscience suggests that these areas are a 'work in progress', and pliable, until well into the third decade of life. In conclusion, emerging understanding of the adolescent brain show it as a time of enormous potential. We now know that the brain develops not through getting bigger but by dynamic reorganisation, specifically in frontal regions during adolescence. These changes in neural structure and function offer an exciting 'window of opportunity' to shape productive learning dispositions and capabilities linked with the 'football brain'. These include higher order cognition such as decision making, judgement and empathy as well as behavioural and emotional control. Coaches working with adolescent players can structure environments that work with these natural motivations, instincts and drives and that take advantage of this 'second window of opportunity' for learning.

Chapter 2 - Decision-making and the adolescent brain

Main findings:

- Taking risks, seeking out novelty and exploration are part of the adolescent condition and should be encouraged by coaches. Adolescents are uniquely motivated to find rewards in new experiences and learn better from these than at any other stage of development. 'Fear of failure' can compromise these natural drives
- There appears a paradox of adolescent decision-making where, although capable of mature judgment and thought, this is not yet consistent and is particularly influenced by context. Adolescent decision-making appears uniquely impacted by environmental factors such as stress, fatigue and the social and emotional climate to a greater extent than children and adults
- In adolescence, a speculated imbalance between faster developing emotion and reward centres, compared to later developing control regions, can make adolescents prone to an 'emotional bias' in decision-making. In certain aroused contexts they may perceive more reward and less risk in their evaluations. These drives can be nurtured by the informed coach to enhance learning
- Increased dopamine and amplified reward centres make the adolescent brain particularly motivated by new and novel experiences. This increased motivation has been linked to more efficient learning and suggest that coaches create environments that help exploit such learning potentials. This might include a 'developmental mindset' encouraging process rather than outcome goals
- Adolescent players may take longer evaluating decisions compared to adults, less able to utilise the 'gist' or 'gut feeling' of a situation. Coaches can help scaffold a better sense of 'knowing' for the adolescent player by facilitating encouraging, trial and error environments that gradually build their experience and decision-making abilities

Adolescent decision-making (1): Heightened Reward/Emotion

Rewards 'shine brighter' for the adolescent

Last minute of the game, the teenage player is through on goal. Just the goalkeeper to beat. If he can just stay composed and pass the ball into the corner of the net, he can win the game for the team. As the 'keeper narrows the angle, the player's emotions seem to get the better of him; there appears to be a 'rush of blood to the head' as the player, seemingly unable to control his excitement, loses composure and blasts the ball over the bar.

As coaches we've witnessed these scenarios many times as the occasion seems to get the better of the player, and he or she finds it difficult to control their emotions and makes a seemingly 'rash' or 'reactive' decision. In the above example, it seems as though the excitement of scoring the goal, the reward of seeing the ball hit the back of the net, outweighs and overwhelms the necessary self-control needed in such heightened situations, such as calmly slotting the ball into the corner.

Of course, this scenario can happen across all age ranges (and abilities), and there will always be individual differences; however, new understandings from developmental neuroscience suggest that the way the brain remodels and reorganises after puberty mean that adolescents might be calculating and making choices in distinct ways that are only just beginning to be understood. Having a working knowledge of this science might help coaches shape environments that help cultivate these natural drives and motivations to enhance player development.

Decision-making starts to change after childhood. Adolescents begin to evaluate and calculate choices in different ways. Motivations change with a tendency toward seeking new and novel experiences, testing limits and pushing boundaries. Linked to a dynamic increase in the availability of the brain chemical dopamine and early development of emotional systems, rewards start to be experienced more intensely for adolescents with an increased motivation to pursue them. Dopamine is a neurotransmitter (chemical messenger) that, amongst other things, is responsible for signalling our experiences of motivation and feelings of pleasure. A release or 'squirt' of dopamine activates reward circuits in the brain that give us those feelings of pleasure when we either anticipate a reward (the dessert trolley being wheeled over, the roulette wheel spinning) or when we actually experience a reward (eating the chocolate cake, receiving the money). We now know that the availability of dopamine increases substantially after puberty impacting how adolescents process and are motivated toward rewards. It has been suggested that a peak in the availability of dopamine and hypersensitivity of the brain's reward centres during this period ensures that adolescents will find the quest for new experiences especially rewarding; natures way to propel us to leave the comfort of the family unit and engage with the wider environment on the journey toward adulthood (Siegel , 2014).

Part of the exaggerated reward signal means that adolescents tend to perceive more of the positive and less danger when weighing up options with a comparative disregard for the negative consequences, compared to their younger selves or the adults they will become (Palminteri et al, 2016). It is as though the temptation of immediate reward outweighs the ability to control those powerful urges.

This increased bias toward perceiving advantage when weighing-up decisions means that adolescents are more willing to try things, discover and explore, hang on in there, despite uncertainty, in a way that gets lost as they enter into adulthood. Underpinned by new scientific insights, a 'reframing of the adolescence' now recognises its potential, as a period of amplified learning, where the brain seems designed to seek out and absorb new experiences. It is only in recent years, however, that adolescent choices have been seen in this positive, adaptive light and invariably such novelty seeking and impulsivity has been linked with negative behaviours, such as reckless driving, fighting, binge drinking or 'sexting'. 'In the moment' choices with little regard for the consequences.

A salient example of 'typical' adolescent decision-making, in a football context, can be found in newspaper articles reporting on England's performance in the World Cup in Brazil a few years ago. Reports in The Times and The Telegraph remarked that Ross Barkley's decision-making was an area of his game that needed to mature. Ross Barkley was a late-adolescent at the time of the World Cup. He was described in his play as 'too impulsive', 'too reckless', and likely to 'take risks in the wrong areas of the field'. As we'll go on to discover, the heightened emotional context of a world cup finals might have impacted Ross Barkley's decision-making in a unique way relative to his more mature England teammates. Specifically his ability to use the frontal control circuitry in his brain to regulate the powerful drives of his reward and emotional systems, seated deeper in sub-cortical areas (towards the centre of the brain).

Recent findings from developmental science are beginning to offer a fuller picture of adolescent motivations and behaviours, suggesting differences in the way that decisions are perceived, evaluated and processed compared to children or adults. This appears to be linked to differences in the pace of development for emotion, reward and regulatory systems in the brain (Casey and Caudle, 2013).

Specifically there appears a developmental variation in the timelines between early maturing emotional and reward circuits (limbic) and later developing control systems (frontal) that make adolescents more susceptible to reactive, impulsive and instinctive decision-making (see Figure 2a).

Dual-Systems Model

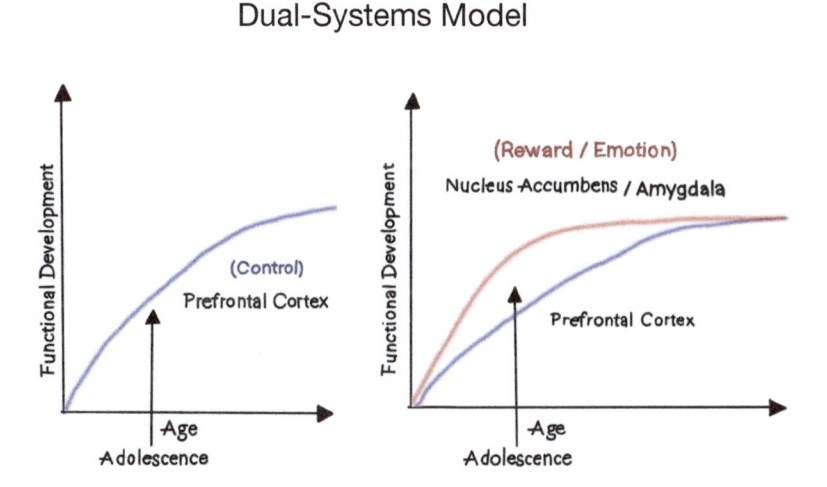

Figure 2a - Dual systems model illustrating earlier emotion/reward processing development in relation to cognitive control in adolescence. The gradual maturation of the PFC (control/judgement) shown on the left picture, contrasted with early maturation of Nucleus Accumbens (reward) on the right

Let's dig a little deeper into the theory and science behind adolescent decision-making and explore how such new knowledge might usefully impact coaches' understanding and practice.

'Storm and stress'

Adolescence as a period of development seems to conjure up certain assumptions and stereotypical behaviours. Public opinion around these years tend to shine a negative lens on adolescent decisions, suggesting that they are generally reckless, risky, easily influenced and characterised by poor choices (Frameworks, 2020). Indeed adolescence has historically been characterised as a time of emotional upheavals and impetuous, rash behaviours, notably coined by early psychologist Stanley Hall as a period of 'storm and stress' (Hall, 1904). It has traditionally been portrayed as a time of thoughtlessness and impulsive decision-making. Shakespeare famously remarked:

"I would there were no age between sixteen and three-and-twenty, or that youth would sleep out the rest; for there is nothing in the between but getting wenches with child, wronging the ancientry, stealing, fighting"

And Aristotle, two thousand years ago, commented that Greek teenagers were *'crazy'* and different from adults because they were more *'passionate, irascible and apt to be carried away with their impulses'*. Indeed, there appears some truth in this characterisation of adolescence. Despite being in better physical shape than at any other stage of life, adolescents are more likely to make preventable choices that put them in harms way. In comparison to adults and children they are more likely to engage in high risk behaviours including reckless driving, illicit drug use, and violent and non-violent crimes (Steinberg, 2015). They are even more likely to drown compared to children or adults! Scientific understanding of the developing mind and brain is beginning to shine a light on what might be happening during this period of dynamic change that make adolescents' uniquely responsive to the promise of immediate rewards which can significantly impact their judgment and decision-making.

This new knowledge, focusing on the underpinning science on how adolescents think, feel and behave has potential value for those working with young people. It can begin to reframe adolescence as a time of flourishing and opportunity rather than one of risk and vulnerability. For coaches working with adolescent footballers it will add an extra layer of understanding. It can offer coaches an understanding of why it might be important to cultivate certain conditions that work with and exploit adolescent-specific drives and motivations. This can support existing thinking or in some cases challenge assumptions about adolescence and the best ways to help them thrive. It can help build a holistic picture of development that, through shining a lens on the mental side of maturation, can scaffold coaches' understanding and potentially inform practice.

Adolescent risk-taking and novelty seeking have traditionally been linked with negative outcomes as the Shakespeare quote, above, implies. Adolescence was something to endure and 'survive' without suffering too much harm (Jensen, 2015). However, recent theories suggest 'a paradigm shift' in the way adolescent behaviours and choices are viewed (Busso and Pinneau, 2020). Adolescent decision-making, especially motivation toward novelty, risk and exploration are increasingly seen as having an adaptive, positive function, that needs to be cultivated to take advantage of the opportunities and motivations of this unique learning phase.

An opportunity for learning and the acquisition of new ideas, skills and interests (Crone and Dahl, 2012). Indeed UNICEF has recently identified adolescence as the 'second window of opportunity', linked to the powerful ability of the brain to make new connections during this developmental phase, similar to the first few years of life. However, this period of heightened brain plasticity (changeability) has both potentials and vulnerabilities. The window is open for both positive and negative influences to 'blow in' and impact brain development. As such, adolescence represents a fertile period of growth, an inflection point for constructive interventions that can set up positive developmental spirals (Dahl, in UNICEF 2017).

The paradox of adolescent decision-making

It is received wisdom that adolescence is a time of volatility, especially for mood swings, emotional highs and lows and passionate but sometimes rash, impulsive behaviours. However, this does not apply to all adolescents or in all situations. On occasions, adolescents appear perfectly capable of showing sound judgements and calculated, 'thought through' choices. Impetuous decisions can be made at any age but statistics suggest that adolescents are particularly susceptible to impulsive and risky choices, especially in 'aroused' or 'emotionally heightened' contexts. This impulsive and reactive behaviour has been found especially in the face of obtaining immediate rewards, in aroused contexts or in the company of friends (Casey, 2015).

In scientific studies, adolescents, in comparison to adults, show a heightened propensity toward risk-taking, novelty seeking, a comparative disregard for negative consequences and are more influenced by social context (Crews et al, 2007). In football we may have witnessed the adolescent player who's decision-making has been adversely affected by heightened emotions, whether that's anxiety, aggression, fear or over-excitement.

For adolescents, long term goals appear more likely to be hijacked by short term impulses. Controlling the urge to answer a text message when studying for an exam or being tempted out by friends on the night before a match. We intuitively know that adolescence is a period of heightened emotions where temptations are hard to resist. Developmental science, through recent imaging technology, is beginning to help us understand why this might be so. Much has to do with the different developmental timings for emotion and control systems in the adolescent brain.

The adolescent brain literature suggests an apparent paradox or contradiction in adolescent decision-making. On laboratory tests of reasoning and behavioural control adolescents tend to show a steady improvement and can function at adult levels by about sixteen years of age (Hartley and Somerville, 2015). However, this is not always the case in real world contexts, where adolescents show an increased propensity toward impulsive behaviours and risky decision-making compared to adults. Especially in the company of friends where respect and status might be at stake or in instances where there is the possibility of gaining immediate rewards, either financial, social or romantic. Think of the skateboarder attempting 'dare devil' tricks in front of their friends or the class clown who plays a joke despite the consequences.

It appears that the environment, especially socio-emotional aspects, has more of an impact on the adolescent brain, and hence behaviours, than for a child or an adult. As we'll find out below, the amplified emotion and reward circuits in the brain, combined with less developed control and judgement circuitry mean that the environment can impact adolescent thoughts, feelings and behaviours more than at any other time. This is important for coaches to be aware of as they are largely responsible for setting the motivational climate for players. In what scientists call 'cold' contexts, such as the laboratory, or where socio-emotional factors are not involved, adolescents are more likely to make consistently 'adult-like' decisions and show mature levels of self-control. This is attributed to the relative dominance of frontal brain circuits which are associated with reasoning, judgement and self-control over emotional systems seated deeper inside the brain (see figure 2b).

Cognitive Control

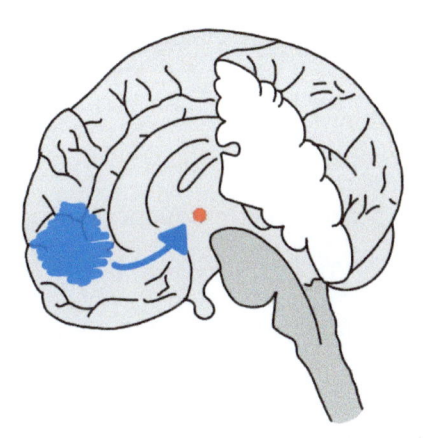

Figure 2b: In 'cold' contexts - where there is minimal interference of emotion, fatigue or peer groups, adolescents tend to show mature levels of emotional and cognitive control. This is characterised by stronger influence of prefrontal (judgment/control)(blue) compared with emotion (red) brain circuitry. It shows the potential capabilities and capacity for adolescent self-regulation in 'neutral' contexts

In football contexts, the coach talking to an adolescent player one-to-one after training might not recognise the same player that was 'acting up' in front of his teammates earlier in the session. Or the teenager who, during an important game, explodes with rage at a poor refereeing decision but is completely calm when you discuss it at the end of the match. The emotional climate seems to affect the adolescents' judgement and decision-making to a greater extent than at any other period of the life span. This is potentially important information for coaches to be aware of and might inform how and in what context the coach communicates to players. A recent suggestion by FA coach educator Paul McGuinness appears salient to this discussion where he suggest to 'praise in public and chastise private'. This advice intuitively understands the strong emotional reactivity such as shame, anger and embarrassment that might be experienced by an adolescent player who is chastised in front of their peers, where conserving status is paramount. The emotional reaction might be felt stronger than at any other developmental period due to the hypersensitivity of emotional circuits.

In interesting research carried out in the USA, Boston police officers were educated about the adolescent brain in an attempt to bring down a spike in juvenile crime. They were taught about the powerful impact of peers on the adolescent brain, especially when status was under threat. They were also told about the difficulties for forethought during this time. After the two day programme they found that arrests went down by 80% when they changed strategies such as reprimanding adolescents on their own, rather than in front of peers and deliberately talking through consequences of potential actions (if you do this then this is likely to happen) (Bostic, 2014). The police had previously found that an adolescent suspect would almost do anything not to 'lose face' in front of peers, including resisting arrest and aggressive behaviours.

Teachers and coaches have probably experienced such 'adolescent' behaviours when friends are present. As a teacher I learnt long ago not to conduct an argument with a pupil in front of their friends especially in emotionally charged contexts where they might be angry or embarrassed. They are often completely different when you can talk to them afterwards, on their own, where they are likely processing information more through frontal circuits which enable self-control, self-awareness and judgment capabilities. In front of friends the 'rational thinking' part of the brain is likely hijacked and suppressed by the powerful activation of emotional circuits (see figure 3).

The importance of environment for adolescent decision-making

Let's delve into the science of why context impacts adolescent decision making and the implications for constructing environments that maximise the unique motivations and learning potential of the adolescent period. In terms of knowledge and understanding there appears to be a general steady improvement in cognitive functions during adolescence. These abilities are associated with the prefrontal cortex which has been likened to the conductor of an orchestra or the CEO of an organisation, responsible for so called 'executive functions' such as planning, co-ordination and decision making (see Figure 2c).

Cognitive control abilities including reasoning, working memory and inhibition (stopping yourself doing something) show steady improvement and reach mature levels during adolescence (Huizinga et al, 2006). Overall, the literature speculates that throughout adolescence there is a gradual increase in the capacity to regulate emotions and preferences for immediate rewards and focus on the long-term consequences of decisions (Van Leijenhorst and Crone, 2010). This is useful for coaches to understand as it shows that adolescents have increasing capacities to take on board information, such as technical or tactical detail; to reason and make choices in relatively mature ways. However, the paradox appears to be that, at a time when adolescents are capable of making sound judgments and rational choices, they are also prone to making impulsive, risky decisions with little regard for future outcomes. It seems as though the ability to make reasoned, 'thought through' choices becomes hijacked by more powerful emotional drives at this stage of development. They have the *capacity* but it is not yet consistently applied during adolescence because of greater *demand* placed on reason and regulation at this stage by powerful emotions (Luciana and Collins, 2012).

Prefrontal Cortex

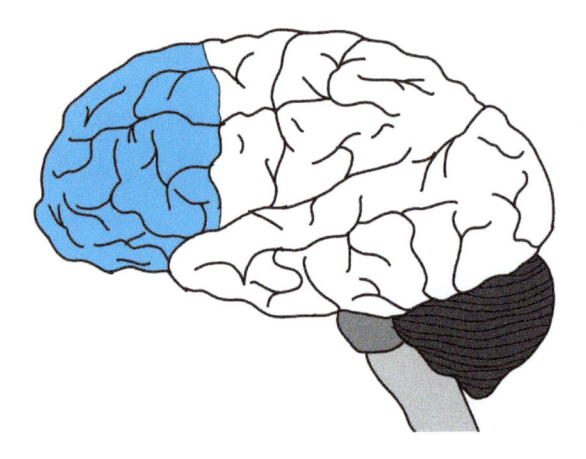

Figure 2c - The prefrontal cortex (blue): Responsible for executive functions including; reasoning, woking memory, inhibition and regulation of emotions and behaviour. Shows gradual development throughout adolescence

When decision-making tasks involve emotional stimuli, such as in the presence of risks and rewards or in emotionally salient contexts, like in the company of friends or other 'real-world' contexts, differences between adolescents and both adults and children begin to emerge (Crone , 2017; Casey et al, 2010; van Duijvenvoorde et al, 2016). That is, the context and the socio-emotional conditions impact decision making more than for other stages of life. This makes sense as, if children have the least mature reasoning skills and cognitive control abilities, then childhood risk-taking should be greater than adolescents but this is not the case (Casey and Jones, 2010).

Heightened emotion and reward in adolescence

Decision-making can be understood as involving the ability to not only reason about a decision problem but also to control emotional responses elicited by that problem (van Duijvenvoorde, 2010). As we've seen, the ability to reason about a decision problem is considered relatively mature by mid-adolescence, whereas the capacity to control related emotional responses are comparatively immature (Steinberg, 2007, Casey et al, 2011, van Duijvenvoorde et al, 2016). As such, there appears a tension between early developing limbic circuitry located deep inside the brain, associated with the processing of emotions and rewards; and later developing prefrontal circuitry that underpin reasoning, judgement, consequential awareness and control of emotions and behaviour (Duckworth and Steinberg, 2015).

Research shows that the responsiveness of circuits linked to emotion (amygdala) and reward (ventral striatum) increase rapidly from puberty onwards. In contrast, the cognitive control circuits mature along a slower developmental pathway over the adolescent period into young adulthood (Steinberg, 2008) (see figure 2a).

This difference in maturational development is proposed to result in a developmental 'imbalance' or 'mismatch' between the two systems during adolescence, with the affective (emotional/reward) network being characterised by heightened reactivity, for example, to rewards (Crone et al, 2017) and in the presence of peers (Steinberg, 2008). The heightened sensitivity of the emotional system appears not yet counterbalanced by the still maturing cognitive control networks. During this period of neural imbalance adolescents are proposed to be susceptible to risk taking, impulsive behaviours, especially in situations of heightened emotional arousal (Figner, 2009).

In football, which is often associated with aroused contexts that are emotionally significant for the adolescent player ('hot' contexts), we might think of a number of scenarios where emotions might 'win out' and result in risky, impulsive and reactive choices and behaviours. This might include, for example, anger at poor refereeing decisions; shame at making a mistake in front of teammates or lack of composure in front of goal; as the amplified emotions and reward centres hijack the frontal control circuits needed to calm an over excited adolescent player (see figure 3).

A number of recent models that have been offered to help understanding of the unique changes in the developing adolescent brain. These have been termed 'dual systems' and 'imbalance' models because they suggest that decision-making can be understood in relation to the different developmental trajectories of emotional and control circuits in the brain.

Decision-making and the adolescent brain
Emotional Hijack

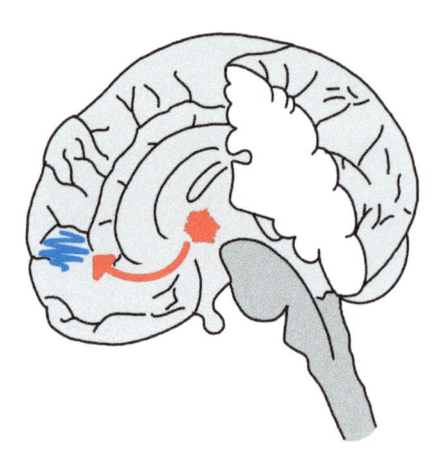

Figure 3: In 'hot' contexts such as in moments of strong emotional arousal, when peers are present or when fatigued - emotional circuits (red) have a stronger influence than prefrontal control circuits (blue) in decision making. This has been linked to an 'emotional-hijacking' for adolescents when making choices.

The triadic model (below) suggests that the reward circuits in the brain (nucleus accumbens/ventral striatum) linked to approach behaviours, exert more power over the amygdala which is linked to detecting stimuli in the environment that should be avoided. At the same time, the prefrontal cortex is insufficiently developed to regulate this imbalance (see Figure 4, below).

So when calculating choices, adolescents might perceive more reward and less danger in situations, which might in turn promote risk-taking, novelty seeking behaviours. We know that with maturation, neural pathways strengthen between frontal and limbic circuitry. This process, which includes strengthening of neural tracts through a process of myelination, matures throughout adolescence and enables better top down regulation of emotional reactivity. This connectivity is more fragile during adolescence (Mercurio et al, 2020) It is likely that these processes can be supported and strengthened by coaches who model positive behaviours and provide nurturing environments where adolescent players have autonomy to practice making decisions and learn from the outcomes, where successes and failures guide their own learning. Repeated practice in supportive environments likely strengthen neural circuitry in the adolescent players' brains, where opportunities for independent decision-making, and learning through real-time experiences, help build brain connectivity.

Dual-System and Triadic Model

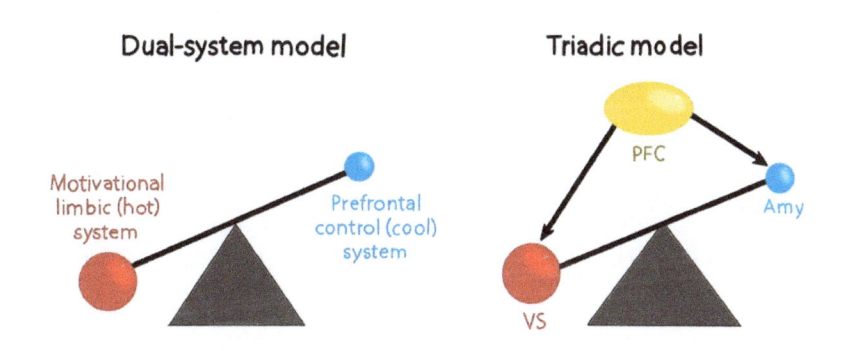

Figure 4: Dual-System and Triadic model: Imbalance models illustrating different timelines in frontal and sub-cortical adolescent development

'Learner driver in charge of a Ferrari'

The adolescent brain has been likened to 'all gas pedal and poor breaks'. This characterisation is rather simplistic but does highlight the strong drivers and motivators during adolescence, that might be too powerful to be kept in check by a slower developing control circuit.

We know that adolescents are more willing than adults to lean into uncertainty and explore situations with the promise of reward. Immediate rewards seem to 'shine brighter' for adolescents. For example, in experiments where there is a prospect of winning a reward, such as money, the reward system (including the ventral striatum) shows heightened activation for adolescents (13-17) compared to children and adults (Galvan, et al, 2006).

Professor Eveline Crone, from Leiden University, carried out a casino style experiment where participants had to play a 'one armed bandit' type task, in which images of fruit were sequentially displayed on a screen. A monetary reward was given when three of the same fruit appeared. If the second fruit did not match the first then it was obvious that no money would be won. However, when two images of the same fruit appeared this indicated the prospect of gaining a potential reward. Interestingly the reward centres in the brain were most active in this condition for mid-adolescents compared to adults and children. It appears that the chance of winning an immediate reward is more rewarding during this adolescent period. Similarly, as well as the anticipation of gaining reward, the receipt of reward activated the reward centres more for adolescents (Crone 2017).

Indeed science shows that, when making choices, for adolescents' the benefits and positives of a decision seem to outweigh the negatives, compared to adults. Monique Ernst and colleagues carried a 'wheel of fortune' task where decisions involving risk were studied. In this task adolescents and adults spin a wheel and the number it lands on determines whether you win a reward (money). Participants were allowed to indicate whether they wanted to choose between a small chance of winning a large reward (risky decision) or a large chance of winning small reward (less risky decision). The study found that adolescents were more likely to opt for the risky decision. Adolescents also indicated that they were more happy with their winnings and less affected by their losses compared to adults. The adolescents seemed more focussed on the advantages of a risky decision and less concerned about the disadvantages (losing money). Interestingly, during the task the adolescents showed more activity in the nucleus accumbens (reward and pleasure centres of the brain) compared to adults. Adults showed more activation in the amygdala (emotion areas that are linked to dangerous situations) and the prefrontal cortex (associated with control and long term consequences). This suggests that when calculating decisions, adolescents' reward centres are amplified and might outweigh centres which evaluate the disadvantages of a decision.

At the same time, the parts of the brain which regulate behaviour and evaluate the consequences of decisions are less influential. Money was used in these tasks but the same circuits which are sensitive to monetary rewards are also responsive to chocolate, attractive faces, praise, friendship and cooperation, suggesting that adolescents might be hypersensitive to rewards in general. Dr Ron Dahl at the 'Centre for the Developing Adolescent' suggests that this natural tendency to perceive the positive over the negative has potentially evolutionary, adaptive purposes. It means that adolescents are more likely to venture out and try things, to persevere with a desire to master new abilities despite the possible downsides, which has benefits not only for the person but also the community and, in a wider sense, the species.

What does this signify for adolescent football players? It might be that their natural condition is to try things, to see more upside in a decision, to have a go despite uncertainty, such as shooting from distance, attempting difficult long range passes or driving out from the back with the ball. Experimenting with new ways to beat an opponent or break a defensive line. All of these are potentially adaptive behaviours. From a coaching perspective, in order to take advantage of these natural drives, certain conditions might be more facilitative and supportive than others. Perhaps as coaches we can be aware of and praise young players' intent and not perceive adolescent choices as just 'poor decisions' but rather give them opportunity to 'figure it out' for themselves through trial and error (with some guidance), or at least be mindful of potential biases on their behaviours.

This enhanced motivation to experiment, to take action despite uncertainty, to 'have a go', is how adolescents' learn and can be cultivated by coaches through developing supportive, 'psychologically safe', coaching environments. On the flip side, if a coaching environment is results driven, characterised by 'fear of making mistakes' or a culture which emphasises outcomes over process then this may thwart natural adolescent motivations toward action in the face of uncertainty. Findings from sports psychology which suggests that balancing challenge and support optimises youth development, appears especially pertinent when coaching with the adolescent brain in mind (Nesti and Sulley, 2015; Gilbourne and Richardson, 2006; Richardson et al, 2004).

Social decision-making

Recent experimental research has shown that adolescents are significantly more likely to make risky decisions when they are in the company of peers compared to adults (Steinberg, 2015). In a simulated driving game, called the 'Stoplight Task', participants drive (virtually) as fast as possible around a circuit and have a number of traffic lights to negotiate. Decisions need to be taken, such as whether to gamble on an amber light, to save time, however, this is more likely to result in a crash and lose time penalty points. In the first condition of the task all participants drive alone. In the second condition participants are accompanied by a friend that they can bring along to watch their performance and can call out supportive advice (same script for adults and adolescents). The study found that in the presence of peers, adolescents (13-16) are three times more likely to take driving risks than when driving alone; young adults (17-24) are twice as likely to take risks and for the adult group there was no difference between the first and second attempts; that is, for adults their friends made no difference to their decisions (Chein et al, 2011, Gardner and Steinberg, 2005), (see figure 5).

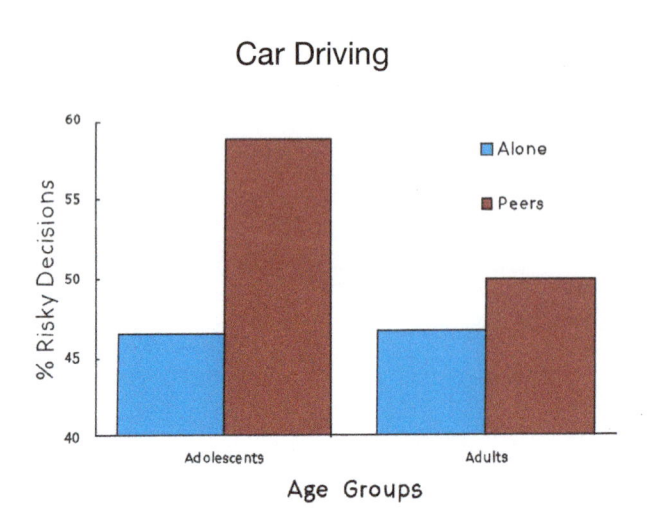

Figure 5- Graphic representation of heightened adolescent risk-taking in comparison to adults in a simulated driving task. Informed by (Chein et al, 2011)

At the same time it was found that the reward centres in the brain were significantly more active for adolescents in the 'social condition' (friends present) compared to adults. For adolescents the social brain areas and the reward circuits show a heightened sensitivity, possibly making social situations feel more exciting and potentially impacting abilities to control behaviour (Steinberg, 2015). This links with crime statistics which show that adolescents are more likely to commit crimes in the company of peers whereas adults are more likely to commit crimes on their own (Albert et al, 2103). Even adolescent mice drink significantly more alcohol they are with their peers compared to adult mice (Logue, 2014). The spike in reward activity and dopamine release in the company of friends can have negative implications but also a potentially positive, adaptive function. In the right conditions it can promote amplified learning and enable positive interventions.

Implications for coaches

These findings suggest that adolescent decision-making is qualitatively different from that of children and adults and, given the right conditions, is prone to experimentation and exploration, seeing more promise and less danger in situations that adults. Coaches need to be mindful that adolescent players learn through taking risks, testing abilities and pushing boundaries. This new science suggests that this is a fertile time to discover and learn, especially through trial and error processing. Science has shown that that brain systems linked with processing rewards and memories are at their most sensitive during the adolescent period and that this exaggerated reward (learning) signal in the brain helps adolescents learn and remember new information better than at other times in life (Peters and Crone, 2017). It represents an ideal time for adolescents to practice and refine their decision making abilities. Environments can be created which cultivate these natural drives and motivations toward novelty and risk, that enable players to practice making decisions and gradually balance their own perceptions of risk and reward. Arguably a more informed appreciation of how decision-making develops and the environments that might best enhance it, are important for producing elite young football players.

We now know that adolescence is characterised by an 'emotional spark', where passions, drives and feelings become intensified (Siegel, 2012). In football contexts, which are often characterised by heightened emotions and arousal, this might manifest as an 'emotional bias' in decision-making, as frontal networks aren't sufficiently developed and interconnected to manage more powerful emotions. Coaches who appreciate this new science might better empathise and connect with adolescents, as well as modelling how to interpret and react in given situations. As neuroscientists Jensen (2015) and Willis (2010) suggest, 'be the frontal cortex' for the adolescents. For example, adding perspective to situations, such as encouraging the re-appraisal of mistakes as opportunities for learning and development. This serves to bolster 'core capabilities' and resilience for adolescent players and can be cultivated by emphasising mastery over performance goals so that 'errors are seen as the routes to mastery' (Dweck, 1999).

Research shows that young people who are taught about the plasticity of the brain, its ability to change and strengthen with practice, are more to likely to be 'mastery oriented', show more perseverance in the face of setback, see challenges as opportunities to learn, have more self-efficacy and have less fear of failure (Dweck et al, 2006); and further, that adopting this incremental or 'growth mindset' can act as a psychological buffer for young players against many difficult challenges (Caro et al, 2016). Coaches can strengthen these learning dispositions, emphasising that abilities are changeable and within the locus of control of players, through the feedback and language they use. This might include emphasising and praising process over outcome to young players, recognising intent in players' decision-making and situating feedback within longer term developmental goals.

Adolescent decision-making (2): 'Gist' based choices
Teenagers 'think too much'. Fuzzy Trace Theory

A brain-based theory that has relevance for football coaches is the idea that as we mature, we use more automatic processing for decision-making that relies on feelings generated from prior experience, rather than reasoning and calculation. 'Fuzzy trace theory' advocates that advanced judgment and decision making is a reflection of simple 'gist' or 'gut feeling' representation of choices ('fuzzy' memory traces) as opposed to more calculated, quantitative representations (verbatim memory choices) (Rivers al, 2011). 'Gist', in this context, can be understood as the memory trace that an individual extracts from information (semantic meaning) which reflects the individual's knowledge, understanding and developmental level (Reyna and Farley, 2006). The theory suggests that, with development and greater experience in a domain, decision-making is increasingly informed by semantic (general meaning) representations rather than literally, 'weighing up' of costs and benefits.

'I didn't see (or feel) that coming!'
Neuroscience research shows that adolescents, compared to adults, have a less developed sense of a 'gut feeling' when making choices and also fail to conjure up a mental image of the possible outcomes of that choice (Baird and Fugelsang, 2004). This is especially the case in emotional or risky contexts. In short, the suggestion seems that they 'think' too much, weighing-up possible alternatives rather than relying on an instinctive gut or 'gist' feeling. That is, as the brain matures there is a shift in processing from frontal to sub-cortical (inner) regions in the brain, linked to more automatic and less calculated processing.

Fuzzy trace theory proposes that processing less information, and relying on gist representations (gut feelings), reduces risk-taking and is associated with more mature judgements. Rivers et al (2011) contend that when adolescents engage in 'rational' decision-making involving 'weighing-up' costs and benefits, then risk-taking increases. Brain scanning research has attempted to identify the neural mechanisms used by adults and adolescents that may suggest differences in decision making, especially where risk is involved (Baird et al, 2005). In this study, participants were presented with 'risky' or 'safe' scenarios and asked to indicate if something was a 'good' or a 'bad idea' (such as 'eating a salad', representative of a good idea and 'swimming with sharks' or 'setting your hair on fire', representative of bad ideas). Findings showed that adolescents took significantly longer than adults on the 'not good ideas' as compared to the 'good idea' scenarios. The research also found that adults showed greater activation in the insula (gut feeling) and right fusiform face area (images) compared to adolescents, during the 'not good ideas'. In contrast adolescents showed greater activation in the frontal cortex (thinking part of the brain) during the 'not good ideas' and there was a significant correlation between frontal activation and reaction time.

    The research proposed that when faced with 'risky' scenarios, adults used a more efficient response, driven by mental images of possible outcomes and a visceral response to those images, in line with 'gist' representations associated with more mature decision-making. Adolescents, however, relied more on reasoning capacities and, as such, activated frontal networks, indicating a more effortful response and analytical calculation in comparison to adults and indicative of a less mature decision-making system. So it seems that adults seemed to 'know' that setting your hair on fire is not a good idea, they don't have to work it out. The same part of the brain (the insula) is activated that remembers when we've have food poisoning or if we see a snake; a gut reaction that is fast and efficient. So the bottom line is that young players may have a less developed sense or feeling of risk and may not be able to sense, or 'know' the dangers in certain decisions. This may manifest itself in risky decision making as the 'gut feeling' sense of knowing that something is not right is not yet developed.

'Fuzzy trace' theory for football

What might this new knowledge suggest for adolescent football players. Firstly, this research suggests that the processing of decision-making might be qualitatively different for adolescents as opposed to adults. This may be particularly the case in contexts that might be considered dangerous or risky. Adults might be able to act more intuitively, automatically, instinctively knowing that something feels right. A faster, more efficient reaction based on a visceral feeling. Adolescents may not have developed this 'gist' process, they are more likely to be 'working it out' and, as such, the decision-making process takes longer, is more inefficient, and might not be as consistently accurate or successful as adults. Coaches need to be aware of this for football when working with adolescent players. Players are making decisions all the time and figuring out how to balance risk and reward. This knowledge, that the processing of decision-making for adolescents might be different from adults', can enhance how coaches might be better able to evaluate and interpret players' decisions and act accordingly. Always in a context of support in which errors are seen as the 'routes to mastery'.

How might this developing sense of 'knowing', play out in football coaching contexts? It might mean that for some adolescent players, it takes more time to work out what to do, something that might seem instinctive for a mature adult player; something that the adult player knows 'feels right'. This might include - risky passing across the penalty area as a defender; dribbling inside your own box; dwelling, and getting caught on the ball, instead of making an 'automatic' quicker decision. Tactically it might mean; not managing the game by pushing too many players forward when you are 1-0 up; over celebrating after scoring a goal and not retreating quickly into shape. For coaches, having a deeper understanding of what might be happening for the adolescent player is important. Give players time and allow them to make mistakes in non-judgemental contexts so that they can construct and build their own understandings, through trial and error sampling of the environment. In this way, it will help players develop their own experiences which will scaffold their own sense of 'knowing', shifting processing from more deliberative to more automatic functioning.

In conclusion, the dynamic reorganisation of the adolescent brain has a profound impact on judgement and decision making capabilities. The increased dopamine at this age, and drive toward risk-taking, novelty seeking and pushing boundaries, offers both opportunities and vulnerabilities. Adolescent players may not be thinking and feeling the same way as the adult coach, using different brain processing systems to calculate choices. Coaches need to be mindful and patient with this. Empowering adolescents to practice making decisions, in supportive climates, enables them to strengthen the connectivity between reward and control circuitry in their brains allowing for optimal development. Coaches who are aware of these changes and motivational differences can capture the unique learning potential of this developmental stage.

Chapter 3 - Creativity and the adolescent brain

Main findings:

- Neuroscience findings suggest that creativity involves differentiated patterns of activity across multiple regions of the brain. Creative thinking appears to engage more complex neural networks than everyday modes of thought
- Neuroscience suggests that creativity is improvable and that environments can be cultivated to help foster creative thinking and behaviour
- Creativity is the product of differing modes of thought including 'generative' and 'analytical' forms. Generative ideas are best fermented in 'soft' environments with reduced stress and judgement. These can then be analysed in more focussed contexts to calculate their usefulness and value
- Developmental neuroscience suggests that the emerging connectivity, integration and coordination of the adolescent brain make it a fertile time to encourage creative, original thinking and behaviours
- Football coaches can utilise these findings to help construct 'generative' and 'analytical' environments that help foster creativity and take advantage of the unique potentials of the adolescent period of brain development

Creativity has been advocated as a vital learning disposition for the 21st century. Developing creativity is not only a goal of schools' education but also a fundamental aspiration for football. The English FA, for example, aspires to develop independent, creative decision-makers (Future Game) and suggests that creativity involves a number of processes including; imagination; originality, the ability to generate ideas that are both unusual and of value; and the generation of ideas through divergent thinking. However, what is creativity? Is it improvable? If it is improbable, what are the conditions that help foster creative thinking and behaviour? Neuroscience is starting to engage with some of these questions and, importantly, suggests that adolescence might be an opportune period in which creativity can flourish (Crone, 2017). The desire for risk and thrill-seeking, a seeming fearlessness to try new things and the ability to learn from rewards, mean that adolescence represents a developmental window to help foster creative expression (Galvan, 2020).

Creativity and the brain

In recent years, with the advent of new imaging technologies, neuroscientists have enquired into the nature of creativity, investigating what constitutes creative processing and which environments might best cultivate it (Howard-Jones, 2010). These studies suggest that, not only is creative thinking different than other modes of cognition using different brain networks, but also that certain environments are more conducive to fostering this type of 'outside of the box' thinking and behaviour. Neuroscientist Kenneth Heilman and colleagues suggest that creative thinking involves co-activation and communication between brain regions that are seldom strongly connected (Heilman et al, 2003).

This chimes with Dr Dan Siegel's contention that adolescence is a ripe time to develop creativity, as brain regions are starting to connect and integrate, enabling new capacities for conceptual and abstract thought processing; as well as the generation of new and innovative ideas and 'out of the box' strategies for problem solving (Siegel, 2014). As such, adolescence might be an opportune to foster creativity in players. Indeed, adolescents are developing the ability to think and make decisions in faster, more complex and creative ways. Information processing becomes quicker as stronger and more efficient brain connections are insulated enabling messages to travel thousands of times faster compared to children.

This streamlining process enables increased capacity for complex and abstract thinking as neurons become interconnected across larger brain areas and basic thinking skills become more automatic. This frees up capacity and provides opportunities for adolescents to think in new ways and grapple with more complex problems, with new found capacities for creative exploration. Indeed it has been shown that, given fertile conditions, adolescence is an opportune time to develop creative decision-making.

Creative thinking is different

Neuroscience findings suggest that creativity involves differentiated patterns of activity across multiple regions of the brain. Creative thinking appears to engage more complex neural networks than everyday modes of thinking. In studies, creative thinking has been linked with '… remote associations. Novel ideas. Benefit from less focus. Allowing attention to drift toward concepts (actions) not primarily associated with the topic' (Howard-Jones, 2010). Neuroscience research has also shown links between loss of inhibition (stopping yourself from doing something) and creativity. Brain imaging studies reveal that during improvisation (inventive or creative behaviour) there is a deactivation of lateral pre-frontal cortex, a brain region associated with focus, self-regulation, self-monitoring and inhibition (see figure 7).

The Lateral Prefrontal Cortex

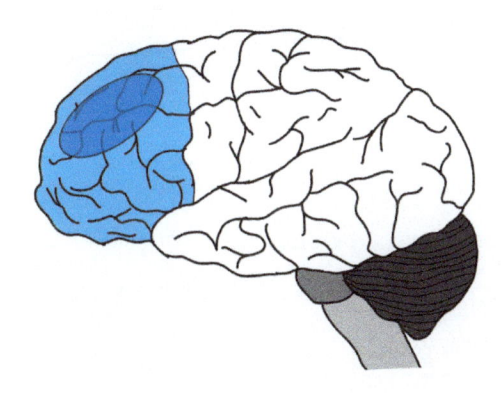

Figure 7 - The lateral prefrontal cortex. Associated with focus, self-regulation, self-monitoring and inhibition

Turning these 'regulation, monitoring and control circuits' off may be associated with 'free floating attention, spontaneous unplanned associations and sudden insights and realisations' (Limb and Braun, 2008). Research with patients who have suffered brain damage to these areas associated with inhibition (frontal areas) has been linked with bursts of creativity (Kraft, 2007).

This research implies that calm, relaxed and 'carefree' environments, where judgment is limited, helps foster mental states or mindsets that are conducive to inventive thinking and behaviour. Further, this might suggest that reducing stress and establishing a positive emotional environment is important for developing creativity (Hardiman, 2010). This is especially important for the adolescent learner because feelings of stress and anxiety are more powerful during this developmental phase, compared to adults, possibly related to the relative dominance of early maturing, subcortical emotion systems (Galvan et al, 2014).

As we have suggested in this book, adolescence is a time of both vulnerability and opportunity. With this in mind, and possibly linked to the heightened activation of the limbic circuits in the brain, adolescence has been suggested as a unique period of 'creative exploration', that can be cultivated given the right conditions (Siegel, 2014). In certain studies, for example, spacial awareness tasks, adolescents show more creative thinking than adults (Crone et al, 2017). Thus adolescence is potentially an opportune time to develop creativity.

Can we create environments that encourage and develop creativity?
Research suggests that creativity can be fostered and developed. Indeed, just by informing learners at the outset of a task that 'creativity is improvable with practice' has been shown to increase creative behaviours; especially in adolescents compared to adults (Kleibeuker et al, 2013). So, for football coaches, informing players from the start that 'everyone can become more creative with practice' can help develop creativity in players.

Neuroscientist Paul Howard-Jones suggests that certain strategies and environments are more conducive to fostering creativity than others. He suggests that creativity is a product of two processes, 'generative' and 'analytical' thinking. Two different modes of thought. One generates ideas, the other analyses those ideas. Generative ideas are best fermented in 'soft' environments with reduced stress and judgement. In this environment there is an express encouragement of divergent thinking. That is, where multiple solutions to problems are recognised. Learners however need some boundaries. There needs to be an element of constraint. Too much freedom and it becomes uncomfortable and stressful, he suggests, whereas too much regulation tend to stifle generative ideas. Balance is needed. Once the ideas are generated learners need to switch to an 'analytical' mode of thinking. Analysing whether the ideas are valuable? Are they useful? Will they work?

Divergent thinking in football

For football coaches, this might involve empowering adolescent players to experiment with different ideas and strategies in a non-judgemental way, for example, generating multiple strategies to penetrate the defensive back line; or combine to break the lines in midfield.

The players' explore these ideas practically, in a supportive environment. Following this, they can discuss which creative attempts were more appropriate. For example, which were most realistic and useful (analytical processing). They may conclude, for example, that flicking the ball over your own head to beat the defence, although creative, might not work in an actual match. In this way we might help foster a 'generative' and 'analytical' approach. Further, empowering players to undertake analytical processing of this kind offers a sense of autonomy and ownership, linked with intrinsic motivation (rather than coach saying this is wrong!). It also resonates with the natural drives and motivations towards independent decision-making during the adolescent phase of growth.

Schools based neuroscience perspectives, similarly suggest that creativity is best cultivated with the encouragement of divergent thinking, where multiple solutions are recognised as appropriate. 'Teachers need to design instructions to engage students in divergent thinking to generate multiple and varied approaches to problem solving' (Hardiman, 2010). This suggestion for developing divergent thinking, in classroom contexts, is also appropriate for developing creative behaviours in football contexts.

To develop divergent thinking and behaviours for football, the coach may want to set problems and tasks and then let go of the outcomes. Encourage multiple solutions, try not to limit outcomes with the coaches' own pre-conceived ideas. The coach can design problem solving practices and then empower players to use their imagination to find solutions in supportive, non-judgemental environments.

For coaches, this suggests constructing an appropriate context for developing creativity. An example of a session encouraging creative play whilst utilising the concept of divergence might consist of scenarios including; edge of the box, quick combinations to free runners behind the opposition defence; making explicit to players that there is no single way to solve the problem and that there could be multiple solutions. Encourage combining using different techniques and different surfaces. For example, one touch play, the use of 'air space' to out manoeuvre the opposition.

As a coach, aim to limit verbal instruction, just general guidance such as; 'combining to release a player beyond the opposition defence' then let the players experiment with different solutions; some innovations might be attempted that you, as the coach, had not thought of. Research shows that verbal instruction is more likely to break down under pressure whereas embodied understanding (construction of learning through engaging with the environment) is more robust and provides for deeper learning. As a coach, aim to establish 'relaxed focus' with young players, modelling a 'confident uncertainty' approach (Claxton, 2005).

Fear of making mistakes undermines creativity

Coaches can develop environments where experimentation and improvised play are explicitly welcomed and encouraged. The coach can reduce pressure from the start by suggesting to players that inventive play and pushing boundaries is 'difficult' and that there are probably going to be more 'mistakes' during such sessions (Claxton, 2005). This creates more of a 'challenge' (rather than 'threat') state for players; particularly important for adolescents. In such coaching climates, errors are framed as a necessary part of the journey.

A positive emotional environment is essential for creative development. There may be, for example, a designated 30 minutes of 'experimental' work in the session where players can improvise, beyond threat or judgement. We know that for adolescents, stress might be experienced more powerfully than adults and children, in which case it might be especially important to construct a relaxed environment for the adolescent player, where the frontal control circuits are toned down, and where mistakes are tolerated, even welcomed.

Professor Guy Claxton suggests that by explicitly informing players that a session is 'experimental', where we are looking for invention, innovation and 'out of the box' thinking, it is more likely to foster creative play. This explicitly gives players the 'licence' to try things and incentivises and rewards invention and creativity. In such supportive, nurturing environments there are no 'mistakes', as such, just consequences that we can learn from (Claxton, 2005). In these facilitating contexts, errors need to be seen as an inevitable, but constructive part of the journey (Dweck, 1999, Beswick, 2000). Such facilitating sessions might include, a designated period of 'experimental work' in the session where players can improvise, push boundaries and take risks without threats of judgement. Research shows that expert players (Brazil) have developed in peer led games without the judgement of coaches and where they are free to express themselves (Aruajo, 2010).

In this light, giving adolescent players autonomy to make decisions away from the scrutiny of adults might help the creative process. We know, for example, that the mere presence of an adult can dampen down the production of dopamine, a neurotransmitter linked to reward, learning and creativity. So for football coaches, adolescence might represent a sensitive period to try to foster and develop creative, inventive play. Michael Beale, former Chelsea and Liverpool youth coach and now assistant to Steven Gerrard at Rangers talks about introducing 'playfulness' into training and enabling players to 'rehearse' their skills ('Ask the coach' podcast, 2020). He suggest that although it's right to 'train like we play', 'breathing space' also needs to be created in training programmes where players can work on developing their individual skills, without explicit judgement from the coach; in a way not dissimilar to street football. He remarks that he discovered this approach while coaching Brazilian players at Sao Paulo earlier in his career who requested this time to practice individual skills and techniques.

In conclusion, adolescence represents an opportune time to facilitate the development of creativity. Coaches can construct learning environments that help foster creative expression, including 'experimental periods' which foreground autonomy supportive behaviours, limit judgement and utilise divergent questioning techniques. These potentiating environments might help encourage innovative, 'outside the box' thinking and behaviours in young players.

Chapter 4 - The emotional spark of adolescence

Main findings:

- Early development of emotion circuits in the brain make adolescence a time of peak motivation, passion and drive. Coaches can take advantage of this new understanding to create environments which help exploit this natural enthusiasm, intensity and propulsion for new experiences
- Amplified emotions in adolescence offer opportunities to help develop reflection and management strategies and techniques. This heightened processing offers a ripe period to develop self-control and emotion regulation strategies
- Coaches should be aware that elevated stress levels can uniquely impact adolescent behaviours which can affect decision making, emotions and behaviours
- Coaches should be mindful that negative emotions can be experienced more powerfully for adolescent players, including for late adolescents and to create environments that take this heightened processing into account
- 'Calculated pressure' environments can be developed for adolescent players where coaches can 'act as the prefrontal cortex' and scaffold emotional management for players which in turn helps them develop their own emotional control circuitry

Adolescent behaviours are often characterised by mood swings and heightened emotions; happy one minute and sad the next. In popular culture the adolescent condition is often portrayed as comprising a roller coaster world of emotional fluctuations. This stereotype of mood swings is actually confirmed by research which shows, for example, that adolescents tend to experience greater lability; that is, ups and downs of emotions, compared to adults. Dr Dan Siegel in his work on adolescence talks of an 'emotional spark', where emotions and passions are 'on fire', with an amplified intensity compared to other stages of the life span. At the onset of puberty hormonal changes 'kick start the engines' in the maturational process toward becoming an adult. A cascade of sexual hormones start a process of physical, emotional and psychological development that ignites the motivations and passions needed to engage with the outside world and develop toward independence. Evolutionary wise it has been suggested that an amplified emotional system drives the needs to venture out and connect with others, try new experiences, providing the energies to push boundaries on the road toward adulthood and the important job of eventually finding a mate. As we've seen above, during adolescence the emotional circuits contained within the limbic system mature faster, and can exert more influence over the later developing cognitive control systems (see figure 8).

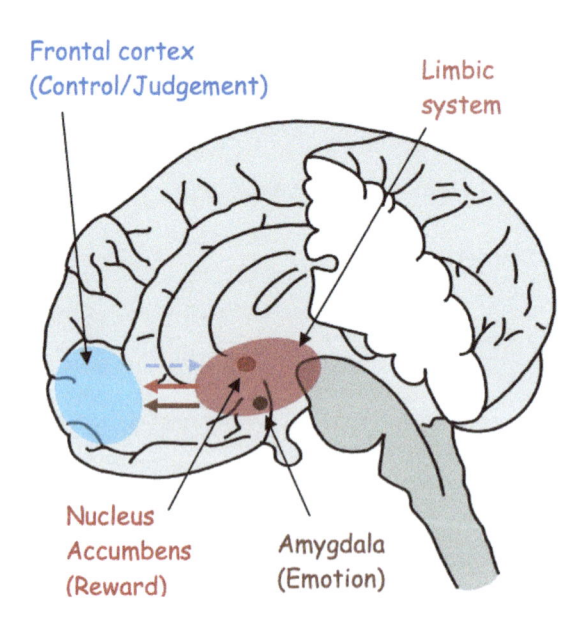

Figure 8 - The early maturing and more powerful limbic system (reward/emotion) can exert more influence over frontal circuitry (judgement and control) in adolescence, especially in aroused contexts or in the company of peers

This has been linked to an emotional bias in decision-making and behaviours, where a powerful limbic system can outweigh and override the prefrontal cortex (linked to judgement, reason and control). These changes present both vulnerabilities and opportunities. Negative influences, for example, can impact maturing neural circuitry and has been linked to maladaptive and pathological behaviours including depression, eating disorders, self harm and addiction. However, we now know that neural reorganisation during adolescence also offers a period of great potential; a time to harness and guide strong passions and drives, enabling adolescents to fine tune connectivity and fulfil their potentials at a time of particular neural adaptability. Coaches can take advantage of this pivotal point in adolescent maturation. A fuller, holistic understanding of player development can help scaffold this fertile phase of growth.

Linking thoughts and feelings
Research is beginning to offer a more nuanced understanding of emotional development during adolescence, where feelings and thoughts are interrelated in ways that is only now beginning to be understood.

How we feel has a direct and integral connection to how we think. Emotion and cognition are bound together in ways that are only now being shown by cognitive neuroscience (Immordino-Yang, 2010). We now know that emotions are important in guiding our decision-making. Recent brain research shows that emotions act as a hidden hand in our 'rational' choices and that when we have trouble feeling emotions, then we are prone to making poor decisions, especially in real world contexts (Bechara et al, 2005).

Neuroscience research has found, for example, that when patients suffer damage to their orbifrontal cortex, a brain region at the interface of cognition and emotion, that integrates thoughts, emotions and actions, then this interferes with their abilities to make decisions in every-day contexts. Emotions are now understood as an integral part of the decision making process. Similar to a rudder that guides a ship, below the surface, but still in charge of the direction of travel, emotions steer our decision-making even if we are not aware of this when we calculate our choices (see figure 8b). This is particularly the case for the adolescent, where early developing and intense emotions might hold more sway in decision-making than at any other time.

The emotional spark of adolescence
The powerful 'adolescent rudder'

Figure 8b- Emotions have been compared to a boat's rudder (Immordino-Yang). Beneath the surface yet strongly influencing the direction of travel. The 'rudder' is suggested as more powerful during adolescence

From recent research focussing on the developing brain, it appears that, for adolescents, this emotional rudder which stealthily guides our choices, is more powerful and influential than at any other stage in our lives. It was found, for example, that in decisions involving risk and reward, teenagers' unconscious emotional reactions, used to guide decision-making, is more powerful than that of adults. Neural imaging found that activity in limbic circuits, linked to the processing of emotion and reward was stronger for adolescents. Further, this more potent emotional reaction was correlated with teenagers' making riskier and less optimal decisions (Cauffman et al, 2010). As such, adolescent decision-making may be disproportionally influenced by strong emotions and the emotional climate. This is likely the case in football contexts.

We know, for example, that in negative emotional contexts the hypersensitivity of the amygdala (linked with fear) is stronger for adolescents compared to adults (Peters and Crone., 2017). That is, adolescents might experience the emotion of fear stronger than adults in the same emotional context. In a football context, for example, adolescents introduced to an adult first team environment, might not experience situations such as admonishment (after losing a game) in the same way as their adult teammates. The amygdala, which detects and monitors stimuli in the environment, likened to a burglar alarm, may be more sensitive with a 'louder volume' for the adolescent compared to an adult. At the same time the frontal circuits used to dampen the emotional reactions, to calm down powerful feelings, are not fully developed and connected with the emotional system. We have seen, above, that adolescence is a time of heightened emotionality. We now know, with the advent of new imaging technologies, that brain systems linked to the processing of emotions and rewards mature earlier than those responsible for judgement and control.

Adolescent behaviours have been described as 'all gas pedal and no brakes'. The situation is a little more nuanced than this but it appears that emotions are experienced more intensely and rewards experienced more powerfully for adolescents. Research has found, for example, that when viewing faces showing the emotion of fear, adolescents (12-14) show heightened activation in the emotional circuits (amygdala, linked to processing fear) compared to children and adults (Sommerville et al, 2004) (figure 9).

Strong Emotional Reaction in Adolescents

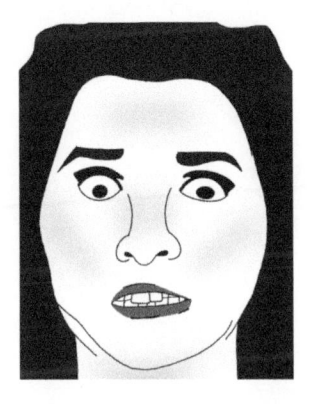

Figure 9 - Adolescents (12-14) were found to show heightened activation in emotional circuits (amygdala) when looking at fearful faces compared to children and adults

Interestingly adolescents are also more likely to perceive neutral emotional faces as fearful relative to children and adults, possibly linked to neural reorganisation at this phase of development. This heightened reactivity to negative emotional contexts has also been found late adolescence, including the early twenties (Silva et al, 2015). This suggests that on the pitch or training ground, emotions, especially negative ones, might be experienced more significantly, and hold more sway for adolescent players, especially in aroused contexts or during moments of fatigue, stress or in the company of friends (where cognitive controls are compromised). At the same time the ability to calm emotional reaction (through frontal brain connections) is still developing.

That is, emotional experiences can feel more intense, not only because of the potency of adolescent emotions but also because it is more difficult to regulate them, compared to when they reach adult levels of brain maturity. Coaches need to be mindful of these developmental differences, especially monitoring adolescent behaviours in negative emotional contexts, such as if they have made a 'mistake', concede a goal or lose a game. That is why focusing more on process goals rather than outcomes at this stage of development is important.

Managing Emotions

Figure 10 - Coaches can help young players manage strong emotions through creating supportive yet challenging coaching environments

The ability to consistently manage emotions and behaviour is still developing in adolescents, linked to a strengthening of connectivity between limbic and prefrontal circuitry. We know that the ability to regulate emotions and behaviour has been implicated in a range of successful outcomes, and those who are better at managing their emotions at a young age achieve more success later in life across a variety of different domains (Duckworth and Steinberg, 2015). As such, helping adolescent football players to better understand and regulate their emotions will likely strengthen their ability to perform at a higher level.

The developmental plasticity (malleability) of the brain during this period offers potential opportunities to support self-regulation strategies that might strengthen connectivity between frontal (control) and limbic (emotion) circuitry. That is, the adolescent years, because of the unique changeability of neural connectivity, might represent an opportune time to strengthen pathways linked to controlling and managing emotions. In research undertaken in elite football academies, findings suggest that young players who possess the most effective coping strategies are more likely to transition into the professional game (Mills et al, 2012). For the coach it might be fruitful to create environments that are sensitive to this 'emotional overshoot' and provide adolescent players opportunities to reflect upon, manage and direct heightened emotions and impulses, particularly in aroused contexts (see Appendix). In this way coaches can use this 'window of opportunity' to help scaffold important self-regulated behaviour patterns.

This might include, for example, offering strategies and techniques to help manage emotions during play, underpinned by a message that mistakes and challenges are a useful and necessary part of the developmental process. These abilities to rationalise and 'put into perspective', provided by prefrontal circuits, are not yet fully mature and consistent in adolescents but can be supported and developed in potentiating learning environments by coaches (and parents).

Brain messages helping improve emotional control

In a recent psychological intervention, undertaken at a professional football academy in England, the authors explored how communicating brain messages about emotion and cognition might assist reflection and emotional control in adolescent players (see Appendix). Simplified 'red-brain/blue brain' models, drawing on neuroscience, were introduced to players that represented how emotions and cognition might interact in certain football contexts. Pictorial representations of limbic (red) and cognitive control (blue) systems were introduced to adolescent players and coaches. Players were said to be 'in the unhelpful red' if they appeared to be losing control of their emotions.

That is, where emotional reactions were detrimental to their thoughts, feelings and performance. This was represented in the models as an enlarged limbic system dominating a smaller prefrontal cognitive control system (See figure 11).

"The Unhelpful Red"

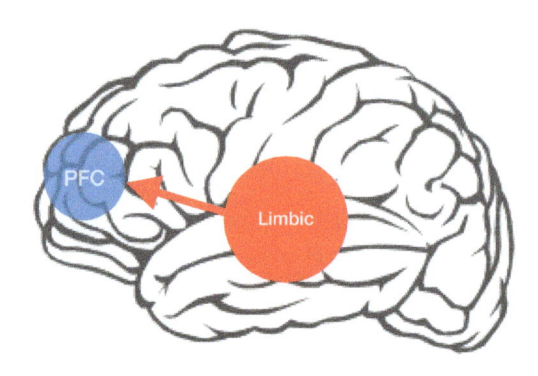

Figure 11 - The above illustrates stronger inputs from earlier developing limbic circuits (emotion/reward) compared to the later developing prefrontal cortex

Examples explored with players included; 'Unfair' refereeing decisions that provoke strong emotional reactions, such as frustration or anger, which might detract from the player's game; a player making a 'mistake' and this provoking emotions such as anger and shame, impacting the player's behaviour including not wanting the ball or generally losing confidence; a player becoming 'over excited' in front of goal, losing composure and missing a chance to score.

The authors worked with players (and coaches) on strategies that they might use to 'get back in the blue'; an emotional state that corresponded with calm, composed, 'in the moment' thinking. These strategies included: positive self talk, such as 'I'll get the next one'; playing simply to 'get back in credit"; talking and organising others around you to regain composure; and an overarching appreciation that mistakes are part of the journey and an inevitable aspect of playing the game. Some of these strategies were delivered by current professionals at the club (via edited video) who had been through the club's academy system and, as such, might better able reinforce the messages (Yeager et al, 2013). The concept of 'key messages from key messengers' underscored this approach.

These simplified brain models appeared to help players and coaches both recognise and reflect on their emotions and also help facilitate strategies to help manage emotions in the context of the game. As we have seen, this is particularly important during adolescence where emotions can become heightened and strategies that strengthen connectivity with control regions are open to manipulation.

Managing threat

Adolescents respond differently to stress. Stress is an automatic reaction to a physical, psychological or emotional threat and the ability to respond effectively is crucial for survival (Galvan and Rahdar, 2013). One of the brain's primary functions is to detect stimuli in the environment that may pose risks to wellbeing and safety. This is an evolutionary bias that prioritises attention toward those things that are potentially dangerous to our wellbeing.

The Reticular Activation System (RAS) is responsible for this filtering process and acts like a gatekeeper channeling incoming information. Threats will take precedence of incoming stimuli and will be sifted through to the amygdala, part of the emotional brain system, and processed in readiness to respond (fight or flight). If feeling threatened or anxious, these cues will take priority and any information that might help learning (for example, technical or tactical football information) will not pass to the cortical, thinking part of the brain to be processed. Fear or threat will be prioritised and hijack other less immediate information. Research suggests that the amygdala's reaction to threat is elevated in adolescents (Willis, 2012). If an adolescent player is anxious about making a 'mistake' or perceives the environment as 'threatening', on the field (or in the classroom or changing room), then they are less likely to be able to focus on the technical or tactical information being delivered by the coach. All their attention is fixated on the threat. That is, learning opportunities may be missed if the environment is overly fearful for the heightened emotional processing of the adolescent brain. Related to this, Pippa Grange, former England FA performance psychologist recently remarked:

'... attention is finite, and the more you spend your time worrying about scary negative consequences, the less attention you have to give to your actual performance. If you are playing for your place in the team, you are not focussed on playing to win'
(Pippa Grange, 2020)

Linked to an amplified emotional system this might be especially pertinent to adolescent players and suggests that coaches be mindful of the coaching climates they help create.

Stress and the adolescent player

Research suggests a heightened stress response in adolescents compared to children (Stroud eve al, 2009) and that adolescents who are more stressed tend to make poor health choices and more risky decisions compared to peers who are less stressed (Galvan and McGlennan, 2012). Coaches can be mindful of this as adolescence is a challenging developmental period characterised by many different stressors including; demanding school work, peer group and romantic pressures as well as establishing autonomy and independence (Galvan and Rahdar, 2013).

Further, findings show that stress can accentuate the personality characteristics of adolescents, such that if an adolescent is usually apprehensive or shy then anxiety exacerbates this characteristic. Alternatively, if a teenager is generally confident and forthright, the anxiety can enhance this characteristic. In addition, acute stress may exacerbate teenage decision-making (Porcelli and Delgado, 2009). Players who show a tendency toward risky decision-making may be more prone to such behaviours when under stress. Alternatively, those players who tend to be risk-averse become more cautious in their decision making under stress. Research has also shown that in moments of stress, teenagers are less likely than adults to consider all relevant information and can rush to judgement. As has been emphasised in this book, the environment is especially important for the adolescent player and how coaches model and react to unsuccessful outcomes can have significant impact on the brain's ability to learn: 'Disrespect, shame and humiliation shut down learning in the brain in the same way as physical attacks' (Cozolino, 2013). So, environmental stressors created in the coaching climate might be counterproductive to optimum learning, particularly for 'emotional' adolescent players. That is, emotions such as anxiety, shame or threat might have a more powerful impact for adolescents compared to adults. As we've seen, this might be because the connectivity needed to contextualise and 'dampen down' heightened emotional reaction provided by the frontal circuits in the brain are not sufficiently connected in adolescence. This situation is compounded by the amplified emotional intensity experienced at this stage of development. A potential 'double whammy' of heightened emotions alongside still developing judgement and control circuitry.

Reframing anxiety

We know however, that anxiety can also prove beneficial for elite players, in terms of motivation and performance. Elite adult players have suggested that anxiety is often a facilitative state for optimal performance. The key appears to be how stressors are perceived by the athlete (Nesti, 2011). As such, coaches might facilitate the interpretation of anxiety as an indication that we care and are passionate for what we are doing, and that this is an indication of readiness for competition (Alred, 2016).

In view of the unique vulnerabilities of the adolescent brain, coaches need to create 'emotionally secure' and psychologically safe learning environments. If a player feels threatened either psychologically or physically he/she will not learn optimally. For example, the player might be less able to process higher order information such as technical and tactical detail if they are unduly stressed. Coaching environments need to offer secure contexts where players are treated with care and respect (Jones, 2009). Adolescence is a developmental period of particular emotional sensitivities. Excessive pressures or threats may be experienced differently by teenagers compared to adults.

For the coach this might mean explicitly creating 'experimental' sessions, as suggested previously in the book. These might be foregrounded as 'psychologically safe' periods where, for example, adolescent players are encouraged to take risks, test limits and experiment in ways that will not be judged as in 'normal' practice. In this way success criteria focuses on pushing boundaries, being inventive and creative; more of a spotlight on the process and less on the outcome.

For example, this might include encouraging creative play, one touch passes, extended dribbles with the ball, adventurous runs or playing in different positions. For coaches this might also include a reassessment of success criteria; less on outcomes, such as winning and losing, and more focus on mastery criteria. In turn, this exploits the positive aspects of heightened emotion in adolescence including strong passions and intensities, curiosity and a natural propulsion for new experiences.

Managing the emotional climate

A potential dilemma for coaches is how to balance challenge and support. How to cultivate a secure, potentiating environment but also mindful that in the 'real world' of elite football there are pressures and stress. Being able to perform under pressure is part and parcel of the professional game and exposing players to these environments in a 'calculated' and 'scaffolded' way is arguably the task of coaches and the development programme. Indeed, some of the most successful clubs in the world strive to drip feed more and more responsibility (and potentially pressure) on academy players as they mature, a developmental process that, ultimately, they believe will help foster coping strategies demanded at the elite level of the game (Nesti and Sulley, 2015).

The framework appears to include meaningful challenge accompanied with player support. The question for football development programmes appears to be: how to strike a balance between providing a safe nurturing environment, whilst at the same time exposing developing players to the stressful and pressurised environments that they will need to perform in? Learning appears compromised by pressure and anxiety at the neural level, where too much cortisol (linked with anxiety) actually hinders how neurons connect to each other; but at the same time, anxiety is part and parcel of the game. We know that a certain amount of pressure is optimal for motivation (Nesti et al, 1999). Just enough for players to be aroused and 'up for the game' but not too much that it has a negative impact on development. The challenge is getting the balance right. Too much pressure, especially with the amplified emotional reactivity in the adolescent brain, can result in players becoming overwhelmed and not in an optimal state for learning and performance.

A solution might be to create environments of 'calculated anxiety' or 'supported pressure', where adolescent players are gradually acclimatised to more and different pressures to prepare them for the adult game. That is, exposure to stresses that they may face as part of a deliberate developmental programme, where 'traumas' or 'speed bumps' are built into the curriculum (Collins and Macnamara, 2012). This may involve a deliberate games programme that exposes players to different challenges and levels of stress.

Consisting, for example, of playing games against older and younger players; playing against elite and grassroots opposition; playing on different surfaces; players' playing in different positions within the game. In this way, a varied games programme provides the 'speed bumps' and challenges for adolescent players, providing an incubation period to enable them to manage a range of emotions. This appears to have been the nurturing environment, for example, experienced by Deli Ali at M K Dons under the tutelage of former England youth coach Dan Michiche (now at Arsenal FC), where a varied games programme was used to provide differing challenges and learning opportunities (FA conference, 2015).

Research shows that at the elite level, anxiety is often perceived as a positive state, indicative of a player's psychological readiness to perform (Nesti, 2011). This has been echoed in recent applied work, highlighting elite performance in Rugby and Cricket (Alred, 2016). Football has been accused of leaning too far either way; either too much pressure too early or not enough pressure, 'too fluffy'; which does not prepare players for the real game. It is a conundrum. Do we teach the oars man how to row by putting him in choppy waters far from shore? Where he either rows or drowns or do we start him nearer the shore and gradually introduce more challenging conditions when he is ready? Some adolescent players will survive the intense environment (the choppy waters) but we will certainly lose some later developers, perhaps some of Kris van der Haegen's (Belgian FA) 'green bananas', along the way.

'Calculated pressure' or 'Scaffolded anxiety'
As a means to prepare adolescent players for the pressures they might later face it is important to explicitly create contexts within which they will experience such intense environments. Sometimes in elite academy football, staff, players and parents can find themselves feeling the pressure; all finding themselves 'in the red'; that is, where their thoughts and feelings are hijacked by the emotionality of the occasion (see Appendix). This is especially when there is an emphasis on the outcomes, such as winning matches, at the expense of the developmental process. From a developmental perspective it is potentially more conducive if the players experience the pressurised atmosphere of intense competition (for example, an important match), with the coach 'on the outside', psychologically and emotionally, less swept away by the occasion. The coach needs a long-term developmental perspective rather than caught up in short term outcomes. In this way the coach can 'be the prefrontal cortex' for the player; scaffolding the thinking, rational, deliberative part of the brain. The adolescent is more likely to be driven and processing the game through their emotional system whereas the coach, the adult, on the side of the pitch, can function differently, utilising their more mature frontal circuits. That is, in control of emotions, more composed, more 'in the blue' (see Appendix). On the side-line, the coach can be a role model which at the same time helps scaffold self-regulation and emotional control in adolescent players.

The importance of positive and composed role models on the side-line is inferred by the Head of Coach Education in Belgium, Kris van Der Haegen. He talks about getting the outside of the pitch 'right'. Levels of intensity and competition, he suggests, take care of themselves on the football pitch. It's part of the adolescent player's condition, he suggests, to be driven by emotion and have a competitive disposition in the context of a football match. This competitive energy takes care of itself. The coach, on the other hand, needs to be the 'cool head' on the outside, using their experience to help the players' acclimatise to the increased intensity of competition, modelling how to react and behave (see figure 12).

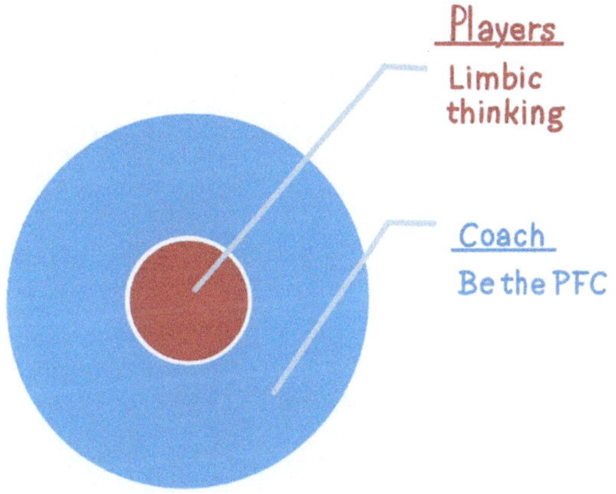

Figure 12- Adolescents are processing information more through their emotional (limbic) regions in comparison to adults who recruit more frontal (control) circuitry. Coaches can 'be the prefrontal cortex' for adolescents, modelling behaviours and helping strengthen neural connectivity

This is not always the case and sometimes, due to external pressures, the coach can get caught up in the occasion, losing the long term objective of optimising player development. We might have witnessed coaches, for example, who experience and show heightened levels of arousal depending on the score of the game, the level of competition or whether a senior member of staff is observing them. This can affect their own emotional systems and they can be operating in the 'red' rather than the 'blue' that is; their own composure and reasoned thinking might become hijacked and they might behave in a reactive, impulsive manner which may not be in the best long term interest of their players' development.

The underlying concept is to provide 'speed bumps' in the road for players; that is, create environments for them where they are exposed to contexts that they may later experience in the adult game. This might include introducing young players to more intense emotional environments, such as playing in the potentially pressurised atmosphere of a competitive match in front of a crowd. The recent introduction of the u15 floodlit league in elite English academy football can be understood to serve this purpose. For the player, they experience the intensity of a pressurised game where there is a valued outcome within which they can experience success and failure. This might help them acclimatise to the sorts of environment they will experience as they progress in the game. The important point is for the coach and club to see this as part of the player's long term development, something factored in to the developmental programme. Trial and error learning in this 'aroused environment' will help players' decision-making skills and help them manage their emotions, connecting and strengthening their own neural circuitry. The coach and the club might, ideally, have an objective, detached perspective where, even though the result of the game might be very important for the players, different success criteria are used by the staff.

They are on the outside looking in. Not caught up in the emotional intensity. The match can be the 'classroom' or the 'experiment', where the coach can manipulate the conditions depending on the purpose of the 'exercise'. Is an objective of the game, for example, 'how to learn to constructively react to defeat'? Losing 2-0 at half time can be grasped by the coach as an opportunity to make valuable learning points (see vignette below).

It might be an opportunity to challenge central defenders by playing two defenders at the back, empowering them to defend 1 v 1 to test their abilities. It might mean playing 9 v 11 in the game to put extra pressure on players. In the above examples, the results of the game are incidental to the objective of the lesson, to test boundaries and foster productive learning dispositions. Nesti and Sulley's investigations into 'the worlds best football academies' talk about developing psychological dispositions such as 'commitment' and 'persistence' through creating 'calculated trauma situations'. These might include, they suggest, playing with one player less in a team our playing against bigger, stronger boys (Nesti an Sulley, 2015).

This might be thought of as generating supported or 'scaffolded anxiety/pressure' where coaches can explicitly talk about how different challenges might affect certain players. The concept of anxiety can be explored with players and reframed as 'expected', 'normal' and even welcomed with further conversations around how we respond constructively or harness the energies of pressure for positive performance; 'getting butterflies (nerves) to fly in the direction you want'. This is the challenge for coaches; to get the message across that 'mistakes' or 'set-backs' are part of the journey toward maturity and how we cope with these challenges is the most important.

Another important factor in the development process is that adolescent players' feel a sense of security and belonging. Dr Dan Siegel's work on the adolescent brain talks of the need for a 'safe harbour' that provides a secure 'launch pad', enabling adolescents to propel into the world, giving them the foundation to develop their natural drives toward exploration and risk-taking. Bielsa, the Leeds Utd and former Argentina manager, talks about the need to 'love your players'. I think if players feel that their coach prizes them, as people, over and above their performances then they are more likely to express themselves in challenging contexts. Related to the developing brain this is especially important for the adolescent player.

**A potential team talk for an adolescent team:
Using the match as a 'learning lab'**

Your team are losing 3-0 at half time. As a competitive person, you (as coach) are as passionate as your players and as such you may well feel angry, frustrated and even embarrassed at the way the first half went. You may want to say (which the authors have heard) 'that was absolutely useless, you are an embarrassment to the club and if you do not improve in the next 5 minutes I'm going to replace each one of you with a younger team!'.

To say these things may make you feel better in the moment. It may be a method of alleviating your frustrations. However, is it the best way to either, get the best out of the players for the second half, or model how we respond to set back for the longer term? Despite these feelings of frustration, a more productive response by the coach might be to grasp this as a learning moment and frame the challenging situation as an opportunity for the players. As such, in an attempt to change the lens on the situation you might say something similar to this:

'OK we can't change what has happened; the past is the past. In fact this gives us a great opportunity. I've been waiting for a moment like this. This is a great opportunity for me (and yourselves) to see how we respond in a situation like this. Anyone can play well when we are 4-0 up but I want to see how we respond when things haven't gone as we may have liked. How resilient are we? How much 'bounce-back-ability' have we got? I want to be able to go back to the academy manager and say – 'young Tom didn't have the best of games in the first half but, by gosh, he showed fantastic character in second half. He ran his socks off, gave great encouragement to his teammates. You can really rely on him when the chips are down'. It's all part of the learning curve. Forget the score for the moment and focus on your game. So the characteristics we need are; encouraging team mates, wanting the ball, whether you feel you are having a bad game or not. Don't worry about mistakes, they are the routes to mastery. See this as a great opportunity to show your character in action'.

As a coach you need to give young elite players, some who may not have had many opportunities to flex their resilience muscles (because they have generally been successful in their football careers) the opportunity to respond positively from setback. They need to be given the opportunity to respond constructively to challenge. This is especially the case with adolescents, who may have a particularly heightened emotional response around, for example, a negative half-time score or a defeat. Similarly, over-reaction on the pitch to a word or gesture from an opponent may feel particularly salient for the adolescent. If a player finds it difficult to control his emotions in the 'heat of the battle' this might be related to their adolescent developmental phase and such self-regulation abilities can be supported and strengthened by the coach.

The challenge for the coach is to reframe negative emotions when things don't go according to plan. To scaffold positive strategies for the adolescent player and to dampen down any 'excessive' negative reactions. We are all disappointed when we lose, but what is the most productive reaction from the coach? The authors believe that the key is to harness the potential heightened adolescent emotions and redirect them into positive process goals for the player. Emphasising the positive will help take advantage of this unique remodelling period of development, characterised by amplified drives in passion, creativity, discovery and exploration. A pivotal point that can set in motion positive spirals for life. At the same time be mindful that this is potentially a period of heightened anxiety and emotionality that, left unchecked, and in unsupportive conditions, can hinder long term development.

In conclusion, coaches need to be aware that emotions are 'on fire' during adolescence. This offers great opportunities where players' passions, drives and energies can be shaped and guided. However adolescents might find it difficult to mange their emotions consistently, especially in highly charged contexts where 'rational', 'thought through' behaviours can be hijacked. During this time coaches can 'lend' their own frontal cortex, modelling more mature judgement and self-control abilities, to help scaffold players' own self-regulation development.

Chapter 5 - The emerging 'social brain' in adolescents

Main findings:

- Coaches should be mindful that the 'social brain' is reorganising during adolescence and marks a period of 'social reorientation'. These changes evoke an increased drive to contribute, connect and belong, especially to peers; along with a heightened sensitivity for status and respect
- Social skills such as empathy and compassion for others, cooperation and leadership skills are all 'coming on line' during adolescence and can be modelled and nurtured by the coach. Enabling adolescent players to contribute both on and off the pitch embraces natural drives at this stage of development
- Coaches can play pivotal roles for adolescents as role models or sources of advice and inspiration. This is especially at a time when there can be a temporary 'push-back' against parental figures
- Empowering adolescent players to work autonomously, beyond the obvious scrutiny of coaches, can trigger increased dopamine which is linked to enhanced motivation, focus, pleasure and learning
- Adolescents are primed to focus upon and respond to peers, especially popular ones. This can be utilised by coaches who can involve popular or slightly older 'influencers' to deliver and reinforce key messages, character traits and values desired by the club
- The ability to take someone else's perspective is still developing in adolescence. Coaches can help build this capacity through a patient 'developmental' approach and utilising coaching techniques such as playing players in various positions so they experience the 'lived world' of the other

Sport, when experienced in positive environments, has been found to contribute towards the development of fair-play, leadership and teamwork (Larson, 2000) as well as helping develop social, emotional and behavioural skills (Lerner, 2005). This is particularly important during adolescence where neural reorganisation involves profound changes in 'social brain' circuits (Blakemore, 2018). Many research studies show that specific brain regions, including the dorsal medial prefrontal cortex (dmPFC) and the temporoparietal junction (TPJ) are activated in social situations, involving other people or thinking about other people (Blakemore, 2018).

This might involve taking the perspective of someone else, seeing things from their point of view, evaluating the emotional state of another person or predicting their intentions. Social brain areas undergo prolonged maturation during adolescence as the brain adapts to profound and complex social changes needed to navigate new relationships and emerging changes in identity. These alterations have been linked to differences in adolescent cognition and behaviours compared to adults.

Part of this process involves changes in the way adolescents relate to their peers. The adolescent brain is especially primed to find increased salience in interactions with other adolescents. There is a drive to connect and belong, especially amongst their own age group. Indeed the adolescent brain shows more activation in pathways linked to pain when socially ostracised compared to adults.

'Cyberball'

Sarah Jayne Blakemore has shown, for example, in a simulated computer experiment, termed 'Cyberball', that adolescents show a uniquely strong activation in brain areas linked to social (and real) pain when 'left out' of a virtual ball game. That is, there is increased activation in pain circuitry compared to adults when the ball is not passed to them, even if they are playing with strangers. Feelings of rejection and social isolation appear particularly intense for adolescents in this study. Participants also reported stronger negative feelings around rejection compared to adults.

Cyberball

Figure 13 - 'Cyberball': Passing game where players are 'socially ostracised'. Adolescents show stronger negative emotional reaction (linked to pain) compared to adults and less activation of prefrontal circuitry associated with rationalising and perspective taking

Using the same 'Cyberball' method researchers have also found an interesting difference between the way that adults and adolescents are able to cope when they are socially ostracised (Gunther Moor et al, 2010). When they are left out of the game, adults were found to activate the prefrontal cortex, linked to rationalising and contextualising information, putting things into perspective thus helping them deal with the negative feelings. For example, saying to themselves that it's not possible for everyone to like each other or that they weren't too interested in the game anyway. Activity in the prefrontal cortex, likely helps them put feelings into perspective and at the same time modulates emotional reactivity. Calming down the negative emotion. Conversely, this study found that there was no activity in prefrontal regions for adolescents. It appears that negative emotions of rejection were left unchecked for adolescents, they had less ability to deal with the negative emotions rationally.

These findings are potentially important for coaches to understand and to appreciate the deep 'belonging' motivations for adolescents. The need for connection and a sense of relatedness, to be part of the group and the possible amplified emotions of being ostracised or not 'fitting in'. Coaches might need to scaffold certain decisions, such as leaving a player out of the team, with empathy and a 'long term explanation', contextualising the decision for the player. For example, a coach might offer a developmental reason the player is not selected or that the player will play in the next game but the squad needs rotating. In this way they are acting as the 'player's prefrontal cortex' by rationalising and situating the context, giving it a sense of perspective. These abilities, to contextualise and see things form others' point of view, are still developing in the adolescent brain. We know from research that in some contexts the heightened reactivity of the limbic (emotional) system is not yet regulated by the prefrontal cortex to the same extent for adolescents as it is for adults (Crone, 2017). The raw feelings of emotion trigged by an emotional event or thought might not yet be modulated by the later developing prefrontal systems, allowing unchecked emotions to 'run wild'. In this way the coach is also helping scaffold development of the player's own top-down processing, helping the adolescent player to develop their own neural connectivity, strengthening capacities for self-control.

Fitting in

Linked to increased hormones (testosterone) and changes in social brain areas, adolescents show an increased sensitivity towards social status and evaluation from self and others. That is why it is especially important for them to fit in and be accepted by friends. Having the latest designer trainers might not seem so important when you are an adult but, for an adolescent, evolutionary wise it feels crucial to be accepted and blend in with their friends and peer groups.

From an evolutionary perspective it is potentially a matter of life and death whether you are integrated into and protected by the group and this is still part of our DNA. Adolescents are especially attuned to the norms and values of the group. This can be for good or bad. For example, achieving acceptance and status in a street gang might involve different values and behaviours compared to achieving status in a sports team. Sports environments might profitably be designed to explicitly honour these developmental motivations through offering opportunities for positive social interactions with peers and adults.

This might be through foregrounding social behaviours such as empathy for teammates, respect and consideration for others (including opponents) as well as facilitating cooperation and leadership opportunities. These social capacities are 'coming on-line' during the adolescent period, and might be an opportune time to shape and develop, particularly in safe positive environments such as sport contexts.

Adolescents are motivated to spend time with their peers and less time with their family unit, possibly with evolutionary underpinnings; conceivably to help form attachments away from the immediate environment for autonomy, reproductive and 'safety in numbers' reasons. Fitting in and being accepted by their friends is part of the adolescent condition.

Despite a potential 'push away' from parental figures, adult influences are still important in adolescents' lives however, especially significant adults such as a sports coach. Football coaches have been found to play an important part in adolescents' lives. They can exert a powerful influence as they are involved in activities that adolescents are generally motivated to engage in but do not fulfil a teacher or parent role (Bowley et al, 2018). In this case they can act as positive role models for adolescents and help shape positive developmental spirals at a time where the brain is especially 'plastic' and ripe for positive interventions.

Rewarding friends - part of the adolescent DNA

We intuitively know that adolescents enjoy 'hanging out' and spending time with their mates. Enjoying the company of friends evokes strong positive emotions and research is now suggesting why this might be the case. Science is showing that the mere presence of friends and peers primes the reward centres in the adolescent brain, increasing subcortical activity and the release of dopamine, linked to pleasure, motivation and learning (Chein, 2011).

This sensitivity to being around their own age group, where social brain areas seem to overlap with parts of the reward circuits, has been linked with changes in adolescent behaviours such as an enhanced motivation to trying new things, explore novel situations and push boundaries. We know that adolescents find experimenting and seeking out novelty especially rewarding and has been linked to increased risk-taking compared to adults, especially if such behaviours confer status and admiration from the peer group. Traditionally this has been associated with negative actions such as dangerous driving, excessive drinking or generally reckless behaviours. However, an emerging perspective suggests that such a heightened sensitivity to rewards (amplified by the presence of friends) may also offer opportunities for productive, socially positive risk-taking, such as in sports contexts, that also honour adolescents' motivations for status, respect and social acceptance.

The amplified reward centres and increased dopamine (linked to motivation and learning) triggered by peer interactions might offer a potential rich learning resource. For example, giving adolescent players autonomy and responsibility to work independently, where adult coaches' presence is perceived to be less involved, might nurture natural drives and motivations toward novelty and creative play. Paul Holder, English FA coach recently remarked, that when adolescents are left alone 'a sort of magic happens' and that the coach shouldn't be too overbearing (FA seminar, 2020). The science is suggesting why this might be the case. It has been shown, for example, that the presence of adults can dampen down the reward centres (dopamine) in adolescent brain and decrease risk-taking and novelty seeking behaviours. This might be welcome if you have a teenage party next door and having an adult in the vicinity prevents undesirable outcomes. However, the presence of adults, such as football coaches or parents, might also stifle certain positive, desirable drives and behaviours, including taking risks, experimenting and pushing boundaries; behaviours that coaches' might want to encourage in adolescent players.

This understanding has potentially significant implications for adolescent learning environments. A coach that is aware of these neural developments, that to encourage certain types of play it might be appropriate to take a back seat with a more 'hands off' approach, might chime with the natural motivations at this stage of development. This also resonates with natural drives toward independence and empowerment at this stage of development. Reinforcing this point, senior English Football Association coaches recently remarked on the creativity and experimentation that can occur when teenage players are granted more autonomy. Particularly in playful, less judgemental environments which has been show to broaden the focus of attention and the ability to take on new information (FA webinar, July 2020). As such, empowering players to work independently in groups, transferring power to adolescents to make decisions (and 'mistakes') beyond the scrutiny of adults (similar to 'street football') can honour adolescent motivations. With the coach's role as one of a facilitator, formulating the structure of practice but letting go of outcomes. This chimes with recent remarks about street football by former England head rugby coach Brian Ashton MBE, reminiscing about playing football as a child:

> *'I was brought up in the era of street games. No adults, no coaches, no one to interfere and no one to inhibit what you were doing. We looked after ourselves and self-learned techniques to adapt to ever changing situations' ... 'By street games I mean giving players a sense of engagement by encouraging experimentation ... So the coach is not a looming figure dominating the landscape'*
> (Training Ground Guru, 2019)

The above remarks by Brian Ashton intuitively seem to make sense and now science might offer a theory as why this might be the case. Further, this new understanding around the adolescent brain appears to support and strengthen pedagogical theories such as Teaching Games for understanding and Games sense theory, which suggest that autonomy supportive behaviours are associated with more effective learning outcomes compared to 'traditional', more didactic forms of coaching (Light et al, 2012)

Key messages from key 'adolescent' messengers

The changing motivations of adolescents, becoming increasingly attuned and influenced by fellow peers, can be utilised as a method to help deliver key messages from coaches.

Adolescents are especially sensitive to influential and popular peers and are more receptive to the social norms that are set by such role models. Educational research shows that messages, such as eradicating bullying, when delivered by popular peers, is more successful than if delivered by adults (Yeager et al, 2013). Similarly, recent research undertaken in the context of adolescent behaviours during the 2020 Covid pandemic, explored the unique way in which the adolescent brain calculates risk and reward and the powerful influence of peers to modify adolescent behaviours (Blakemore et al, 2020). The study suggests that the unique sensitivity of the adolescent brain, particularly the strong desire to take risks and spend time with friends might make it more difficult for adolescents to abide by social distancing rules. The study proposes that key messages for helping adolescents to change behaviours and abide by lockdown rules has more success if delivered by peers and adolescent 'social influencers'. Linking with previous research it suggests that adolescents are more likely to listen to their peers or 'valued influencers' rather than adults, particularly if the messages are developed by adolescents themselves and not imposed by adults.

This is potentially important knowledge for football coaches to understand and to incorporate in their coaching practices. Coaches might use influential and admired members of the group, for example, to deliver and reinforce key messages that the coach wants to bolster. These could include general learning dispositions, such as determination and perseverance, or values such as respect or humility as well as technical and tactical information. This also might include empowering slightly older adolescent players, such as scholars, working with schoolboy players, to model and reinforce the kinds of attitudes and behaviours that the coach wants to foster. This taps into the natural inclinations to orient attention and focus to admired peers. As such, positive social and cultural norms can be influenced by key messengers in the club who might reinforce desired character traits. This might be through, for example, foregrounding social behaviours such as empathy for teammates, respect and consideration for others (including opponents) as well as facilitating cooperation and leadership opportunities. These social capacities are 'coming on-line' during the adolescent period, and might be an opportune time to shape and develop, strengthened by being delivered by fellow adolescents.

'Mentalising' – reading other peoples' minds

The ability to read other peoples' emotions and mental states allows us to predict what they might be thinking and feeling; anticipate what they might want and allows us to modify our own behaviours accordingly. These capacities are vital for effective social interactions (and might not be functioning optimally in certain conditions, such as autism). Science is now suggesting that the regions that are responsible for these 'perspective taking' capacities are developing throughout adolescence.

Brain regions associated with integrating the intentions and perspectives of others, something termed 'mentalising' or 'Theory of Mind' (Baron-Cohen, 2001) is still developing in mid to late adolescence (Dumontheil et al, 2010). A number of research studies have identified specific brain regions that become activated when we are involved in social situations or take on the perspective of another person. These include the dorsal medial prefrontal cortex (dmPFC) and the temporoparital junction (TPJ).

These brain regions show development in terms of structure and function during adolescence. One such study used the paradigm of a 'director task' (Dumontheil et al, 2010) to investigate potential developmental differences between adolescent and adults in their ability to see things from others' perspective and make decisions accordingly.

In the director task the participant is asked to take the perspective of the 'director' and move objects between various shelves. The director cannot see all of the objects that are visible to the participant. An instruction might include 'move the highest triangle across one square'. In figure 14 (below), from the perspective of the participant, this might be the 'red triangle' on the third shelf down, that is not visible to the director. The highest triangle for the director is the 'dark triangle' on the bottom shelf. So to perform the task correctly the participant must take on the perspective of the other person, the director. Put themselves in the others' shoes. Interestingly when the rule is changed to simply 'do not move an item with a card behind it' there was no difference between adolescents and adults.

However, when the instruction requires taking the perspective of the other person (the 'mentalising' condition) adolescents performed significantly worse than adults. This difference in behaviours seems to link to the structural differences in brain regions between adults and adolescents. This research might be interpreted to suggest that adolescents are less ready than adults to take on others' perspectives as well as their intentions, beliefs and feelings. That is, the ability to put yourselves in others' shoes, see things from their angle, is still developing in adolescence. In the adolescent brain, this area, known as the 'social brain network', is still maturing and not consistently functioning at adult levels yet.

Director's Task

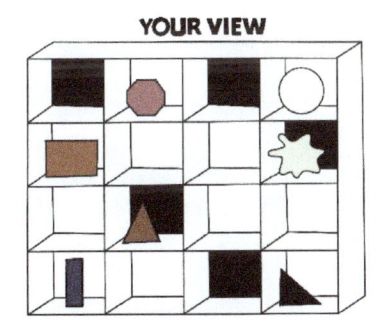

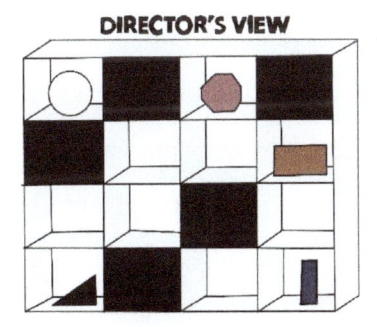

Figure 14- The Director task: The participant is asked to take the perspective of the 'director' and move objects between various shelves. (Left side front view, right side view from behind)

The ability to anticipate what others are thinking and feeling is arguably a very important skill for footballers. This might include 'reading the game', through anticipating what teammates or opponents are going to do next or helping a team mate who might be about to 'lose emotional control'. In other football contexts these brain changes might manifest themselves behaviourally as a player not understanding the intentions of the coach, such as not understanding the role that is required of them. Adolescent players may also find it difficult to accurately perceive the emotions of the coach. They might experience negative contexts as especially intense. Interestingly, we also know that adolescents, more than children or adults, perceive neutral expressions as threatening. It is worth bearing in mind for a coach that an adolescent player might perceive an environment as more threatening and hostile than it actually is, as a result the coach might go out of their way to make it as nurturing and secure as possible.

As we have seen, adolescent players might still be developing the ability to 'read' the intentions of team-mates and build the capacity to take on others' perspectives. This might be aided by the coaches through scaffolding an adolescents' understanding through patiently walking through patterns of play. Help the players to 'paint pictures' through slowly reinforcing key messages and explicitly voicing that 'if you do this then this might happen; whereas if you do this this might happen', This helps build consequential awareness in players. Research with police forces in the USA, for example, show that when police officers are taught about the adolescent brain, in particular the need to give explicit information about the consequences of future actions (for example, 'if you resist arrest or walk away then this will happen whereas if you listen and follow instructions this will happen), then arrests reduce dramatically (Bostic, 2014). Coaches should not assume the player knows what the coach means first time. To help build 'mentalising' capacity in adolescent players it might be fruitful to explain explicitly, in a detailed manner, what the coach is thinking and give reasons for actions, methodically talking through a decision. Coaches can utilise different mediums for presenting information and also allow players to construct understanding for themselves. Utilising a 'construction' rather than 'transmission' method for learning.

A further method to scaffold 'mentalising' capacity might include playing players in different positions so they can 'construct' for themselves what it feels like to play in that position. For example, play a forward as a full back so they can appreciate what a full back 'sees' or a striker as a central defender. So they can appreciate the 'lived world' of the other player. This is reminiscent of Denis Bergkamp's recollection of early work at Ajax academy, where he was asked to play in the position of a defender in order to gain the perspective of that player and see what he sees and feels.

Contribution

New research is suggesting that we can help adolescent motivations and general well-being by creating opportunities where they are able to contribute to others, to individuals, groups and to the wider community (Fuligni, 2018). In football contexts there are potentially numerous ways that we, as coaches, can facilitate contribution for young players, from simply empowering them to offer an idea to the group, to helping organise a practice session or facilitating a talk to a younger age group. It will be useful to dig a little deeper into the theory behind why providing opportunities for contribution might be positive for adolescent football players.

It has been suggested that helping others resonates with psychological and social motivations such as the fundamental psychological needs of autonomy, relatedness and competence as identified in self-determination theory (Deci and Ryan, 2000); and the social need for 'belonging'. Voluntary contribution to others can fulfil the basic agentic feelings of autonomy, increase social affinity and connection necessary for relatedness, and promote the sense of influence and usefulness that feed into competence. Contribution can enhance the need for belonging and a sense of group identification and has been associated with many psychological and general health benefits. For example, volunteering, and offering social and financial assistance and support has been linked with less stress, reductions in depression, reduced cardiovascular risk factors and lower mortality rates.

Although the drive toward giving and assisting others is a prevalent throughout the lifespan, adolescence appears a prime phase for the development of capacities and skills needed for contribution. The expanded social world of adolescence mean that adolescents have more opportunities to offer support to others. There is a natural drive to spend less time with the family unit, and to connect and integrate with peer groups, at the same time navigating an increasingly expanded and complex social world. This social reorientation is facilitated by enhanced abilities for empathy and recognising the needs and perspective of others and means that adolescents can offer more nuanced support linked to specific needs. There appears a development in the calculation for giving to others, from more simple equality evaluations in childhood, to assimilating more complex reasoning linked to an increased understanding of others' feelings, concerns, situation and needs.

Brain changes during adolescence indicate that this is a ripe period for the development of contribution. Brain areas found to be activated during contribution include reward pathways (striatum), social cognition (social brain areas) and cognitive control (prefrontal cortex), all of which are all developing during adolescence. Heightened reward activation linked to a peak in the availability of dopamine suggest that adolescence might be a prime time to support contribution. Pro-social behaviours such as offering support or ideas to the wider group have been found to activate reward pathways in the brain, conferring pleasure and reinforcing behaviours.

Being able to contribute to the group confers status and acceptance for adolescents and is linked with successful integration in the wider group. This resonates with one of the main motivations during adolescence; that of acceptance and connection with groups beyond the family unit, possibly for evolutionary purposes. Those who offer positive contributes to the group whether that's proposing an idea or providing support for others in distress are generally more popular that those with a negative influence, such as bullies. Especially where this contribution is recognised by the group. Further, reflecting on contribution enables adolescents to nurture their identities, reinforce that they matter and have effect, and helps develop the basic psychological needs of agency and volition as well as strengthening connection within the group.

During adolescence there appears an increasing capacity for complex conceptual understanding and abstract thinking. Linked with faster neural processing and stronger connectivity between brain regions there appears an increased tendency to contemplate other possibilities, an increased social awareness, a developing sense of meaning beyond the self and a growing sense of purpose. Associated with this, adolescents are often involved in larger community causes such as climate activism or political movements or community volunteer organisations. Research has shown that such contribution predicts positive health outcomes such as 'eudaimonic' well-being - a sense of meaning and purpose. It appears that adolescence represents a ripe time to develop these pro-social capacities.

Obviously not all people give all the time, and some people will contribute more than others depending on a host of individual differences. However, it does appear that, as a social species, there is a prime motivation to contribute to the wider group and that confers benefits to the giver and the receiver. Adolescence appears to be a ripe period for the development of capacities linked to contribution and that being given the opportunity to contribute does have positive social, developmental and well-being outcomes. To be able to offer ideas, support and advice to others strengthens the development of basic psychological needs such as autonomy, relatedness and competence, all associated with improved intrinsic motivation. These psycho-social aspects feature heavily in coaching pedagogy and creating the conditions where adolescent players can have opportunities for contribution, whether small (offering an idea) or large (planning and designing a practice, visiting a school in the community) can help develop adolescents both on and off the pitch.

In conclusion, adolescence is a period of social re-orientation where attention and focus is on connection and belonging, especially with peers. Being 'left out' is particularly hard for adolescents. Coaches can play a pivotal role in player development at a time of 'push back' against authority figures such as teachers and parents. Coaches need to be mindful of the amplified reward centres that are sparked when adolescents are empowered to have ownership and work with autonomy, and are encouraged to contribute both on and off the pitch. That might mean reflecting on the traditional view of the coach, of 'stepping off' the centre stage' and, at times, work as a facilitator and co-participant in the learning process rather than 'font of all knowledge'.

Chapter 6 - Coaching with the late adolescent brain in mind

Main findings:

- Adolescence starts earlier and lasts longer than previously thought. New research shows that 'late adolescence', that extends beyond the teenage years (18-22), represents a distinct phase of development with unique learning potential
- Peaks in learning signals during the late adolescent phase predict that players can learn and remember new information more efficiently than at any other age. However, the environment needs to be conducive for emerging capacities such as planning, decision-making, self-control and inhibition to flourish.
- Research suggests that the inclusion of non-judgemental, problem solving, creative, experimental environments might be optimal at this stage of development and can be blended into the young professional programme
- Training programmes that seek to extend individual skills and learning dispositions align with neuroscience findings suggesting this as a particularly fertile time for development
- Natural drives toward independence at this stage suggest that environments that support autonomy and independent decision-making especially motivate late adolescent players. Empowering late adolescent players in encouraging, problem solving environments can help develop their own self-regulation, judgement and decision-making capacities

Adolescence is often equated with the 'teenage years' however research is suggesting that adolescence constitutes a longer period, beginning at the onset of puberty and lasting well into the third decade of life. Indeed some are suggesting that this period is extending, with puberty starting earlier and entry into adulthood becoming more delayed with each generation (Steinberg, 2014). As such, this developmental period, where the brain is ripe for nurturing and growth, provides protracted opportunities that extend well into the late teens and early twenties. Football might previously have not grasped these opportunities for continued development but recent changes in approach, which is backed by brain science around the unique possibilities of the late adolescent brain, are seeing changes in coaching philosophies.

Developmental coaches

Elite English football clubs have recently appointed 'developmental coaches', tasked with working with younger professionals players, often in individual and small group contexts, aiming to optimise abilities and potentials. The appointments of individual development coaches at a number of English Premier League clubs seem to suggest a movement toward specialised programmes for young professional players, tailoring training to specific individual needs. A recently appointed development coach suggests such roles 'give them them that little extra attention and detail that they need'. These emerging coaching roles appear particularly appropriate as they chime with the latest findings from developmental neuroscience suggesting late adolescence (18-22) as a unique time for learning and development. Research has found that late adolescents' brains are both more plastic (adaptable to new information) and more sensitive and vulnerable to negative emotional environments compared to mature adults. 'Late adolescents' or 'emerging adults' might appear to be fully developed physically but science is suggesting that they are still a 'work in progress' in terms of emotion and cognition, offering both vulnerabilities and opportunities. These findings are potentially important for coaches working with players in and around the professional developmental phase and have implications for coaching environments constructed for this developmental period.

As has been noted earlier in this book, adolescence has been described as the 'Second window of opportunity' because of the unique learning potential for this period, equally as important for development as the first few years of life (UNICEF, 2016). The most recent research suggests that this window of opportunity can be optimised and kept open for longer to grasp the unique potential of the late adolescent phase of learning. (Steinberg, 2014). Traditionally, football has viewed the earlier developmental phases as the prime time for exploration and experimentation, with freedoms for players to express themselves and make mistakes in supportive environments. This freedom arguably starts to diminish as players mature, with more external pressures such as a growing emphasis on performance, results and contracts. Emerging research from developmental neuroscience suggests that such exploration, risk taking and problem solving might be equally as valuable for late adolescent players, to take advantage of this unique period of growth.

Late adolescence has been suggested as an optimal time for learning through problem solving, decision making and exploration in the environment. Recent research has shown that late adolescents (18-22) learn from feedback, in terms of trial and error engagement with the environment, better than adults (25+) and mid adolescents (13-17) (Davidow et al, 2016). The plasticity of the brain, that is, the ability of the brain to change, rewire and adapt to new environments is most pliable during this late adolescent period, particularly in frontal circuits. The late adolescent brain has been described as 'an adaptive life period during which the brain is optimally responsive to learning signals and new information' (Peters and Crone, 2017). The prefrontal cortex, that sits just behind the forehead, goes through most change during adolescence and is linked to high level cognitive tasks such as planning, decision making, inhibition and self-control. Part of what drives this dynamic brain reorganisation are adolescent-specific motivations to inquire, take risks and experiment in the environment, linked to increased levels of dopamine (a neurotransmitter associated with motivation and learning).

This is thought to have evolutionary underpinnings related to adolescent drives towards independence with motivations to inquire and adapt to new habitats. Traditionally, this propensity to take risks, push boundaries and test limits has been associated with maladaptive behaviours in late teens including excess drinking, taking drugs and fast driving. Indeed, research show that the main cause of injury and death in late adolescence is through preventable choices and actions (Jensen, 2015). However, an emerging narrative suggests that late adolescence is also a time of enhanced learning, where the brain is at its most efficient for information gathering; primed to seek out new experiences and to learn better from those experiences, than at any other time. Recent neuroscience findings state that reward activity in the brain, indicating heightened sensitivity to learning signals, peaks in late adolescence and that this 'can predict better current and future learning performance' (Peters and Crone, 2017). This unique phase of development might be an opportune time for coaches to design learning contexts that optimise late adolescents' abilities.

Recent research, for example, has shown that sub-cortical brain systems linked with processing reward (striatum) and memory (hippocampus) are at their most sensitive during the late adolescent period and that this exaggerated reward (learning) signal in the brain helps late adolescents learn and remember new information better than at other times in life (Davidow et al, 2016). Reinforcement learning or 'trial and error' exploration of the environment is how we learn, with the brain adapting to its surroundings through dynamic adjustments linked to increases and decreases of the neurotransmitter dopamine. The brain repeats choices that are successful (accompanied by the release of dopamine) and learns not to repeat actions that are unsuccessful (reduction in dopamine) (Willis, 2010). This research might be interpreted to suggest that the key for coaches is to create conditions where late adolescents are free to sample the environment and learn from their mistakes, which are actually an essential part of the learning process.

However, in elite environments, as younger players progress toward first team environments there might be less opportunities to focus on individual development. A developmental coach at a Premier League club suggests, for example, that 'if you are in that group of players who are young but not involved in the first team squad then where is your development coming from' … 'games come thick and fast and training can be just ticking over, where is the development going to come?'. It might be suggested that football clubs which recognise this potential gap and work specifically to refine the skills of late adolescent players are taking advantage of natural proclivities during this developmental window. This coach comments, 'I always use the example of a winger. Their job is to beat a man and get crosses in. But if they are only ever doing small-sided games in training when are they ever facing up a full-back in that area of the pitch? They are not'. Working with young professional, sometimes individually, to push boundaries and extend abilities, likely harnesses these natural instincts and motivations.

Keeping the 'window of opportunity' open for longer

Neurons are still firing at a faster rate (phasic firing) in the late adolescent phase of development, however this window of opportunity for learning begins to close depending on the novelty and stimulation provided by the environment (Steinberg, 2010). When a player reaches adult maturity and or the environment becomes less nurturing then this heightened period of developmental plasticity decreases, and neural circuits mature (settle down). The rate of firing for dopamine slows when the environment is less challenging or novel, less developmental. This can be a good thing because it consolidates and strengthens existing connections, enabling expertise; however, if the environment is just 'ticking over' then clubs are potentially missing an opportunity for developing players during this ripe period for growth. So if clubs create developmental learning environments for the late adolescent player, including young first team players, then this might keep the window of opportunity for development open for longer. As such the new developmental roles appear to be particularly appropriate in view of recent scientific advances.

Implications for coaching environments

What does this mean for football coaching with young professional players? Firstly, although an 18-22-year-old player might look like an adult they might not be thinking, feeling and acting that way. To harness the unique potentials of this late adolescent period, it might need subtle changes in coaching methods and the relationship between coach and player. Coaches need to be mindful that players learn through taking risks, testing abilities and pushing boundaries and not solely at early stages of development. An understanding of this developmental phase support coaching philosophies that advance the creation of secure, caring, non-controlling environments, where learners are empowered and have choice and volition (Light and Harvey, 2017: Deci and Ryan, 2000). Importantly, emerging scientific understanding around the adolescent brain reinforce and extend some of this coaching philosophy, offering a rationale and theory for practice, something advocated as critical for coach education programmes (Partington and Cushion, 2013). For example, research has shown that in negative emotional environments, the late adolescent brain doesn't function in the same way as an adult but rather reverts to mid-adolescence type processing, characterised by unchecked, heightened emotions (Cohen et al, 2016). As such, supportive environments that facilitate instrumental trial and error practices where players can experiment, and are free to learn from their own feedback, honour these natural drives. To learn by trial and error in a 'stress free environment is not a soft option but is essential for development' (Willis, 2013). As has been suggested earlier in this book, explicitly designed 'experimental sessions' might be cultivated that 'tap into' the unique motivations of the late adolescent period, where there are no 'mistakes' but rather 'interesting outcomes' that can be learnt from (Claxton, 2005).

Coaching conditions might take the form, for example, of 'boundary work', where practices are constructed to extend players to the edge of their abilities and test limits, designed to exploit this optimal period of developmental plasticity. This might include, for example, crossing at full speed for overlapping full backs or central defenders driving out the back, engaging with the environment through trial and error decision making, experimenting when to pass and when to run with the ball. Theory suggests that with the increased drive to take risks and explore, this will ignite a corresponding up-tick in cognitive function such as improved cognitive and emotional control capacities. Conditions that might exploit the potential of the late adolescent brain might include scaffolding this work as 'experimental', encourage pushing limits and taking risks that may be slightly beyond players' current levels of ability and, importantly, within supportive, nurturing environments.

Coaching environments that are mindful of the developing adolescent brain might also suggest a re-positioning of the traditional role of the coach towards more of a facilitator (or co-participant) in the learning process rather than director and transmitter of knowledge (Nelson et al, 2012). This approach echoes the position held in recent coaching pedagogy (Light and Evans, 2017), but extends this understanding by offering an underpinning rationale through developmental science.

This suggests a potentially difficult shift from the traditional role of the coach, with them 'stepping off centre stage' to a more 'co-participant' role that might challenge some of the taken for granted assumptions about the role of the coach and the nature of learning (Harvey et al, 2015). An autonomy supportive approach can empower late adolescent learners to explore and build on opportunities for developing agency through self-directed judgements, with the coach functioning in a facilitator capacity. It chimes more with the view of sports coaching as education rather than training, linked to the aims of developing inquiring and curious learners rather than technically proficient, passive receives of knowledge (Nelson et al, 2012, Dewey, 1938).

In conclusion, even though the late adolescent player may look physically mature, he or she may not be thinking or feeling in the same way as their adult teammates. Their brains are still developing and in negative emotional climates may be functioning more like a 15 year old than a 25 year old. It is still a time of enormous potential where capacities linked to the 'football brain' such as decision-making, emotional control, empathy and creativity are ripe for development, possibly more so than at any other stage. Coaches need to be mindful of this emerging knowledge and construct coaching environments that take advantage of this unique potential.

Chapter 7 - The learning brain and football

Main findings:

- 'Dopamine delight' and 'dopamine disappointment' guide and modify learning. Errors need to be seen by coaches and players as an essential part of the development process. Players need to not feel ashamed or fearful of making mistakes but see 'errors as the routes to mastery'
- Adolescents are particularly efficient at learning from trial and error engagements with the environment. Coaches can design learning practices that are more 'hands off', enabling players to build or 'construct' their own understanding through real-time feedback in a 'psychologically safe' climate
- Coaches can design explicit 'experimental periods' where the emphasis is on the process rather than the outcome. Creating a deliberate, non-judgemental context gives adolescent players a licence to work at the edge of their abilities, where they can push boundaries and gradually build their understanding and skill levels
- Empowering adolescent players to be 'in the driving seat of their own learning' potentially needs a reconsideration of the traditional role of the coach. This power shift from 'font or all knowledge' to 'facilitator' and 'co-participant' may offer challenges to the coach. Sessions might profitably be designed to nurture the natural motivations of the adolescent player, 'challenging' environments that develop a sense of autonomy and independence within a climate of care and belonging

How understanding learning at the neural level might help coaches?

'Dopamine delight and disappointment'

When enquiring into how adolescent footballers learn and how this might relate to how they are coached, it is worth considering how learning happens at the cellular level of the brain. The brain learns at the basic neural level by trial and error (reinforcement learning).

Those actions that are successful are rewarded with the release of a chemical called dopamine, linked to pleasurable experiences and serves to reinforce successful actions. Actions that are successful are repeated as the brain craves the dopamine to reinforce the memory trace of success. Equally important is 'dopamine disappointment'. Actions that are unsuccessful equate to dopamine reduction. The brain dislikes this state and memorises the 'error action' so as not to repeat again. The brain modifies actions in order to gain dopamine release. Successful actions are repeated; unsuccessful actions are avoided. In this way dopamine 'delight' and 'disappointment' guide behaviour. So, through a process of dynamic updates and adjustments, the brain responds to the environment, repeating actions that are preferred and avoiding actions that are not. This is learning. Recent scientific discoveries are suggesting that this learning process, of real-time, trial and error modifications, is most responsive and efficient in frontal parts of the brain during adolescence where '… there is a rich supply of dopamine, especially plentiful to help forge connections in the developing brain; to take advantage of new environments and to learn' (Luciana and Collins, 2012).

A crucial aspect of this process, and something coaches should be particularly mindful, is that the brain is allowed the opportunity to experience both positive and negative outcomes so as to dynamically modify behaviour. The brain has a memory trace of both success and failure, wanting to repeat the former and avoid the latter. In this process, undesired outcomes ('errors') form a useful and necessary part of the learning pathway. 'Errors' are an essential part of the process and should be treated as vital 'learning signals' for development. Self-correction is the key. For example, when a baby learns to walk, many actions might be described as 'undesirable', or a short term 'error', such as losing balance and falling down but these 'unsuccessful' experiences are critical for the baby's development, enabling the long-term goal of learning to walk. The baby, through a series of reinforcements, adjusts and modifies its behaviour accordingly. Importantly, there are no connotations of negativity attached to 'getting it wrong'. It is merely the natural way that a baby learns, through reinforcements of a series of 'successes' and 'failures'.

'Let errors be the routes to mastery' - Dweck
It is important for optimal learning that 'errors' or 'dopamine disappointments' do not carry negative associations such as guilt, shame or embarrassment. At a fundamental level the brain needs the experience of 'getting it wrong' as an integral aspect of the process of learning. In the context of football, the young player, somewhere in their development, needs to experience a series of 'failures', such as a cross going straight behind for a goal kick, a shot going over the bar, a pass being over-hit or a mistimed run flagged for off-side.

The player needs to experience what that feels like as a precondition to be able to modify behaviour; to put it right, to self-adjust. The player must be allowed to make the mistakes in order to build up memory traces, to construct the knowledge to guide future successful behaviours. Importantly, the learner must be allowed to make the mistakes in order to build up memory traces; to construct the knowledge to guide future successful behaviours. Fear of making mistakes will compromise this process. This chimes with social psychologist Carol Dweck's assertion 'let errors be the routes to mastery'.

This perspective demands a vision of learning which tolerates mistakes, indeed which frames them as a necessary consequence of learning, a learning opportunity rather than something to get upset about. It is interesting that recent research suggests that football academies such as Barcelona, Real Madrid and Bayern Munich increasingly encourage autonomy and responsibility for young players' development where they are encouraged to reflect upon and rectify their own mistakes (Nesti and Sulley, 2015). The key for the coach is to create the optimal environmental conditions for this self-regulation to take place. Where there is good balance between challenge and support. What might be termed 'scaffolded pressure' (see below).

Recent research (Walters, 2013) undertaken with academy football coaches gives insight into how this process of trial and error learning might manifest itself in a supportive football context. As part of this research two premier league academy coaches describe what they see as a 'facilitating football-learning context' that emphasises independent reinforcement, (trial and error) learning;

'...4 v 4's, there's a lot of opportunity to practice…killer passes, when to keep it, when to dribble, or when not to and I think you have to put them in, I think the best way of learning is through their own success and failure if you like. You shouldn't hinder that you should just let them.. ...They can work out when to hit it long, when not to, there's no pressure on getting it right or wrong.'

Another experienced academy coach suggests allowing young players time for their own trial and error learning;

'..he actually worked it out for himself, his movement, his mobility was better, so he learnt that himself through the experience of that 20 minutes – does that make sense?.. …and I thought about it after and thought if I would have gone in at the beginning and said.. "bla bla bla.. you do that, that and that", you know, in terms of his learning, I think he's probably learnt that in a more .. because he's learnt that himself, he's learnt it more fully'

These comments by professional academy coaches suggest the facilitation of 'constructionist' environments, that enable players to build their own understandings though engagement with their surroundings (Fischer, 2007). This might be a raiding full back making an overlapping run; being encouraged to attempt a first time cross at full pace. The attempt may end up behind the goal or at least not where intended. The player needs to know what that feels like, the experience of not getting his foot, for example, around the ball to keep it in play; the memory trace of foot connecting with ball. This will inform subsequent decisions. The 'dopamine disappointment', the 'mistake' will builds toward better learning if it is seen as part of the journey; part of a longer term developmental trajectory. The player needs to make the mistake to be able to correct it and modify his/her actions. He/she needs to be encouraged to keep practicing at this cutting edge of ability in positive emotional environments, where learning signals from the brain are at their most powerful. Further, this needs to be viewed as a long-term learning process because this particular skill might take years to perfect. One is reminded of players, like Gary Neville, who's ability to cross the ball at pace progressively improved over the course of his career; reinforcing the point that the adolescent brain is ripe for development throughout the teenage years and well into the mid- twenties. The nurturing environment at Manchester United undoubtedly helped this process. This also echoes John Stone's development at Manchester City, who has been encouraged to drive from the back, learning through trial and error engagements, experimenting when to pass and when to run with the ball. Importantly this appears to take place in a supportive, encouraging environment where mistakes are seen as 'part of the dance' (Beswick, 2000).

Brainy ways of thinking about learning

These football related examples of trial and error learning appear to align with the dominant model of learning espoused within the field of educational neuroscience. A model in which learning is characterised as an embodied process whereby knowledge is built and constructed through embodied action (Fischer and Heikinen, 2010). This also resonates with recent sports science research which advocates the development of decision-making by way of 'embodied learning through engagement with the environment' (Light et al, 2017), learning 'habits of action' through processes of adaptation (Davis and Sumara, 2003).

Further, this concept of learning aligns with a 'construction' rather than 'transmission' metaphor. That is, instead of transmitting information as in 'I possess this knowledge and I pass it to you and then you have it'. It's more of 'you building knowledge yourself through trial and error engagement with the environment'. This resonates with the discourse within the relatively new field of 'educational neuroscience' which seeks to replace the traditional model of learning contained in the conduit or transmission metaphor with an alternative model which understands learning as the active construction of knowledge (Fischer, 2009). Recent research, undertaken at premier league football academies suggest that football coaches primarily use traditional, technique focused, direct instruction in their coaching practice (Ford et al, 2011; Partington and Cushion, 2013) that uses a transmission model of learning, where knowledge is passed as if though the metaphor of a conduit (Fischer, 2007). The receiver is characterised as an empty vessel that is 'filled up' with the new knowledge. Using a football example, coaching a group of under 14s how to combine and play through the midfield may be most effective if the adolescent players are empowered to construct that knowledge themselves through trial and error in a 'psychologically safe' environment; where they can construct embodied experiences in stimulus contexts that replicate the game. Demonstrations, pictures, videos, verbal instruction will help but will not substitute for active learning until the players actively engage with the environment, preferably in supportive conditions that allow for trial and error modifications of behaviour. In this manner, through dopamine delight and dopamine disappointment the player builds that knowledge anew for themselves, with the coach creating a supportive environment (Vygotsky, 1978).

Further, the player needs to strive to improve in an encouraging, caring context. Research conducted in academies has suggested a climate of fear and intimidation can exist (Potrac et al, 2007). It is not a 'soft option' to provide supportive environments that encourage experimentation, rather, from a neuroscience perspective, it is essential for learners to experience their own dopamine delight and dopamine disappointment, fine-tuning their behaviour accordingly. Neuroscientist and educator Judith Willis states that to learn 'in a stress free environment is not a soft option but is essential for development' (Willis, 2010). Fear of making mistakes will compromise this process. The young footballers need to be given the opportunity to build their own memory traces. The young player needs to experience the delights and disappointments themselves with the coach adopting a more facilitative, advisory role. Yes, the coach can guide and it is essential that the coach gives regular advice but the learning process needs to be experienced by the player in a context which is conducive for learning. In an optimal learning environment, permission needs to be given to 'make mistakes'.

In academy settings that means in all contexts, both training and match level. Excessive anxiety, fear and stress are the enemies of learning as cognitive functions (attention, thinking, reasoning) are hijacked by non-conscious emotional systems concerned with fight or flight responses. Recent research has suggested that teenagers are particularly vulnerable to stress (Galvan et al, 2014), in part, related to a robust development of the emotional system during adolescence in comparison to the cognitive control system.

Experimental periods

A practical way in which academy coaches can 'give permission' to make mistakes is to explicitly provide a period of 'experimental' time, for example specific sessions that explicitly enable young players to try new, creative techniques, tactics, skills without the shackle of 'fear of making mistakes'. Indeed they can be encouraged to work at the boundary of their abilities, in the process making 'interesting mistakes' that can be learnt from (Claxton, 2005). These 'psychologically safe' experimental environments can be extended beyond training sessions to include match-play contexts. There may be periods of a match where players are encouraged to experiment with their play and decision-making.

This allows the players to push boundaries and to work at the edge of their abilities. We know from research around the adolescent brain that in such environments adolescents are better at learning from real-time, in the moment, trial and error feedback than both children and adults (this might especially be the case in mid to late adolescence). Coaches can scaffold this through giving licence to try things and make mistakes with communications such as 'I want you to drive out of the back with ball. If it doesn't come off, fine, I'll take responsibility'. Further, coaches can reduce the fear of making mistakes by stating, at the outset, that when players are working at the cutting edge of their abilities errors are to be expected and an inevitable part of the process.

Working at the edge of abilities and trying new things also enables players to practice how to control their impulses in the 'heat of the moment', on the pitch. Research shows that the best way to manage impulses, be it emotions or rewards, are in intense environments that actually push the boundaries of control. In this regard adolescent players are practicing using the frontal brain regions to control their heightened impulses, reactions and risk-taking instincts.

This helps strengthen the neural tracts between frontal and subcortical regions of the brain that are' coming on line' during this period. It is only by allowing this experimentation that players can develop the neural connectivity that strengthens their self-control. A racing car driver, for example, is probably very competent at driving on the road as he has practiced in extreme circumstances. The strong drives and impulses enables opportunity to exercise inhibition and control.

'Hands off' coaching environments

Creating a facilitative structure for learning, echoes Dewey's contention that we don't 'educate directly, but indirectly by means of the environment' (Dewey, 1916/17, p.19) and extending this concept, (Light et al, 2012), suggests that learning to make appropriate decisions is achieved through engaging with the environment rather than being told what to do; with an emphasis for the coach of 'getting the game right' (Thorpe and Bunker, 2010).

This chimes, it would appear, with the English Football Association's stated ambition of developing 'independent decision makers' (Future Game, 2010) and resonates with a 'hands-off approach', in which instructional behaviours are minimised in favour of allowing athletes to solve problems independently, promoting implicit rather than explicit learning (Davids, et al, 2008; Williams and Hodges, 2006). This also resonates with recent insights form the world's best football academies which suggest a 'less is more' attitude from coaches, facilitating autonomous behaviours in young players (Nesti and Sulley, 2015). Indeed research shows that when players learn through their own engagement with the environment, with less verbal instruction, this is less likely to break down under pressure.

The creation of learning contexts in which players feel able to experiment in non-threatening environments, aligns with a number of psychological research frameworks including, Self-Determination Theory (Deci and Ryan, 1985), Achievement Goal Theory (Nicholls, 1989) and Flow Theory (Nakamura and Csikszentmihayli, 2009). These theoretical approaches speculate that the environments created by social agents, such as coaches, that emphasise autonomy supporting behaviours, relatedness and positive feedback, promote intrinsic motivation which is, in turn, associated with promoting interest, enjoyment, persistence in the face of setback and improved performance (Hagger and Chatzisarantis, 2011). Further, positive environmental resources have been found to scaffold self-efficacy and self-belief in young football players (Bakker et al, 2011) and serve to facilitate core self-evaluations of one's psychological capital (Luthens et al, 2007). This view was echoed by an Academy director, interviewed in recent research (Walters, 2013) who argues that:

'You go in circles. To make errors to improve, but you're afraid of making errors because of that emotional attachment to it. That feeling of disappointment, anguish, anxiety… It's the biggest challenge for a coach, to create that environment where they feel free, anxiety-less to make those errors that lead to improvement'

Interestingly recent research has suggested that elite footballers from Brazil have learnt in environments in which there was limited involvement of coaches. These learning contexts involved designing their own practices. Araujo et al (2010) examines the unconventional environmental constraints on the acquisition of expertise in sports including football in Brazil and cricket in India. This research suggests that the development of expertise in Brazilian football is associated with counterintuitive and often 'aversive' environmental constraints including minimal formal coaching, unconventional material facilities (non-standard pitches, footballs, games) and a paucity of parental support. Expert decision-making, in this context, is developed through 'self-generated, non-guided discovery learning during play'.

Learning to play football - 'Just like riding a bike'
A useful analogy might be that of learning to ride a bike. No matter how accurate the description of how to do it, how clear the instructions and how forcefully the communications, there is no substitute for actually riding the bike! Even the best teacher in the world cannot transmit enough knowledge to enable the learner to bypass the actual act of learning, through trial and error, all the necessary skills to perform the action.

The novice bike rider needs to build up, or 'construct', his or her own learning, through immersion in the actual task. Verbal input from the side, however well intentioned, might just 'get in the way' and actually prove counterproductive and serve to 'put the learner rider off'. Indeed, the role of the teacher might be quite limited; provide the best possible environment, good bike, about the right size for the child, an appropriate size area to work in (devoid of unnecessary hazards), non-judgmental encouragement and the odd piece of well-timed technical advice. The rest, leave to the learner. It could be argued that, in many respects, learning to play football and the role of the coach in that process, is similar.

Helping Young People Learn

Figure 15 - Is coaching football like helping someone learn to ride a bike?

Now, that is not to say the role of the coach is not important. The coach needs to encourage regular limited adjustments to behaviour. The coach needs to act as the guiding expert, as in Vygotsky's 'Zone of proximal development'; to be on hand to offer advice and guidance, like a parent, such as steadying a child who is learning to ride a bike. To enable the learner to achieve more than they would left to themselves. However, no amount of verbal instruction or demonstration can substitute for the child actively engaging with the bicycle and likewise, young football players need to construct their own learning, build their own memory traces through immersing themselves in football action. A context where the coach adopts a 'hands off' role. Recent research into the best academies in the world suggest that 'less is more' in regards to coaching.

Responsibility for learning is given increasingly to players. Self-correction is encouraged. Steadily passing ownership for learning to the learner. In addition, we know from research that when the learner has more responsibility and control over what they do; that is when they are supported in having more autonomy in their learning, more ownership, then this has many benefits in terms of development. They are also more likely to perceive difficulties as 'challenges' rather than 'threats' if they have some volition and locus of control in what they do.

Trial and error learning – a football psychologist's message

The author was fortunate to hear an FA conference presentation by a psychologist from a top Spanish La Liga club. Her presentation was visually very effective and made both a lasting impression on me and also reaffirmed some of my own beliefs on learning and how coaches can support the learning process.

To the confusion and concern of the large audience she insisted on getting people to move their tables, set out in the style of a large wedding function, so as to clear a large space in the centre of the room. She was vague about her motives (she said 'deliberately so' afterwards) and we were confused as to what was going on. Why wasn't she just speaking at us like everyone else does! Then she started asking for volunteers! Eventually she picked a number of people and gave them roles; 'you can be a player', 'you a coach', 'you a stadium', 'you a training ground', 'you a parent'. She made a number of important points with these volunteers about how, when one thing changes, say a manager, then this has repercussions for the other people who need to be flexible within the organisation. She illustrated this by showing how when one thing changes the other parts have to change and move/be flexible. Then she got three 'coaches' paired with three 'players'. The players were blind folded. The goal was for players to navigate from one side of the room to the other. She moved around putting obstacles in their way, such as chairs and tables. At first, the coaches physically guided 'their players' across the room to avoid bumping into the obstacles (and possibly hurting) themselves. Then she asked the blind folded coaches to cross the room again but this time unaccompanied, and for the coach only to offer verbal advice.

The third time she asked the blind folded coaches to navigate the journey with no help at all (apart from imminent danger).

The psychologist asked the coaches and players how they felt when coaches were not allowed to give any guidance to their players as they crossed the room.

Coaches admitted feeling anxious by not being able to help their players enough. The players felt anxious about not receiving guidance. Eventually the players got better at navigating across the room. Using their own senses. Guiding themselves, with the coaches saying only absolutely necessary things to stop them hurting themselves. The process of letting go was difficult for the coaches. The point she made very well was that players need to learn by themselves. When they are on the pitch they need to make decisions themselves.

If the coach guides them too much, tells them what to do all the time, then this, in the long-run compromises their ability to make independent decisions. It takes away from their own initiatives and instincts. Short term it might work out but in the long run it deprives them of their own decision making skills.

Is the process of letting players make their own decisions bumpy? Yes. Will they make mistakes? Yes. Will they hurt themselves? Yes. Will they fail? Yes. Will the coach feel frustrated when they fail? Yes. Will they want to intervene? Yes. Will that help? Maybe, but not always. The process for player and coach is not a smooth one. Sometimes the journey will need different coaches with different obstacles but the end goal is to develop a player who has the resilience and grit to make their own decisions, hopefully in the first team. The best the coach can be is supportive when the player fails. Give some guidance but be prepared for the player to venture alone, even if it is frustrating for the coach and problematic for the player. The player needs to construct their own knowledge. It cannot be passed across but needs to built by the player through trial and error engagement with the environment; that is instrumental learning, how we learn naturally. Remember what we said about dopamine delight and dopamine disappointment. The player needs to be able to build their own memory traces of success and failure. They need to bump into the chair to know what that feels like and not repeat it again. The player will bump into things. How we respond as coaches to that and how we interpret and frame these 'mistakes' is important for the player's development.

In conclusion, the brain learns through trial and error engagements with the environment. In this process "dopamine delight' and 'dopamine disappointment' help dynamically adjust behaviours in the pursuit of goals. This is learning. The adolescent brain is particularly efficient at learning in this way. Recent models of learning replace the 'transmission' model with that of 'construction', where knowledge is built through engagement with the environment rather than passively received.

Coaches can help create environments that empower adolescent players and tap into their natural motivations to explore, test boundaries and take risks. Put them in the driving seat of their own learning. This might suggest a more 'hands off' approach for the coach where the main objective is 'getting the game right'; resonating with John Dewey's contention that 'we do not educate directly, but indirectly by way of the environment'.

Appendix - Integrating neuroscience within coaching sessions - utilising the concepts of 'red-brain' and 'blue-brain'

Out of the red and into the blue

Strengthening adolescent footballers' emotional understanding and control through talking about their developing brains

We know that adolescence is a time of heightened emotion which affords both opportunities and vulnerabilities. It is a time of strong passions, drives and impulses. These amplified motivations are part of the adolescent condition to explore, inquire and find reward in new experiences. However, the relative strength of the emotional system compared to the slower maturing frontal control circuitry, makes the adolescent period a time of potential impulsivity and emotional decision-making. Enabling adolescents to better understand their developing brains might help them appreciate and manage their emotions in more profitable ways. This is especially the case in sports environments which are often characterised by heightened emotional arousal.

Helping adolescent players manage their emotions in the context of elite academy football has been cited as a significant challenge for coaches (FA Advanced Youth Award). This chapter describes an exploratory psychological intervention that used pictorial representations of the brain to help foster reflection in academy footballers around their cognitive and emotional processing. The sessions were designed as a metacognitive exercise for academy players to better recognise and manage emotions both inside and outside football contexts. Researchers in the field of educational neuroscience speculate on the possible benefits of sharing new knowledge around their developing brains with adolescent learners (Choudhary, 2017, 2010; Blakemore, 2018). In social psychology this has proved fruitful, especially introducing the concept of neuroplasticity (the ability of the brain to change connectivity in response to experience) and the inference that intelligence and talents are not fixed, but changeable and within the locus of control of the learner (Dweck

1999). In addition to exploring the concept of adolescent neuroplasticity in the context of football (Walters and Hodge, in press), further sessions introduced academy players (9-16) to neural representations of emotional and cognitive systems. These were designed for players to develop a better understanding of their own brain and their emotional and cognitive processes which might, in turn, help scaffold a greater sense of autonomy and agency in their own learning; something advocated amongst elite football coaches (Nesti and Sulley, 2015).

The metacognitive process of 'thinking about their own thinking', including planning, monitoring and evaluation has been suggested as important for adolescent learners in the field of education and might equally be beneficial for academy football players. As such, this intervention aimed to aid self-reflection through offering players pictorial representations of what might be happening in their brains in differing contexts and how they might mediate this process. Consequently, this might be a potentially useful method to help scaffold metacognition in the context of elite academy football.

Into the blue and out of the red

Drawing on recent neuroscience research (Casey et al, 2010; Sommerville et al, 2016) simplified pictorial representations were generated of limbic and prefrontal neural systems as a method to deliver basic concepts of brain functioning (see Figure 16).
These were devised to highlight emotional reactivity and the connectivity between frontal (control) and limbic (emotion) systems that might mediate such reactions.

Although the method in which brain processing was explained inevitably lead to compromise in term of scientific detail, a simplified visual message was adopted to help make it as meaningful as possible for adolescent football players (and coaches). Explanations of processing, where appropriate, were contextualised within practical football examples drawing from both the adult professional game and their own experiences. Drawing on prior neuroscientific illustrations (Sommerville et al, 2010), emotional systems were coloured

Appendix: 'Out of the red' and 'Into the blue'

red and prefrontal systems were coloured blue, symbolically to represent 'hot' (emotional) and 'cool' (prefrontal) processing (Figner, 2011).

Top Down Processing

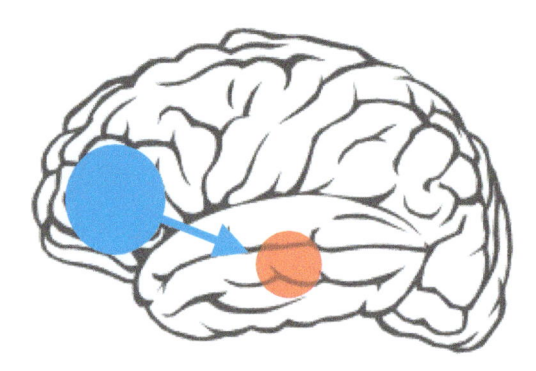

Figure 16 - Prefrontal and limbic regions suggestive of top down processing, calming emotional reactivity

Method

Whole group discussions, utilising PowerPoint, introduced the adolescent players to the concept of differing brain regions and the connectivity between them, simplified to prefrontal (cognitive control) and limbic (emotion) circuits. Players were given various examples, depicting an emphasis on either emotional or cognitive reactivity in the ascendency.

Different shades of colour and size were used to represent the reactivity and strength of brain processing in the two regions (limbic and prefrontal) and arrows illustrating connectivity and the relative dominance of each region. 'Emotional hijacking', where emotional reaction is relatively strong as compared to cognitive processing was represented as a large red shaded area in the limbic region with red arrows emanating from the limbic toward the prefrontal regions. In this way a representation of 'bottom up' processing was characterised in which emotion might be 'winning out' (Casey, 2016) in relation to cognitive control (see Figure 17).

Appendix: 'Out of the red' and 'Into the blue'

Football examples were explored such as players becoming angry, frustrated or anxious and this having a negative effect on performance.

Overpowering Cognitive Control

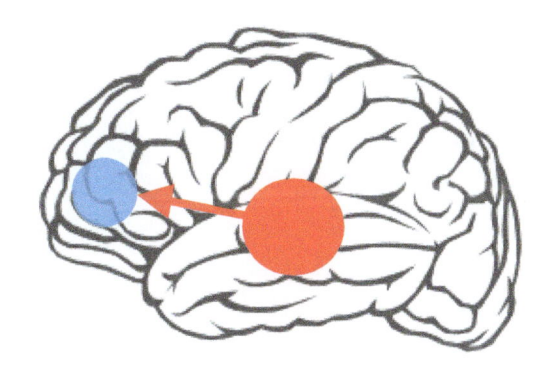

Figure 17 - Powerful emotional reaction overpowering cognitive control

Cognitive functioning in this instance was depicted as a relatively smaller shaded blue area in the prefrontal region, signifying reduced 'thinking' and control and where strong emotions might be dominating the capacity to maintain composure. To contextualise this, players explored football specific situations within which this type of processing might arise. The interpretation generated by players included; 'Zidane striking out in the world cup final', where it might be interpreted as Zidane losing control of his emotions. It was proposed that the heightened emotional response of the provocation (by Materazzi) might have overwhelmed Zidane's ability to control that reaction. Further examples generated from players own experiences included; unhelpful reactivity toward conceding a goal; making an error during the game resulting in not wanting the ball again for fear of making a mistake; becoming over excited in front of goal and losing composure; and becoming anxious before a game that has a detrimental effect on performance.

Pictorial representations were also given of the prefrontal cortex in the ascendency suggestive of 'top down' processing (see Figure 16). This was characterised as a large blue shaded area in the prefrontal cortex in relation to a small lighter shaded limbic system with arrows travelling toward to the limbic regions, suggestive of connectivity between cortical and subcortical brain circuits. The arrows direction of travel, from prefrontal to limbic areas, suggestive that prefrontal (cognitive control) regions hold relative dominance. This representation was framed for the players as the cognitive or 'thinking' part of the brain being in control of emotions. This was interpreted by players as being 'calm 'in control of emotions' and 'thinking clearly under pressure'. In this instance, where cognitive processing might be in the ascendency, players interpreted this as a facilitative state for optimal decision-making.

Strategies to strengthen connectivity

The sessions also focussed on the connectivity (or communication) between the frontal and limbic regions. This is an area that strengthens during the adolescent period and as such it was framed for players as an opportunity for metacognitive reflection that might help facilitate improved performance; that is, to plan and monitor their own strategies to help appraisal and management of emotions. To help frame the process for players it was suggested that parts of the limbic system might be interpreted as an 'alarm system' whose function is to monitor, detect and alert us to things that are important to our functioning such as threats or rewards.

The function of the prefrontal cortex, it was suggested, is to interpret these stimuli and communicate with our emotional system as to the best course of action. In situations where emotional reactivity is detrimental for performance, for example, when we react negatively to a mistake and fear having the ball again (common as suggested by elite academy coaches; Advanced Youth award), then we need strategies to sooth this alarm; to turn down the volume so we can think clearly during the game (get back in the blue). Using the visual imagery of pre-frontal and limbic circuitry the session progressed to explore examples of how communication from prefrontal regions (blue) might help sooth or dampen down emotional reactions (red) if deemed unhelpful for performance. Players were encouraged, in small groups, to interpret these pictorial representations of brain processing in the context of their own football experiences. Examples generated by players, to move from the 'red to the blue' included, using positive self-talk as a rebound strategy after setbacks; for example, after a mistake such as; 'it's gone'; 'I'll get the next one'; 'everyone makes mistakes'. It was also explained to players that emotional reactions are natural, show that we have passion and that we care about what we are doing and further that strong emotions are often facilitative for good performance (Nesti, 2012). For example, anxiety before a game is ubiquitous and sometimes signals a state of readiness for elite players and can be perceived as a 'fuel to aid performance' (Alred, 2016).

It was important for players to realise, we believed, that emotions such as anger, frustration and anxiety were to be expected and could be used productively. It was also suggested that just by recognising and naming emotions ('I'm feeling angry') this can kick start frontal networks which can then begin the process of soothing unhelpful emotional reactions (Siegel, 2013). This might be viewed as a way of helping players monitor and manage their emotions and, in so doing, might help strengthen autonomy and locus of control.

Conversation tools

A variety of visual representations of emotion-cognitive scenarios were given to players as a method for them to explore and discuss differing emotional reactivity within the game. This was also an opportunity to share with peers any of the scenarios that might resonate with their own game, thus aiding metacognitive reflection for players. Visual representations also provided an opportunity for coaching staff to use as a tool to talk individually with players about issues they had observed in their game. One player, for example, had recently experienced heightened and unhelpful emotional reactions that were detrimental to his performance, including 'making mistakes' (and not wanting the ball) and being substituted (becoming upset so he would not want to return onto the field). The pictorial representations were used by his coach (spontaneously in the session) as a medium to explore what heightened emotion might mean for him and strategies that might help manage these situations. In this instance it was suggested to draw on some of the advice given by our first team players to 'mistakes' on the pitch such as positive self-talk; 'it's gone', 'I'll get the next one' 'play it simple and get back into credit', and further core-beliefs such as 'we all make mistakes' and 'to learn we must take risks'; 'everyone gets nervous before a game'. In this case the visual representations became a useful discussion tool for coaches to prompt metacognitive reflection and explore strategies to manage emotions.

'Keeping in the blue and out of the red'

An overarching aim of these sessions was for players to better able understand and manage their emotions. How can we nudge players more into the blue and less in the red? Firstly, we might create environments that are potentiating for players such that emotional reactions are facilitative and not detrimental for performance. That is where heightened emotions are channelled toward challenge and not threat, that tap into the natural proclivity toward risk-taking during adolescence (Blakemore, 2018). Arguably, if we instil an incremental motivational framework (Dweck, 2006) such that mistakes are appraised as part of the journey and risk-taking is perceived as essential for learning; and where success is measured by process goals such as effort rather than outcome goals such as results; then such environments might mean that negative emotional reactions are less intense; the alarm does not go off so frequently or so 'loud'. If it does go off, which is inevitable in football, how can we sooth that alarm to 'bring the player back into the blue?'

Practical applications

Academy coaches who sat in on the psychology sessions appeared to engage with the concepts and were quickly using some of the terminology in their coaching practice. For example, coaches used terms such as 'let's get back in the blue' after players had become frustrated or angry after losing the ball or conceding a goal. One coach suggested to a player that he was operating 'in the red' when remaining upset after conceding a goal and suggested strategies to get back 'into the blue'. Interestingly this narrative of staying in the blue and keeping out of the red was recently reported as being used by psychologists working with the

All Black New Zealand rugby team (see Training Ground Guru, May 2018) which describes players having a 'Red Head' in 'hot' contexts (anxious, inhibited, tense) or Blue Head when 'cool' (calm, composed, in control). The above intervention supports the psychological concept of 'red head' and 'blue head' through offering new scientific understanding of the developing adolescent brain.

The above describes how off-field interventions, drawing on the sciences of mind, brain and education, might aid reflection for players and staff to help better recognise and manage emotions in academy football contexts.

Concluding remarks

The main goal of this 'theoretical' part of the book has been to frame adolescence as a period of unique opportunity, where natural drives and motivations toward novelty, risk and experimentation can be guided by the coach to maximise the learning potential of young players. Long thought of as a 'troubled period' of development we can now see that dynamic brain changes during adolescence have potentially adaptive functions that can be nurtured on the path toward adulthood and maturity. Differences in emotional intensity, decision-making, social relationships and learning mean that adolescents likely think, perceive and behave in different ways to children and adults both on and off the pitch. This new knowledge can hopefully add to the holistic understanding of player development for coaches. Overall, our emerging understanding of the adolescent brain suggests it as a time of enormous potential. We now know that the brain develops not through getting bigger but by dynamic reorganisation and remodelling, specifically in frontal regions during adolescence.

Coaches working with adolescent players can structure environments that work with these natural motivations, instincts and drives. Coaches can to be mindful that players learn through taking risks, testing abilities and pushing boundaries and not solely at early stages of development but also into late adolescence. An understanding of this developmental phase support coaching philosophies that advance the creation of secure, caring, non-controlling environments, where learners are empowered and have choice and volition. An autonomy supportive approach can empower adolescent learners to explore and build on opportunities for developing agency through self-directed judgements, with the coach functioning in a facilitator capacity. It chimes more with the view of football coaching as education rather than training, linked to the aims of developing inquiring and curious learners rather than technically proficient, passive receivers of knowledge.

Underpinning this approach is an unconditional positive regard for the young player, where they are valued as a person first, before their performance as a player. These kinds of coach behaviours strengthen adult-player connections and are linked to increased intrinsic motivation and psychological safety for players. Football coaches are important figures in adolescent players' lives and these relationships are especially important in light of a potential push-back against the family unit during this developmental stage.

The adolescent player needs opportunity to make decisions and hold responsibility in supportive environments where they can learn from the outcomes of their choices. Positive as well as negative. Empowering players to explore responsibilities and provide space for contribution in supportive environments, provides for the basic drives toward autonomy and independence and helps scaffold the player's own learning. Although this might involve more power sharing than is traditionally the case between coach and player it enables the adolescent to adapt to their surroundings through experiential engagement with their environments; to refine their neural connectivity in safe and secure conditions where their brains are more sensitive to reinforcement learning processes. The coach might be seen as more of a 'guide on the side' and co-participant rather than the more traditional didactic, dominant figure. The new science of the adolescent brain offers a rationale for why these kinds of coaching behaviours are especially important and timely.

The first part of this book has focused on recent insights from the science of the adolescent brain and explored where this new understanding might be meaningful and have relevance for football coaches. The next part looks at how practical sessions might be tailored with the adolescent brain in mind.

References

Albert D, Chein J, Steinber L (2103) The Teenage Brain: Peer Influences on Adolescent Decision Making. Current directions in psychological science *APS Vol. 22 Issue 2. p114-120*

Albert E, Trent A. Petrie & E. Whitney G. Moore (2019) The relationship of motivational climates, mindsets, and goal orientations to grit in male adolescent soccer players. *International Journal of Sport and Exercise Psychology*

Allpress J (2006). Managing mistakes to the players' advantage: lessons from coaching in football (soccer). Development and Learning in Organizations. Volume: 20 Issue: 4 Page:6

Alred D. (2016). The Pressure Principle: Handle Stress, Harness Energy, and Perform When It Counts. Penguin Life

Araújo, D., Fonseca, C., Davids, K., Garganta, J., Volossovitch, A., Brandão R and Krebs R (2010) The Role of Ecological Constraints on Expertise Development Talent Development & Excellence Vol. 2, No. 2, p.165–179

Bakker, A B, Oerlemans, W, Demerouti E, Slot, B B, Ali, D K (2011) Flow and performance: A study among talented Dutch soccer players Psychology of Sport and Exercise 12 (2011) 442-450

Baird A, A, and Fugelsang J, A (2004) The emergence of consequential thought; Evidence from neuroscience. Biological Sciences, 359, 1797-1804

Baron-Cohen S (2001) Theory of Mind; Prisme, 34, 174-183

Bechara A, Damassio H, Tranel D, Damassio AR, (2005) Gambling task and somatic marker hypothesis: some questions and answers. Trends Cogn. Sci 9, 159-162

Beswick B (2000) Focussed for Soccer. Human Kinetics Publishers

Blackwell, L; Trzesniewski K H; Dweck C (2007) Implicit Theories of Intelligence Predict Achievement Across an Adolescent Transition: A Longitudinal Study and an Intervention Child Development, Volume 78, Number 1, Pages 246 – 263

Blakemore, S-J., Winston, J., & Frith, U. (2004) Social cognitive neuroscience: where are we heading? Trends in Cognitive Science, 8; 216-222

Blakemore, S.J., 2008. Development of the social brain during adolescence. The Quarterly Journal of Experimental Psychology 61, 40–49.

Blakemore, S.J., Choudhury, S., 2006. Development of the adolescent brain: implications for executive function and social cognition. Journal of Child Psychology and Psychiatry and Allied Disciplines 47, 296–312.

Blakemore S J (2018) Inventing Ourselves: The secret life of the teenage brain. Penguin. Random

Bostic J Q et al (2014) 'Policing the teen brain'. Journal of the American Academy of child and adolescent psychiatry 53 (2): 127-9

References

Bowley C, Cropley B, Neil R, Mitchel I (2018). A life skills development programme for youth football. Sport and exercise psychology review 14 (1), 3-22

Bruner, J. T. (1997). Education and the brain: A bridge too far. Educational Researcher, 26, 4–16.

Casey, B.J., Getz, S., Galvan, A., (2008). The Adolescent Brain. Developmental Review 28 (1), 62–77.

Casey, B.J., Jones, R.M., 2010. Neurobiology of the adolescent brain and behavior: implications for substance use disorders. J. Am. Acad. Child Adolesc. Psychiatry 49, 1189–1201.

Casey, B.J., & Caudle, K. (2013). The teenage brain: Self-control. Current Directions in Psychological Science, 22, 82-87. Cauffman, E., Shulman, E.P., Steinberg, L., Claus, E.,

Chein, J., Albert, D., O'Brien, L., Uckert, K., Steinberg, L., 2011. Peers increase adolescent risk taking by enhancing activity in the brain's reward circuitry. Dev. Sci. 14, F1–F10.

Claxton G and Allpress J Smart Coaching. Insight. The FA Coaches Association Journal. Autumn (2005). 8-9

Choudhary S (2017) Situating the adolescent brain: The developing brain and its cultural contexts. UNICEF 2017: The Adolescent Brain: A second window of opportunity. A compendium. p. 39-45

Cohen, J.R., Asarnow, R.F., Sabb, F.W., Bilder, R.M., Bookheimer, S.Y., Knowl-ton, B.J., Poldrack, R.A., 2010. A unique adolescent response to reward prediction errors. Nat. Neurosci. 13 (6), 669–671.

Collins, D and Macnamara (2012) 'The Rocky Road to the Top Why Talent Needs Trauma'; *Sports Medicine 42(11):907-14*

Crocker, P.R.E., Tamminen, K. A., & Gaudreau, P. (2015). Coping in sport. In S. Hanton & S. Mellalieu (Eds.), Contemporary advances in sport psychology: A review (pp.28-67). New York: Routledge.

Crone E, A,. & van Leijenhorst, L (2010) Paradoxes in adolescent risk taking in Eds. Zelazo, P, D,. Chandler, M,. & Crone E, Developmental Social Cognitive Neuroscience (2010). Psychology Press

Crone, E.A., Ridderinkhof, K.R., (2011) The developing brain: from theory to neuroimaging and back. Developments in Cognitive Neuroscience 1, 101–109.

Crone, E., Dahl, R. Understanding adolescence as a period of social–affective engagement and goal flexibility. *Nat Rev Neurosci* **13,** 636–650 (2012).Crone E. A. (2017) The Adolescent Brain: Changes in learning, decision-making and social relations; Routledge

Cohen J D (2005). The vulcanisation of the human brain. A neural perspective on interactions between cognition and emotion. Journal of Economic Perspectives, 19, 3-2
Cohen et al, (2016) 'When is an adolescent an adult ....": Psychological science vol. 27(4) 549-562

Cushion, C. (2010) Coach and athlete learning, in: R. L. Jones, P. Potrac, C. Cushion & L.T. Ronglan (Eds) The sociology of sports coaching (London, Routledge).

References

Dahl R E, Allen N B, Wilbrecht L, Suleiman A B (2018) Importance of investing in adolescence from a developmental science perspective. *Nature. vol. 554: p.441-450*

Daley C., Wei Ong C., McGregor P. (2020) 'Applied psychology in academy soccer settings' in The Psychology of soccer Dixon J G et al; Routledge

Davidow et al (2016) 'An upside to reward sensitivity .....': Neuron 92 93-95

Davidow et al (2018) 'Adolescent development of value guided goal pursuit': Trends in cognitive sciences vol 22 no.8

Davids, K., Button, C., & Bennett, S. (2008). Dynamics of skill acquisition: A constraints led approach. Champaign, IL: Human Kinetics.

Davis, B. & Sumara, D. (2003) Why aren't they getting this? Working through the regressive myths of constructivist pedagogy, Teaching Education, 14(2), 123_140.

Davis E L, Levine L J, Lench H C, and Quas J A (2010) Metacognitive Emotion Regulation: Children's Awareness that Changing Thoughts and Goals Can Alleviate Negative Emotions: Emotion 10 (4) p.498-510

Deci, E.L. and Ryan, R.M. (1985). Intrinsic Motivation and Self-Determination in Human

Behaviour. New York: Plenum Press.

Deci and Ryan (2000) 'The what and why of goal pursuits': Psychological Enquiry, 11, 227-268

Dewey (1916/97) "Democracy in Education': New York. Free press

Dewey, J. (1925). Experience and nature. Whitefish, MT: Kessinger.

van Duijvenvoorde, A.C.K., Jansen, B.R.J., Visser, I., Huizenga, H.M., 2010. Affective and cognitive decision-making in adolescents affective and cognitive decision-making in adolescents. Dev. Neuropsychol. 35, 539–554.

van Duijvenvoorde, A.C.K, Peters S, Braams B R, Crone E A. What motivates adolescents? Neural responses to rewards and their influence on adolescents' risk taking, learning and cognitive control: *Neuroscience and Biobehavioural Reviews. 70 (2016) 135-147*

Dweck, C. S., & Leggett, E. L. (1988). A social-cognitive approach to motivation and personality. Psychological Review, 95, 256 – 273.

Dweck C. S. (1999). Self-Theories. Their Role in Motivation, Personality, and Development. Taylor and Francis

Dweck C. S. (2006). Mindset: The Psychology of Success. Random House

Duckworth A L, Gendler T S, & Gross J J (2014) Self-control in school age children; Educational Psychologist 49, 199-217

Duckworth A and Steinberg L, (2015) Unpacking self-control. Child Development Perspectives. Vol.9. Issue 1 p. 32-37

References

Ericsson, K. A. (2006). The influence of experience and deliberate practice on the development of superior expert performance. In K. A. Ericsson, N. Charness, P. J. Feltovich, & R. R. Hoffman (Eds.), The Cambridge handbook of expertise and expert performance (pp. 683–704). New York: Cambridge University Press.

Ernst, M., Pine, D.S., Hardin, M., (2006). Triadic model of the neurobiology of motivated behavior in adolescence. Psychol. Med. 36, 299–312.

Ernst, M., Romeo, R.D., Andersen, S.L., 2009. Neurobiology of the development of motivated behaviors in adolescence: a window into a neural systems model. Pharmacol. Biochem. Behav. 93, 199–211.

Figner, B., Murphy, R.O., 2011. Using skin conductance in judgment and decision making research. In: Schulte-Mecklenbeck, M., Kue-hberger, A., Ranyard, R. (Eds.), A handbook of Process Tracing Methods for Decision Research. Psychology Press, New York, NY, pp. 163–184.

Fischer, K. W., Daniel, D. B., Immordino-Yang, M. H., Stern, E., Battro, A., & Koizumi, H. (Eds.).(2007). Why mind, brain, and education? Why now? Mind, Brain, and Education, 1(1), 1–2.

Fischer K, W,. & Heikkinen, K. The Future of Educational Neuroscience. in Ed. Sousa D, A (2010) Mind, Brain and Education. Neuroscience implications for the classroom. Solution Tree press

Ford, P.R, Yates I., & Williams A.M. (2010): An analysis of practice activities and instructional behaviours used by youth soccer coaches during practice: Exploring the link between science and application, Journal of Sports Sciences, 28:5, 483-495

Forde, M (2010) in Nesti, M,. (2010) Psychology in Football. Working with Elite and Professional Players. Routledge p.X

Fuligni A J (2018) The need to contribute during adolescence. *Perspectives in Psychological Science* 1-13. APS

'Future Game' (2010) Document. FA Learning. Wembley Stadium

Galvan, A., (2010). Adolescent development of the reward system. Frontiers in Human. Neuroscience. 4, 6. P.1-9

Galvan, A., Hare, T., Voss, H., Glover, G., & Casey, B.J. (2008). Risk-taking and the adolescent brain: who is at risk? Developmental Science, 10 (2), F8–F14.

Galvan, A,. 'The Washington Post', (March, 2020)

Gardner L A, Vella S A, Magee C A, (2015) The relationship between implicit beliefs, anxiety, and attributional style in high level soccer players. *Journal of Applied Sport Psychology 27:4, 398-411*

Giedd, J.N., 2008. The teen brain: insights from neuroimaging. J. Adolesc. Health 42 (4), 335–343

Giedd J.N. 'The Amazing Teen Brain' Scientific American 312, (2015), 32-37

Gilbourne, D., & Richardson, D. (2006). Tales from the field: Personal reflections on the provision of psychological support in professional soccer. *Psychology of Sport and Exercise, 7,* 325-337.

References

Hagger, M. S., & Chatzisarantis, N. L. D. (2011). Causality orientations moderate the undermining effect of rewards on intrinsic motivation. Journal of Experimental Social Psychology, 47(2), 485-489.

Hardy, L. and Whitehead, R. (1984). Specific modes of anxiety and arousal. Current Psychological Research and Reviews, 3, 14–24.

Hare T, A,. (2007b) Competition between pre-frontal and subcortical limbic systems underlie emotional reactivity during adolescence. In Casey et al (2008) Ibid.

Hartley C A and Somerville L H (2015) The neuroscience of adolescent decision-making: *Science Direct 5: 108-115*

Harvey, S., Light R,L (2015) Questioning for learning in game-based approaches to teaching and coaching. APJHSE. Vol. 6 issue 2 175-90

Harwood, C.G. (2008). Developmental consulting in a professional soccer academy: The 5C's coaching efficacy program. The Sport Psychologist, 22, 109-133.

Heckman JJ and Rubinstein Y (2001) The importance of non-cognitive skills. Lessons from the GED testing programme. American Economic Review, 91 (2) 145-149

Heilman et al (2003) Creative innovation: Possible brain mechanisms Neurocase 9 369-379

Hooper, C, J,. Luciana, M Conklin, H, M, and Yarger R, (2004) Adolescents' Performance on the Iowa Gambling Task: Implications for the Development of Decision Making and Ventromedial Prefrontal Cortex. Developmental Psychology 2004, 40, 6. 1148–1158

Howard-Jones P. A. (2008) Fostering Creative Thinking. Co-constructed Insights from Neuroscience and Education. Bristol. Escalate

Howard-Jones P. A. (2010) Introducing Neuroeducational research. Neuroscience, education and the brain from contexts to practice. Routledge

Howard-Jones P, A,. (2011) From brain scan to lesson plan. Psychologist 24 2 pp.110-113

Huizinga, M., Dolan, C.V., van der Molen, M.W., (2006). Age-related change in executive function: developmental trends and a latent variable analysis. Neuropsychologia 44 (11), 2017–2036.

IDYOMS workshops (2021). Interviews with professional academy coaches exploring how insights around the adolescent brain might be useful for football understanding and practice. IDYOMS website: Idyoms.org

Immordino-Yang, M. H (2007). A tale of two cases: Lessons for education from the study of two boys living with half their brains. Mind, Brain and Education 1, 66-83

Immordino-Yang, M. H (2010) 'The role of emotion and skilled tuition in learning' in Souza D, A,. (2010) Mind, Brain and Education: Implications for the classroom. Solution Tree Press 69-83

References

Jensen F.E. and Nutt A.E. (2015). THE TEENAGE BRAIN: A Neuroscientist's Survival Guide to Raising Adolescents and Young Adults: Harper Collins

Jones M.V. Controlling Emotions in Sport, The Sport Psychologist, Volume 17:3 (2003), 471-486Pages: 471–486

Jones R L, (2009) Coaching as caring (the smiling gallery): accessing hidden knowledge.

Physical Education and Sport Pedagogy. 14(4):377-39.

van Leijenhorst L., V., Zanolie, K, Van Meel, C S, Crone E, A, (2009) What motivates the adolescent? Brain regions mediating reward sensitivity across adolescence. Cerebral cortex 30

Van Leijenhorst, L., Moor, B.G., Op de Macks, Z.A., Rombouts, S.A., West-enberg, P.M., Crone, E.A., 2010. Adolescent risky decision-making: neurocognitive development of reward and control regions. Neuroim-age 51 (1), 345–355.

Van Leijenhorst, L., Zanolie, K., Van Meel, C. S., Westenberg, P. M., Rombouts, S. A., & Crone, E. A. (2010). What motivates the adolescent? Brain regions mediating reward sensitivity across adolescence. Cerebral Cortex, 20, 61 – 69.

Light, R L, Harvey S, & Mouchet A (2012): Improving 'at-action' decision-making in team sports through a holistic coaching approach, Sport, Education and Society 1, p 1-18

Light R L and Harvey S (2017) 'Positive pedagogy for sport coaching': Sport education and society 22:2, 271-287

Luciana M and Collins P F, (2012). Incentive Motivation, Cognitive Control, and the Adolescent Brain: Is It Time for a Paradigm Shift? Child Development perspectives. Vol.6 issue 4

Mangels, J.A., Butterfield, B., Lamb, J., Good, C., and Dweck, C.S. (2006). Why do beliefs about intelligence influence learning success? A social cognitive neuroscience model. Soc Cogn Affect Neurosci 1, 75-86.

Mercurio E et al (2020) Adolescent Brain Development and Progressive Legal Responsibility in the Latin American Context. *Frontiers in Psychology.* Vol 11. Article 627

Mills A, Butt, J, Maynard I & Harwood C; (2012) Identifying factors perceived to influence the development of elite youth football academy players, Journal of Sports Sciences, 30:15, 1593-1604

Nakamura, J., & Csikszentmihalyi, M. (2009). Flow theory and research. In C.R.

Snyder & S.J. Lopez (Eds.), The Oxford handbook of positive psychology (2nd edn.,

pp. 195–206). New York: Oxford University Press.

Nelson L, et al (2012) Carl Rogers, learning and educational practice: Critical considerations and applications in sports coaching. Sport, Education and Society 19(5). 1-19

Nesti M., and Sewell D., (1999) 'Losing it: the importance of anxiety and mood stability in sport'. Journal of Personal and Interpersonal Loss, 4: 257-68

References

Nesti M. (2010) Psychology in Football. Working with Elite and Professional Players. Routledge

Nesti, M. and Littlewood, M. (2011). Making your way in the game: boundary situations within the world of professional football. In D. Gilbourne and M. Andersen (eds), Critical Essays in Sport Psychology. Champaign IL: Human Kinetics.

Nesti M., Sulley C. (2015) Youth Development in Football. Lessons from the World's Best Academies. Routledge

Nicholls, J. G. (1989). The competitive ethos and democratic education. Cambridge, Mass.: Harvard University Press.

Overman W H et al (2004). Performance on the IOWA card task by adolescents and adults. Neuropscholgia 42, 1838-1851

Pain, M. A. & Harwood, C.G. (2007). The performance environment in English youth soccer: A quantitative investigation. Journal of Sports Sciences, 26, 1157-1169.

Pain M. A. & Harwood C. G. (2004): Knowledge and perceptions of sport psychology within English soccer, Journal of Sports Sciences, 22:9, 813-826

Palminteri, S., Kilford, E. J., Coricelli, G., and Blakemore, S. J. (2016). The computational development of reinforcement learning during adolescence. *PLoS Comput. Biol.* 12:

Partington, M Cushion, C (2011) An investigation of the practice activities and coaching behaviours of professional top level youth soccer coaches. Scandinavian Journal of Medical Science in Sports, 1-8

Partington and Cushion (2013) 'An investigation of the practice activities ... ': Scandinavian journal of medicine and science in sports. 23 374-382

Paunesku D., Walton G. M., Romero C., Smith E. N., Yeager D. S., Dweck C. S. Mind-Set Interventions Are a Scalable Treatment for Academic Underachievement. Psychological Science (2015), 1-10

Peters and Crone (2017) 'Increased striatal activity in adolescence benefits learning': Nature communications 18

Potrac, P., Jones, R. L., & Cushion, C. J. (2007). Understanding power and the coach's role in professional English soccer: A preliminary investigation of coach behaviour. Soccer and Society, 8, 33–49.

Reyna, V.F., Farley, F., (2006). Risk and rationality in adolescent decision-making – implications for theory, practice, and public policy. Psychol. Sci. Public Interest, 1–44.

Reyna, V.F.,(2008). A theory of medical decision making and health: fuzzy trace theory. Med. Decision Making 28 (6), 850–865.

Richardson, D., Littlewood, M., & Gilbourne, D. (2004). Developing support mechanisms for elite young players in a professional soccer academy: Creative reflections in action research. European Sport Management Quarterly, 4, 195–214.

References

Rivers, S E., Reyna V., F Mills B. Risk Taking Under the Influence: A Fuzzy-Trace Theory of Emotion in AdolescenceRose L T, Daley, S G Rose D H. (2011) Let the Questions Be Your Guide: MBE as Interdisciplinary Science Mind, Brain, and Education Volume 5, Issue 4, pages 153–162

Rudolph et al (2017) 'At risk of being risky. The relationship between brain age .....' Developmental Cognitive Neuroscience 24 (93-106)

Ryan, R. M., & Deci, E. L. (2000). Self-determination theory and the facilitation ofintrinsic motivation, social development, and well-being. American Psychologist, 55, 68-78.

Samuels, B. (2009). Can the differences between education and neuroscience be overcome by mind, brain and education? Mind, Brain and Education, 3, 45–55

Siegel D J,. Brainstorm: The Power and Purpose of the Teenage Brain (2013). Tarcher

Sigmundsson H, Clemente FM, Loftesnes JM (2020) Passion, grit and mindset in football players. New Ideas in Psychology. Vol.59.

Silva et al (2015) 'Peers increase late adolescents exploratory behaviour and sensitivity to positive and negative feedback': Journal of research on adolescence 26(4) 696-705

Somerville LH, Kim H, Johnstone T, Alexander AL, Whalen PJ: Human amygdala responses during presentation of happy and neutral faces: correlations with state anxiety. Biol Psychiatry. 2004 May 1; 55(9):897-903.

Somerville, L.H., Jones, R.M., Casey, B.J., 2010b. A time of change: behavioral and neural correlates of adolescent sensitivity to appetitive and aversive environmental cues. Brain. Cogn. 72, 124–133.

Somerville (2016) 'Searching for signatures of brain maturity': Neuron 92

Southgate, G (2011) The Boot Room. FA Coaches Journal, Volume 1. FA Learning

Souza D, A,. (2010) Mind, Brain and Education: Implications for the classroom. Solution Tree Press

Steinberg, L., (2004). Risk taking in adolescence: what changes, and why? Ann. N. Y. Acad. Sci. 1021, 51–58.

Steinberg, L., (2008). A social neuroscience perspective on adolescent risk-taking. Dev. Rev. 28, 78–106.

Steinberg L (2015) 'Age of opportunity' Lessons from the new science of adolescence: First Mariner Book

Suleiman, A. B., & Dahl, R. E. (2017). Leveraging neuroscience to inform adolescent health: The need for an innovative transdisciplinary developmental science of adolescence. Journal of Adolescent Health, 60(3), 240–248.

Thorpe, R, Bunker, D (2010) Preface. In: Butler, J, Griffin, L (eds) More Teaching Games for Understanding: Moving Globally. Champaign, IL: Human Kinetics, pp.vii–xv.

Tokuhama, T (2011) Mind, Brain, and Education Science: A Comprehensive Guide to the New Brain-Based Teaching. W W Norton and company. New York

Todd, M. E. (1968) The thinking body (Brooklyn, NY, Dance Horizons).

References

Training Ground Guru Red to Blue: How the All Blacks perform under pressure. May 28, 2018

UNICEF 2017: The Adolescent Brain: A second window of opportunity. A compendium:

Vallerand, R. J. (2007). Intrinsic and extrinsic motivation in sport and physical activity. A review and a look at the future. In G. Tenenbaum, & R. C. Eklund (Eds.), Handbook of sport psychology (3rd ed.). (pp. 59-83) New York: John Wiley.

van Leijenhorst, L., Moor, B.G., Op de Macks, Z.A., Rombouts, S.A., West-enberg, P.M., Crone, E.A., 2010. Adolescent risky decision-making: neurocognitive development of reward and control regions. Neuroimage 51 (1), 345–355.

Vygotsky, L. (1978). Mind in society: The development of higher psychological processes (M.Cole, V.John-Steiner, S.Scribner, & E.Souberman, Trans.). Cambridge, MA: Harvard University Press

Walters P J 'The Teenage Brain and football'. Presentation delivered as part of the FA Advanced Youth Award. 2017

Walters P J (2013) An exploration of how the discourse within Educational Neuroscience might inform developmental understanding of decision-making in the context of elite academy football. Unpublished Thesis: University of Bristol: Graduate School of Education.

Walters P J 'Changing the game for teenage footballers'; The Psychologist online Feb 2017

Ward, P., Farrow, D., Harris, K. R., Williams, A. M., Eccles, D. W., & Ericsson, K. A. (2008). Training perceptual-cognitive skills: Can sport psychology research inform military decision training? Military Psychology, 20, S71–S102.

Williams, A. M., & Ford, P. R. (2008). Expertise and expert performance in sport. International Review of Sport and Exercise Psychology, 1, 4–18.

Williams, A. M., Hodges, N. J., North, J. S., & Barton, G. (2006). Perceiving patterns of play in dynamic sport tasks: Identifying the essential information underlying skilled performance. Perception, 35, 317-332.

Willis J. (2010). Mind, Brain and Education: Neuroscience Implications for the Classroom (Leading Edge (Solution Tree)). Souza D. A. Ed (45-69)

Yeager D., Walton G., Cohen G. L. (2013) Addressing Achievement Gaps with Psychological Interventions. Kappan 62-65

Coaching Football With The Adolescent Brain In Mind

Practical Sessions

SESSION PLAN

The Scrambled Football and Scrambled Brain Game

Coaching The Adolescent Brain Creativity

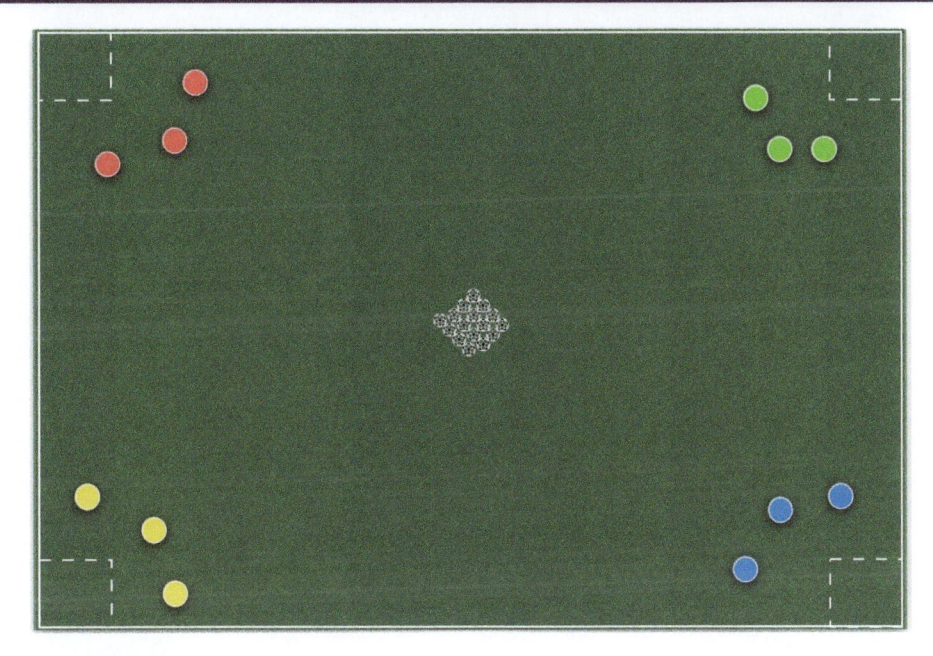

The Scrambled Football and Scrambled Brain Game

THE FOOTBALL COACH

SESSION DETAIL

This is a very simple session to setup. The players work within a 22m wide space and a 18m deep space. In each corner there are four areas, these are safe zones. In the middle of the pitch there are as many balls as you have available, ideally at least 20 balls. The players are then split in to four teams of three (this can be more or less if required).

The idea of the game is very simple, players must steal the balls from the central area and bring them to their safety pen, the team that has the the most balls when the coach blows his or her whistle wins. However, there are some rules to force the players to make decisions during the practice:

- Only one ball can be taken at a time per player

- One player must always be defending their zone

- You must make a decision whether to steal from the central zone or an opponents' zone.

- Defending players can tackle the players who steal from their zone.

The Scrambled Football and Scrambled Brain Game

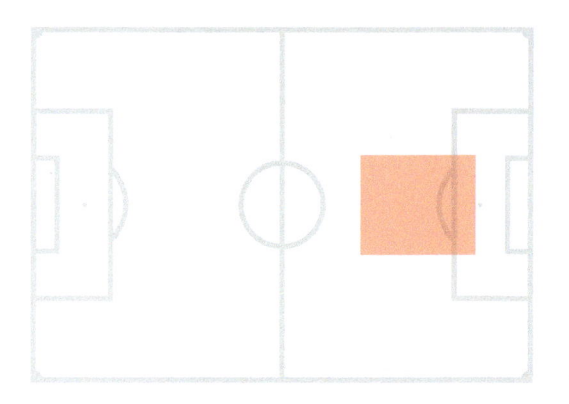

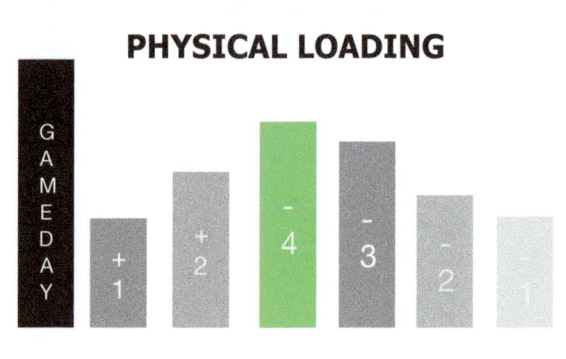

THE FOOTBALL COACH

PHYSICAL LOADING

GAMEDAY | +1 | +2 | -4 | -3 | -2 | -1

WORKING	RECOVERY	BLOCKS	TOTAL
3 MINS	2 MINS	4	20 MINS

- WORKING
- RECOVERY

PITCH SIZE: 22M x 30M

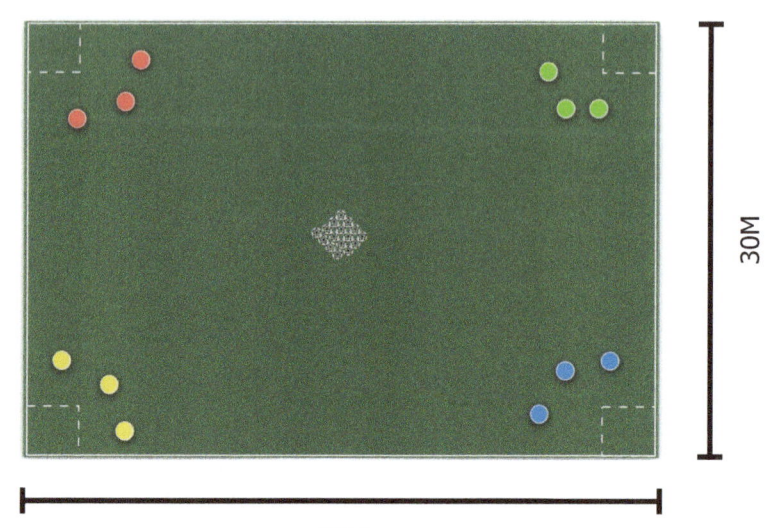

The Scrambled Football and Scrambled Brain Game

DECISION MAKING

Although this session is a highly enjoyable game, players will also be challenged in their decision making processes. We can manipulate and deliver these challenges specifically to ensure we continue this challenge. As the game develops, players will need to make a decision between staying in their own zone and defending, attacking the central area and taking an uncontested ball, or attacking an opponent. This not only forces players to make a decision, but also learn to make decisions on the balance of risk and reward under the pressure of the training game intensity, and the competitiveness of their teammates.

From Dr Perry Walters' previous section on decision making, we know that players struggle to balance the risk against the reward, during the development of the prefrontal cortex. This means we will likely see players attack their opponent because the risk is something they can't fully process, where the promise of reward weighs heavier and tips the balance in their decision-making.

We also know from wider research that stress and anxiety can also have an influence on decision making and the ability to balance risk and reward. With the reward often being seen clearer during stressful situations, the intensity of this practice could potentially create a stressful environment and further increase players' awareness of the reward.

COACHING IMPLICATIONS

For coaches, this type of session does have implications depending on how we deliver and speak to our players. It will become obvious when watching these sessions that players might fail to accurately compare the risk and the reward, we must as coaches be willing to think back to the research shared within this book and allow the players to make these mistakes as they must, understand the risk and the reward for themselves. Although telling them the correct answer maybe tempting, it is a short term fix to the problem and it will limit the players opportunity for long term learning; they will stop making the 'decision' and follow the instruction. Telling them what to do in training sessions like this can be damaging to players in the long term as we know how important decision making is for them and their development.

The Scrambled Football and Scrambled Brain Game

This doesn't mean that as coaches we are redundant and should not speak to players about their decision making, it just means we must use a different approach to challenge and understand the players approach. Taking the player out of the session and asking them to explain their decision, what they were thinking and why they did it, will give you as a coach an understanding into their thought process before putting the player back into the session and seeing if they continue to make the same mistake or become more aware of the risk and reward process. This scaffolding process helps players develop autonomy in their decision-making, strengthening connectivity between emotion and regulation circuits in their own brain.

PLAYER IMPLICATIONS

Whenever we take a session, there are always implications for players, these implications can vary dependent on the challenge the session provides. This session will be high in many areas of the game, the intensity will be extremely high, because of the competitive nature of the practice, whilst the 22M and 30M distances will make sure that the challenge physically is demanding.

The physical challenge will make sure that players become tired, both physically and mentally and this level of fatigue affects decision making, and also makes the session realistic, as these decisions will be made with similar levels of fatigue to that of the fatigue they will experience in games.

SESSION PLAN

3v3 Goal Scoring Transition Game

Coaching The Adolescent Brain   Decision Making

3v3 Goal Scoring Transition Game

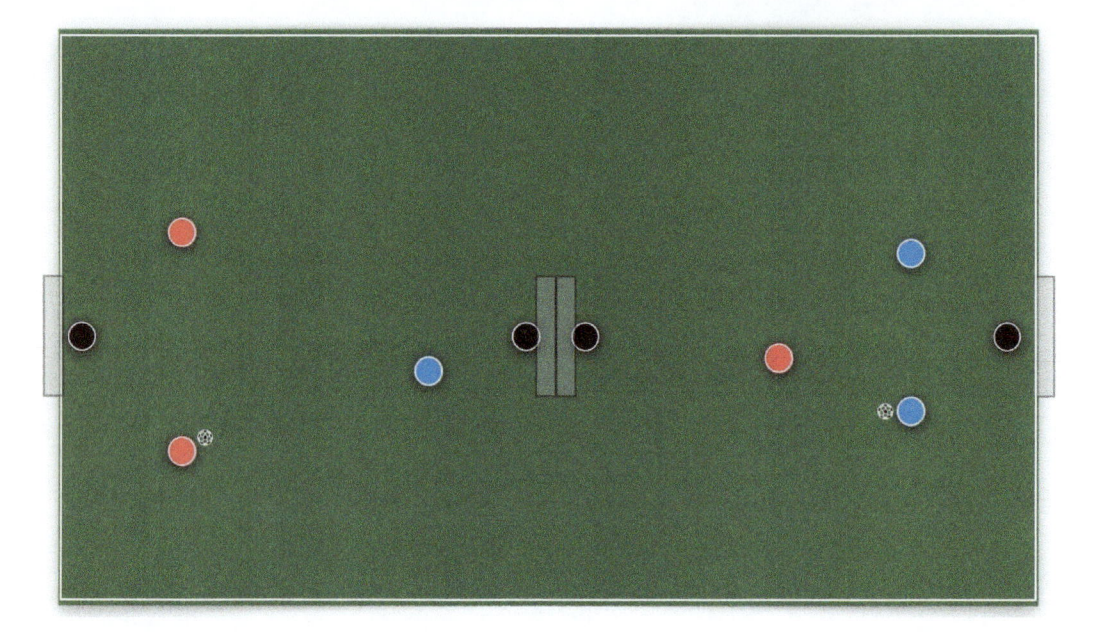

THE FOOTBALL COACH

SESSION DETAIL

This task is a great way of developing players decision-making under pressure. The session is easy to setup and easy to manage. The pitch is two pitches back to back, with the central goals back to back as can be seen above. The session takes place with 4 goalkeepers (or mini goals if you don't have keepers) and 3v3 in outfield players. The numbers can be varied depending on the availability of players you have.

Each team will need to split to create 2v1 on both pitches, on one pitch with the overload, and on the other pitch the team will be overloaded. The decision making will arise through the rules applied to the game. Once a team have scored with the overload, they can chose to stay on the pitch they are on, or cross over on to the next pitch and play in a 2v2 and 1v1, but any goals scored whilst in this format are worth double.

This creates a risk/reward process as the opponents' goals are also worth double at this point, on both pitches, so dependent on the game situation, players might chose to cross the pitch and chase the game. They might chose to stay as they are as they are already ahead in the game. Managing the players and understanding the thought process behind their decisions will help both us as coaches, and them as players.

3v3 Goal Scoring Transition Game

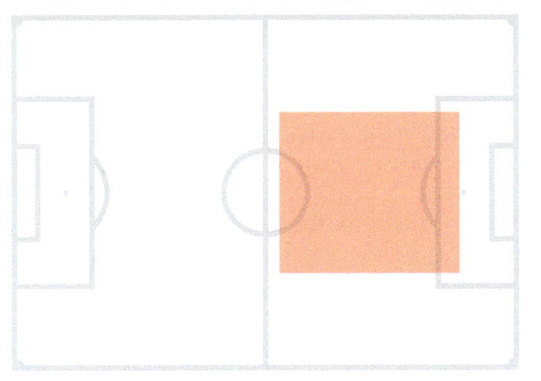

PHYSICAL LOADING

| GAMEDAY | +1 | +2 | -4 | -3 | -2 | -1 |

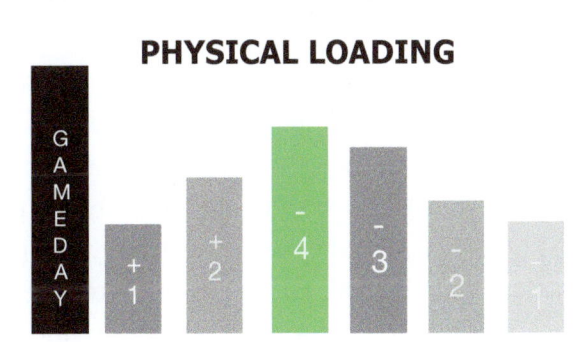

WORKING	RECOVERY	BLOCKS	TOTAL
4 MINS	2 MINS	4	24

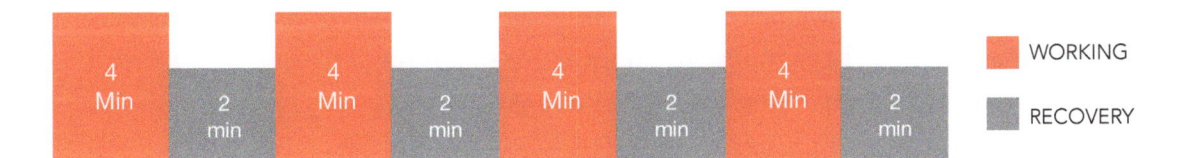

4 Min | 2 min | 4 Min | 2 min | 4 Min | 2 min | 4 Min | 2 min

- WORKING
- RECOVERY

PITCH SIZE:

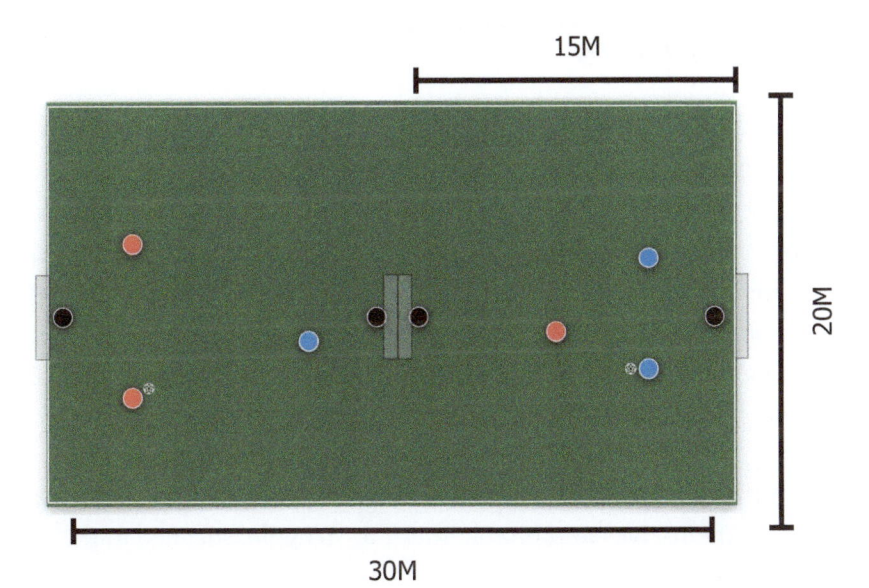

15M
20M
30M

3v3 Goal Scoring Transition Game

DECISION MAKING

Research has suggested that the adolescent period is the optimal time to forge 'The Football Brain'. During this unique phase of brain development, we see that the pre-frontal cortex (responsible for decision making and judgement) is still developing. This is because it is the last part of the brain to link to other brain regions. This means we must always be training the cognitive elements of performance in tandem with the technical, tactical and physical. Having decision making at the heart of the session will help forge that 'football brain' and allow players to understand the risk and reward of specific situations within the game, learning through trial and error adjustments and strengthening their own independent judgements.

The decision-making part of the game is so important to players and it allows for technique to be transferred into the game effectively and allow it to be used against the opponent. The practice will create an element of chaos which will need to be managed by the players. The chaos will be created by the consistent change between a 2v1 (or 1v2) against a 2v2 (1v1). Recognising when the game might require us to 'gamble' and take the risk because we are losing by two or three goals, or when the risk might not be worth it because we are only losing by one, or only winning by one. Being able to make these decision whilst under pressure from the opponent will be the key element to this game.

COACHING IMPLICATIONS

For coaches we must use the evidence to structure the way we deliver our session. Because we know from the science mentioned previously that the pre-frontal cortex might not be fully developed until the mid twenties, we must be accommodating and understanding to decision making that is at times inconsistent. However this doesn't mean that we as the coach are redundant and can't be supportive of the players decisions. We can do this through offering a co-operative approach to coaching, where we create a meaningful environment to the game and use effective communication with the players to understand why they decided to do what they did.

For coaches, we must still be willing to encourage independence and allow players to manage these games themselves and enable them to struggle, succeed and enjoy the occasion. supported with guidance.

3v3 Goal Scoring Transition Game

The prefrontal cortex is also responsible for the control of emotions, so as players make 'poor' decisions, they might at times become emotional and erratic because they find it difficult to stop their emotions hijacking the decision-making process. This lack of emotional control is one of the characteristics we often attach to the adolescent age. This is a time of great developmental opportunity where coaches can provide players with strategies to try and manage their emotions, but must recognise that the inconsistencies of control are linked to brain development and can be supported with guidance.

PLAYER IMPLICATIONS

For players of the adolescent age, sessions like this can be erratic but enjoyable because of the goal scoring element included with them. As players fatigue and become intrenched in 1v1 battles, we will find that their ability to make decisions becomes crowded, because they struggle to think clearly about the game situation and the process of winning the game. This is because the fatigue might have a negative influence on their clarity and composure, whilst their 1v1 battles and conflict with players will make them emotional, meaning they make emotional decisions based on the players they are playing against, not decisions based on their team and the situation.

Players at this age will have a higher level of brain 'plasticity' (changeability). Training in these environments and experiencing these emotional and situational problems, will help create a more football specific level of 'mental strength' as the brain begins to develop and forge towards the end of the adolescent phase.

SESSION PLAN

Four Team Cognitive Chaos Game

Coaching The Adolescent Brain Decision Making

Four Team Cognitive Chaos Game

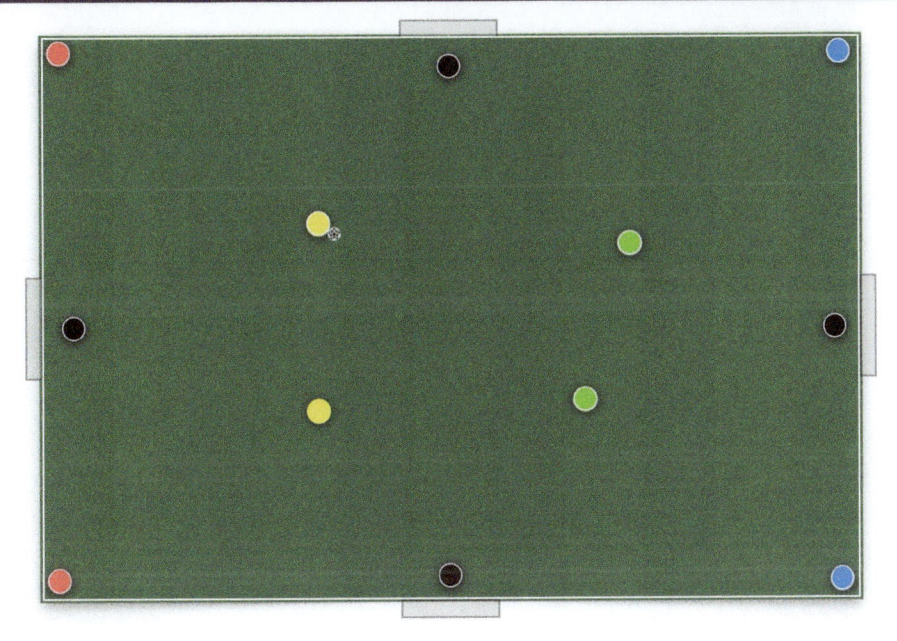

THE FOOTBALL COACH

SESSION DETAIL

This can be an extremely chaotic game, which will challenge players when remembering the score inside the session. The session has four teams, which are obvious by the colour of the player in the session above. Inside the shape, two teams compete within a 2v2 and on the outside there are two more teams of two. Within the session the 2v2 compete as normal, however if they choose to pass in to an outside player, the outside player has a decision, they can;

Pass the ball back in to the same team, like an outside player, and if the team they pass to scores, they will receive one goal.

Or they might decide to drive in with the ball, as this happens the team who had possession will move to the outside and the outside team will move in. With this decision, there is a risk for the players who decide to drive in; if they fail to score or lose possession the three other teams score two points

- Normal Goal = 2 Points

- Passing to a team who directly score = 1 point

- Score when driving in = 3 points / If they miss or lose possession, all opponents get 2 points

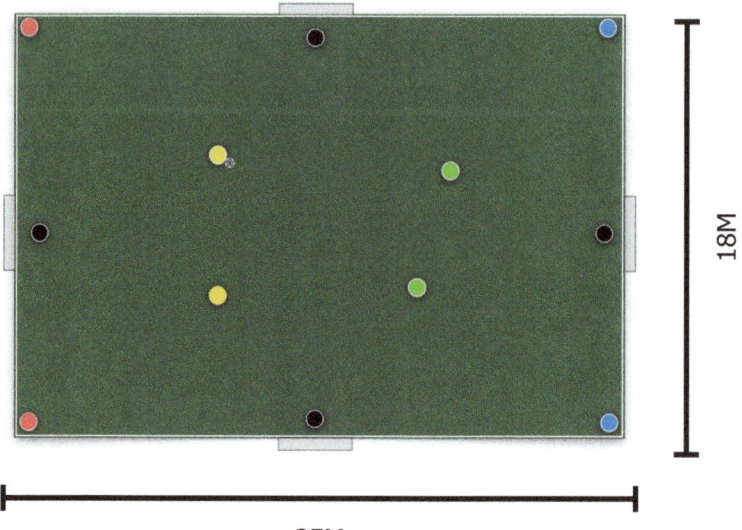

Four Team Cognitive Chaos Game

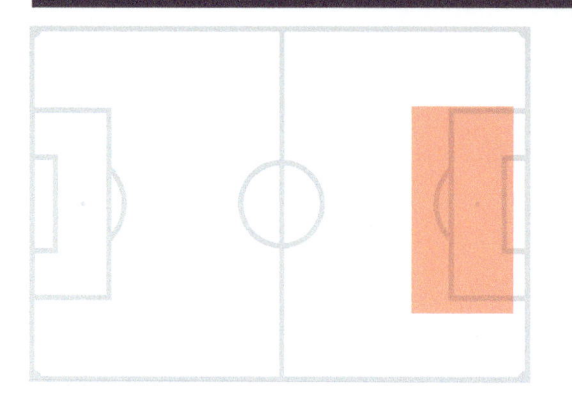

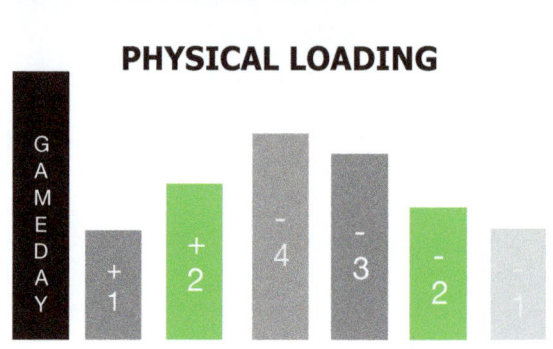

PHYSICAL LOADING

GAMEDAY | +1 | +2 | -4 | -3 | -2 | -1

WORKING	RECOVERY	BLOCKS	TOTAL
4 MINS	2 MINS	4	24 MINS

4 Min — 2 min — 4 Min — 2 min — 4 Min — 2 min — 4 Min — 2 min

- WORKING
- RECOVERY

PITCH SIZE: 25M x 18M

Four Team Cognitive Chaos Game

DECISION MAKING

As mentioned above this session does have a complex goal scoring system that challenges players to remember how to score goals and score points within the system, whilst still playing and performing in a competitive task. The task design will be highly competitive and challenge players to perform under the competitive pressure, with this in mind the coaches will not need to ramp the pressure up, as increased pressure can have a negative effect on players' decision-making and creativity.

Individually, players will need to be aware of what the score is within the game; which team is winning and which team are passing them the ball. This will mean the task has a huge amount of complexity, within a simple setup players will need time during the recovery period to discuss in their pairs, their strategy and plan. Dependent on the team who passes the ball to the outside player might influence the way the decision is made.

The risk and reward element should really challenge the thought process of players, this challenged thought process should allow for intelligent and cognitively aware players to perform to high levels in this task.

COACHING IMPLICATIONS

For coaches, it can be fairly difficult to allow a chaotic game to take place without feeling the need to step in and control the chaos. Chaotic sessions can look unorganised and poorly structured, however great structure can limit player autonomy. In the short term, limiting player autonomy can makes sessions easier to run, more successful and aesthetically more pleasing to watch.

The chaos comes from the complexity of decision making that players have to make, it is these moments that challenge the players to learn in complexity and develop an understanding of the game. They do this through 'embodied cognition' or 'body thinking' where brain, mind and body work together to construct their own learning. This also increases player effectiveness, as players become more confident in the chaotic environment, they will begin to become more comfortable using their technique at the correct times through trial and error.

Four Team Cognitive Chaos Game

PLAYER IMPLICATIONS

For players, chaos can be a challenge for those with less confidence and a welcomed challenge to those who are more self assured. Those who have a greater control of their emotions and behaviours, have either greater prefrontal control or lesser emotional reactivity and might be more consistent in these practices. However, all players can develop with practice in a supportive, caring environment.

Regardless of the rate of development, we must be willing to encourage players to relish the chaos and complexity even if they struggle with the higher end cognitions. It is the opinion of the authors, that even during 'failure', this adolescent period provides such a ripe time to compete in sessions of this type, because of the level of decision making and the opportunity to repeat the task on a consistent level. Immersion in meaningful, game related practices, where players have the opportunity to engage with the environment, are best suited for adolescent learning.

SESSION PLAN

A Race to the Finish

A Race to the Finish

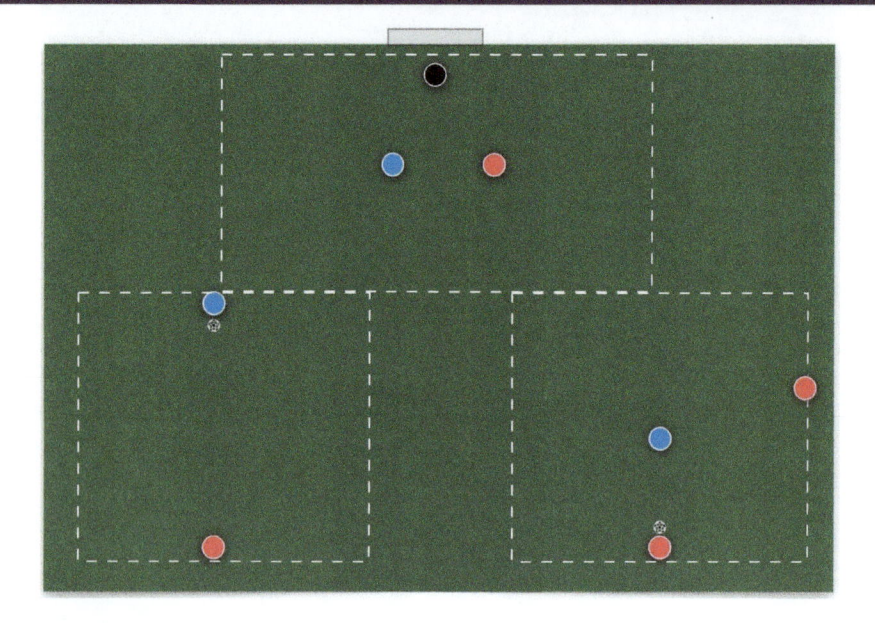

THE FOOTBALL COACH

SESSION DETAIL

This is a very small micro session that involves nine players, within a small space. If needed, the area can be increased and so can the amount of players used. Meaning this can be a very easily adapted session for low intensity days. Each space is roughly 12 meters in size and provides a small space, large enough for players to compete in 1v1's or look to make passes in a 2v1 rondo.

The session is very simple to setup. There are three boxes, the top box is the goal scoring box, the two boxes below are racing to complete their challenge to get in to the final area and score. The reds will have to make a decision; do they want to go into a 1v1 against a blue or do they want to be the attacker within a 2v1 passing rondo. The reds on the right hand side must complete two passes before they can play into the end zone and score with the 2v1, or the red must win the 1v1 on the left side. The first box to finish can progress into the attacking zone.

The players effectively having to make decisions will make us aware of how confident they are at attacking within 1v1 situations. It will also show us how creative they are, and whether the creativity can be transferred from a skill into a technique and be used in opposed situations.

A Race to the Finish

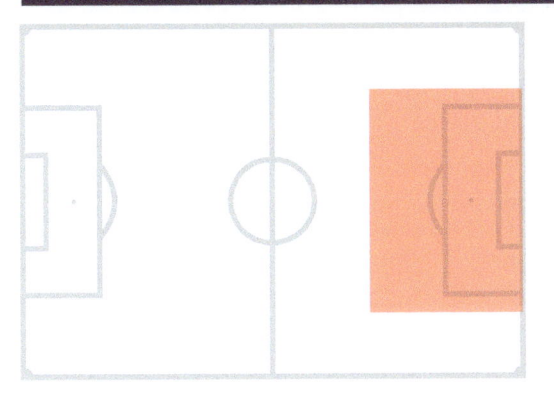

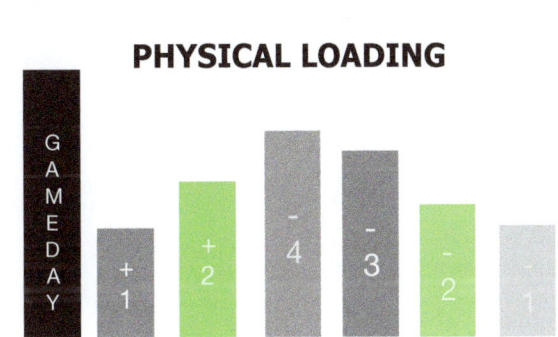

PHYSICAL LOADING

GAMEDAY | +1 | +2 | -4 | -3 | -2 | -1

WORKING	RECOVERY	BLOCKS	TOTAL
3 MINS	2 MINS	4	20 MINS

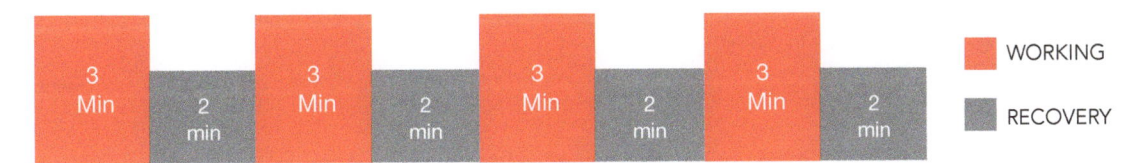

- WORKING: 3 Min
- RECOVERY: 2 min

PITCH SIZE:

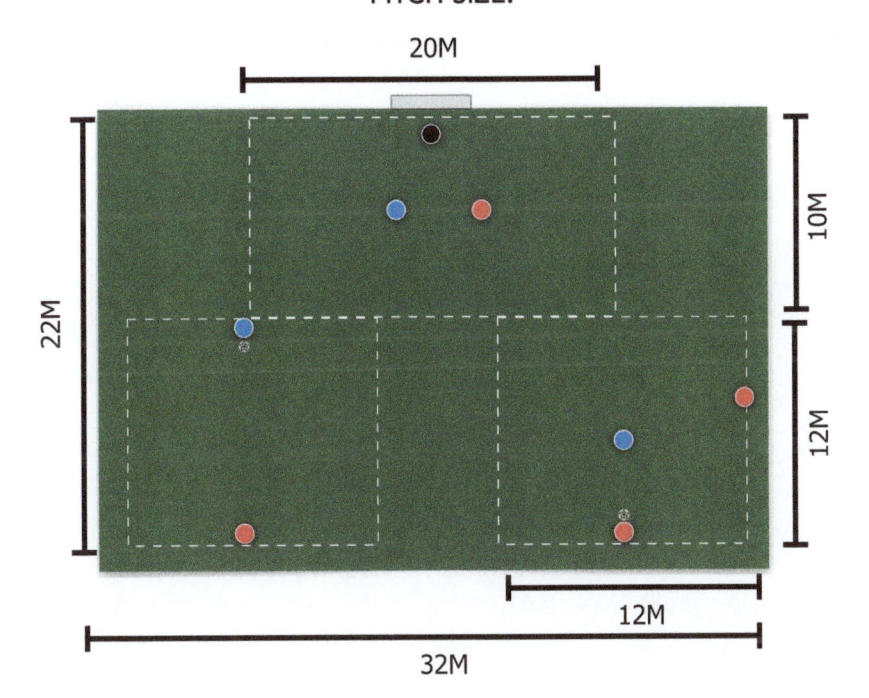

20M
22M
10M
12M
12M
32M

A Race to the Finish

PROGRESSION

This session can be progressed in a few different ways. It is common to find that players will find success in one element of the game, it could potentially be the 2v1 passing option. If this is the case, it can be moved to a 2v2 to create a bigger challenge for the reds. This will naturally make the balance between the 1v1 and the passing section more even.

We might also want to apply a greater challenge and reward to the blue team for preventing the reds attacking. This can be done in two different ways. Firstly, we can change the practice, so when the blues win possession back, they can play into the blue in the end zone, and score. We can add an additional box, like the attacking box on the other end of the practice. This way, when the blues win possession from the reds, they are making an attack in the opposite direction with a realistic directional attack, realistic space and the pressure that would be experienced in a realistic finishing situation.

COACHING IMPLICATIONS

This session will be eye-opening for coaches, as we will likely be surprised by players' decisions. Some players will relish the opportunity to compete in the more complexed and individually pressured 1v1, compared to other players who don't relish this experience and will look to go in to a 2v1 passing square. It is then really important for us to talk with our players and try and work out and understand why they have made that decision. Some players will see the opportunity of a 2v1, and make a positive decision to attack the opponent and score; others might be intimidated by the opposite practice (1v1) and hide themselves in the passing practice to avoid the individual spotlight.

This isn't the end of the world, and actually as players get older, it is important that they recognise their strengths and their weaknesses and play to them, to ensure they're the best player they can be. At adolescent age we are likely still going to encourage our players to be 'brave' and attack the 1v1 situation and dominate the opponent. This practice can have implications for generating strong emotions (such as 1v1 battles) which, as we know, can become heightened in adolescence. As such, it is a great opportunity to scaffold emotional control in young players. The practice also offers great opportunities for creative play which can be fostered in supportive, non judgmental environments.

A Race to the Finish

PLAYER IMPLICATIONS

Within this small practice we will see many implications for players of all ages. With the players involved in the 1v1 situation, we must look to watch with detail and understand the plan from both the defending and attacking player; Are they looking to show them towards goal or away from goal? What is the decision being made in the 1v1 moment? Are the players stepping in and getting beat because they are struggling with their decisions around when to stand up and when to step in?

On the other hand you have the attacker; What is the thought process? Are they dominating the 1v1 centrally? Are they looking to drag the defender into the wide area and then cut inside, or are they running at the defender and standing them up? All of these decisions will be exposed within this fantastic, small little practice.

SESSION PLAN

Player Driven Overloads

Player Driven Overloads

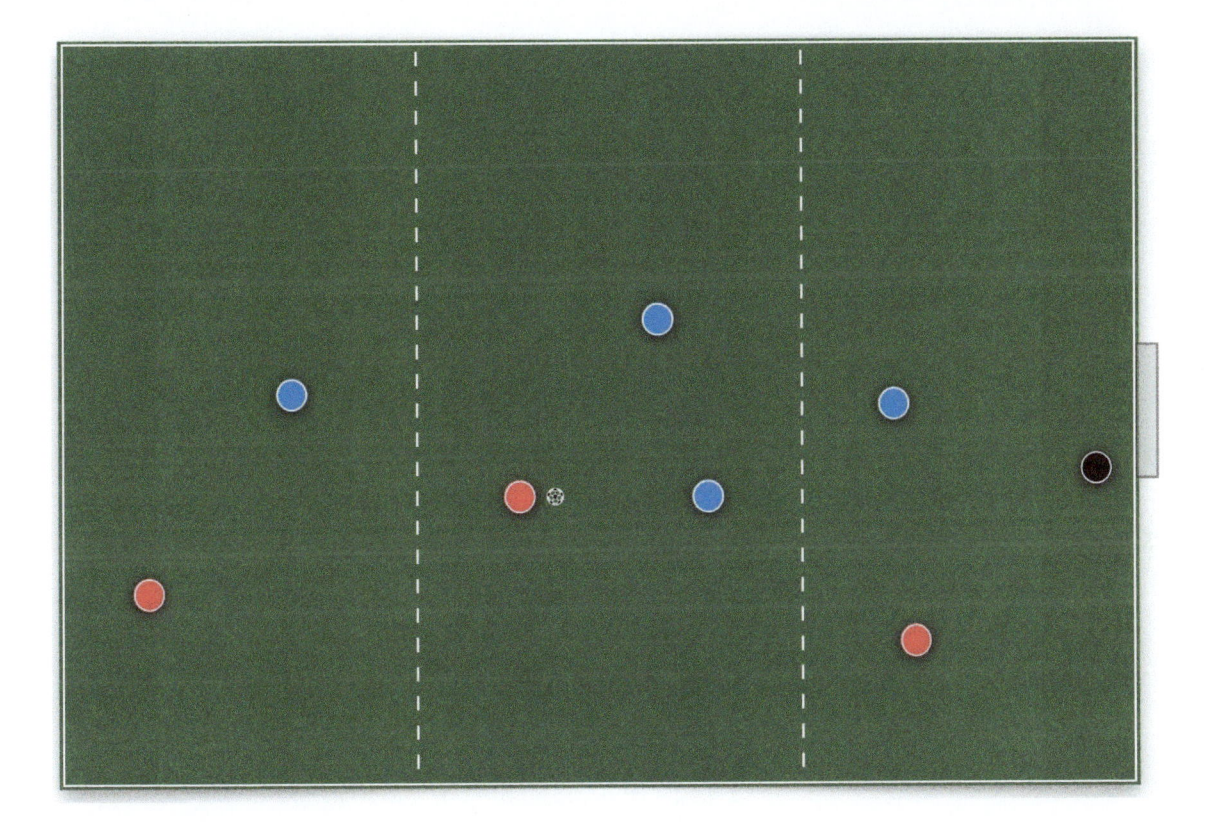

SESSION DETAIL

This session can be very difficult to find success, at times, because the players guide and control the setup of the session. The players setup in an area split into three equal zones, before splitting themselves between the three zones. The players are given the responsibility to decide where players go, and what zones they must play in. This will challenge the decision making, and they will need to think about the thought process behind who is assigned to each zone.

Block 1 - Blues decide the set up for both teams (They decide where they will have an overload and an underload)

Block 2 - Reds decide the set up for both teams (They decide where they will have an overload and under-load)

Player Driven Overloads

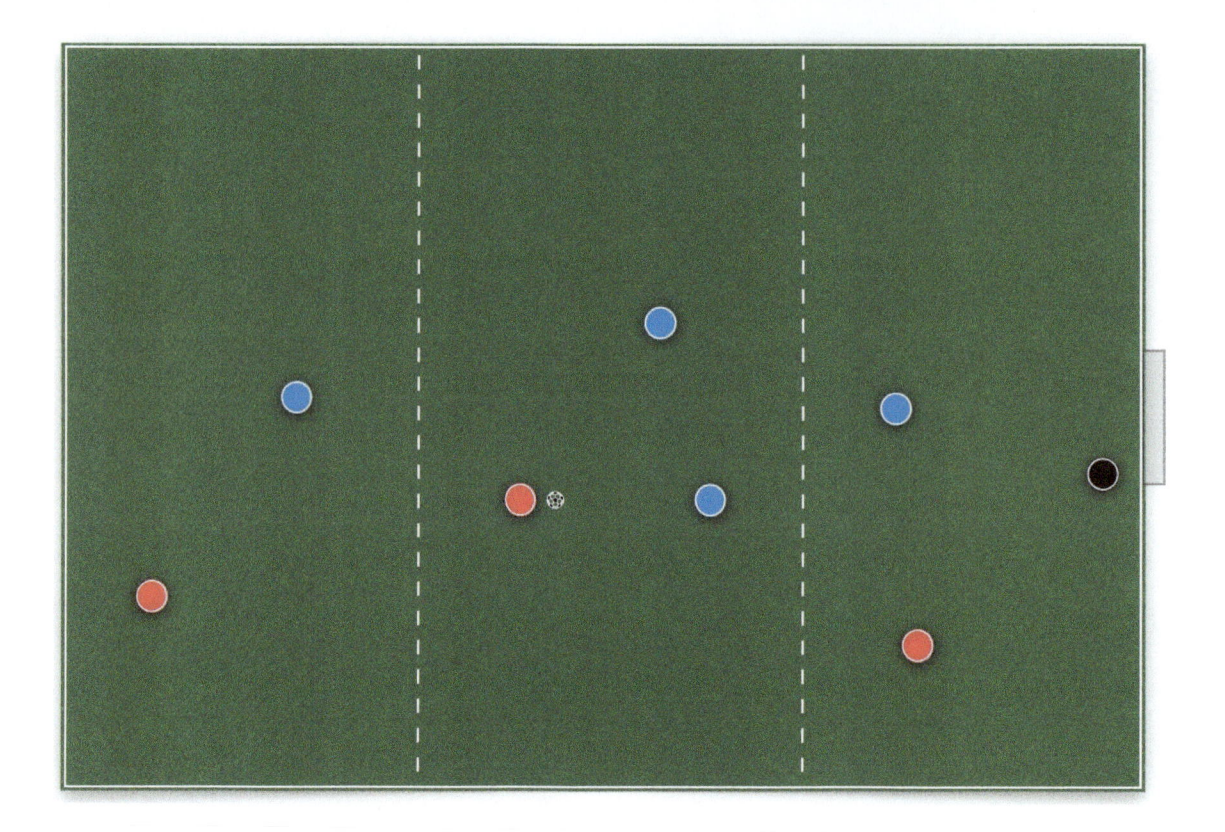

SESSION DETAIL CONTINUED

The next two blocks are controlled by the two teams. The coach can have a great influence on the players during the two minute recovery time, the influence doesn't need to be over powering, but an attempt to understand why each team has made the decision they have.

Naturally the attacking team will find the practice difficult because they are always underloaded with 4v3 in the outfield area. This will be an interesting exercise to see how they set the opponent up, to give themselves the greatest opportunity to score. It is important to remember this is the goal; the team in possession want to score and prevent the opponent regaining possession and playing into the coach who stands at the top of the practice.

Player Driven Overloads

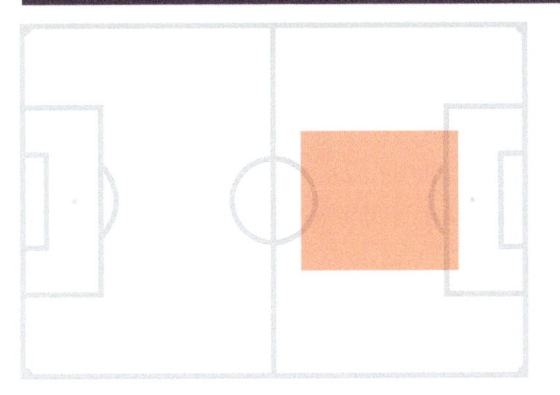

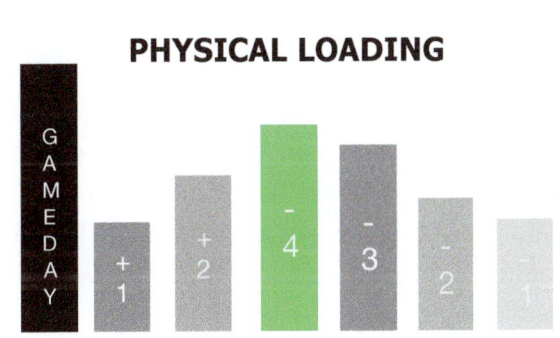

THE FOOTBALL COACH

PHYSICAL LOADING

GAMEDAY | +1 | +2 | -4 | -3 | -2 | -1

WORKING	RECOVERY	BLOCKS	TOTAL
5 MINS	2 MINS	4 BLOCKS	20 MINS

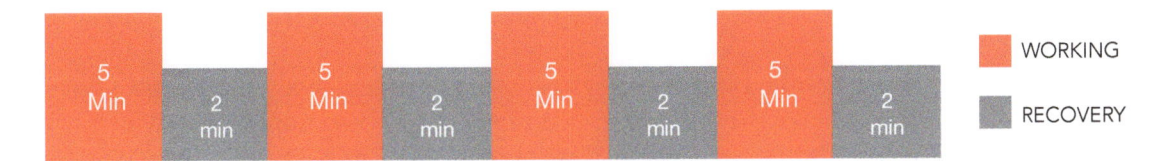

5 Min / 2 min / 5 Min / 2 min / 5 Min / 2 min / 5 Min / 2 min

- WORKING
- RECOVERY

PITCH SIZE:

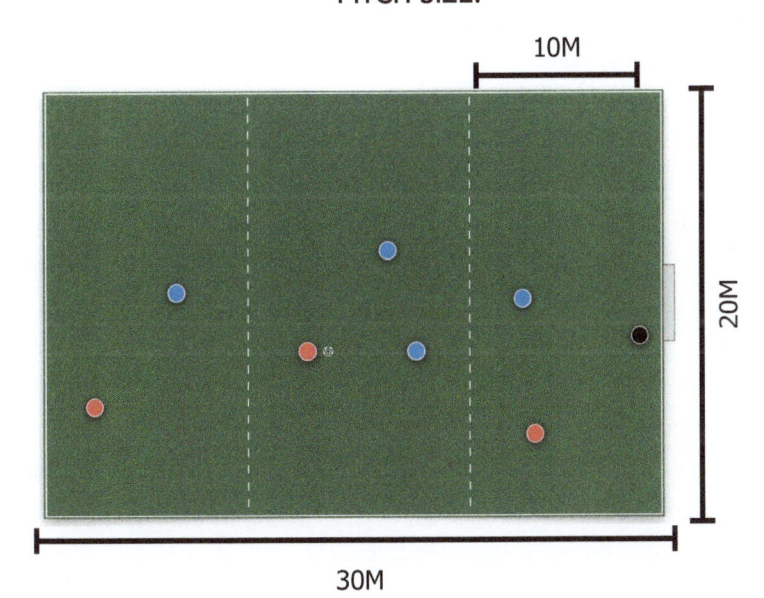

10M
30M
20M

Player Driven Overloads

PROGRESSION

The session can be manipulated in many ways if needed. There is a risk to sessions with high player engagement; that a lack of engagement can lead to a flat and low engaging session. The numbers can be increased, to allow for the practice to have greater influence when creating the overloads. For example, if the practice was 5v4, we might see more tactical decisions by teams, to limit the opportunity for players to be successful in the central area.

Other progressions can be used to manipulate the practice, if the players find the practice too easy, the size of each area can be changed by the other team. For example, the reds might choose what size each space is, whilst the blues might decide the numbers in each area. This approach to autonomy supportive behaviour will drive player engagement, task engagement and have players thinking about the game in a deeper thought process.

Another way this session can be processed, is to add an additional goal at the other end of the practice. This will make the game more contextual and directional. This will allow for end to end transition and consequences to having an under-load and overload in each area of the pitch.

COACHING IMPLICATIONS

These types of sessions can be challenging for us coaches. We need to recognise that we can't always be the fountain of knowledge and sometimes, the players need to learn by doing. It is important for them to trial different situations and find their own solutions, they will not always get it first time. In this way, we are empowering players to construct their own learning through trial and engagement with the environment.

This taps into natural drives during adolescence for autonomy and supports their development of independent decision-making. Of course, as the facilitator in these practices, we as coaches still play a huge role. We have to ensure that the players understand the task, can discuss their thoughts openly and find ways to support them with effectively delivering them into the practice.

Player Driven Overloads

Of course this is not the only responsibility of the coach, we must be proactive in how we deliver the session. The challenges can be vast in sessions where the players are responsible for the setup of the session. We must make sure that the challenge is realistic; the players might attempt to damage the realism of the practice. At this point, the coach might speak to the players instead of instructing them, manipulating the approach they have taken to find success within a framework that allows the session to be successful. Adopting a more hands-off approach can offer many potential benefits, including a greater release of dopamine (linked to reward, focus, learning) which increases when adolescents work independently from the judgement and scrutiny of adult figures.

PLAYER IMPLICATIONS

For players, sessions like this can provide many challenges, first they must focus on the footballing element of being successful in their 1v1s and dominating the opponent, but they must also recognise how to spot the areas of strength and weakness in their defensive and offensive shape.

They must also recognise the opponents' shape, both in and out of possession, along with the players who are strong and the players who are weak in the opponents' system. Recognising this sort of information is important within the real game, but also important in this practice. It will help them to build the framework for creating the structure of the practice. Players who recognise their opponents' shape and strengths are usually those who can effectively and quickly find ways to expose the opponent.

They will also benefit from the social interactions with other players. Their group discussions, unit discussions and paired conversations will lead to the development of social skills within a competitive footballing environment.

Player Driven Overloads

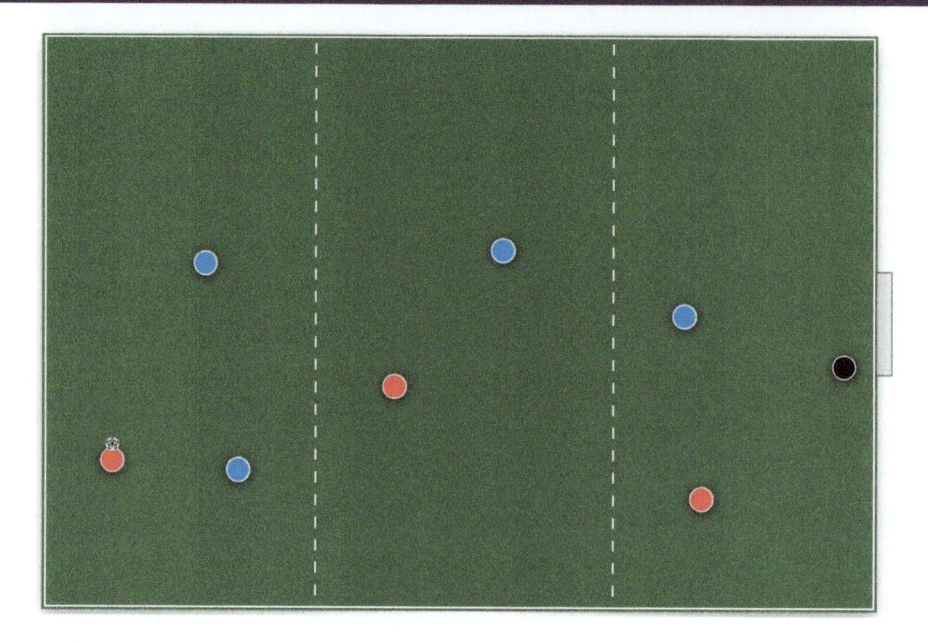

The two images show two different situations or scenarios, and how the opponent might manipulate them to be successful. The second image shows how manipulating the trainer numbers, might influence the practice

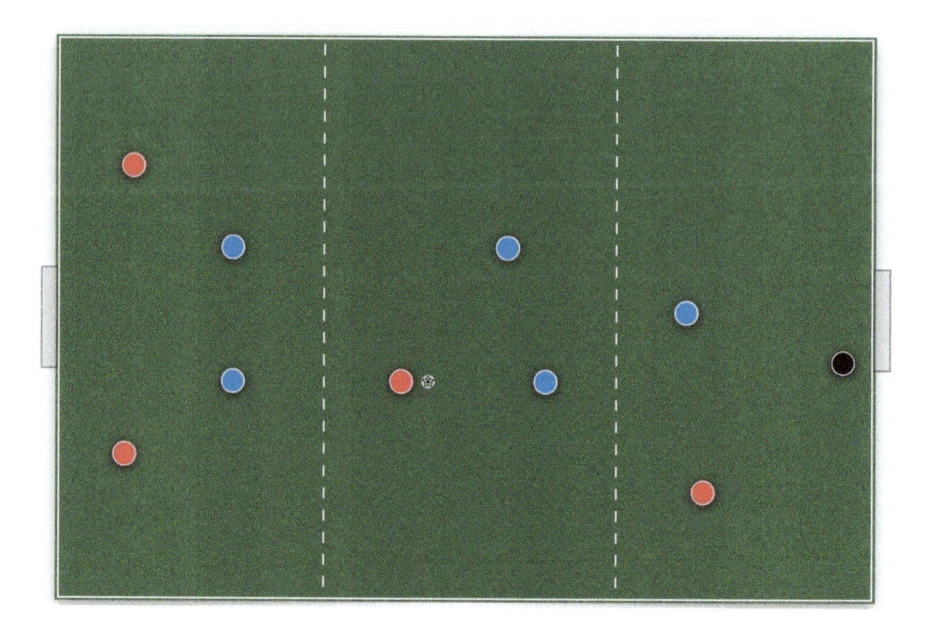

SESSION PLAN

Defending With Emotion

Defending With Emotion

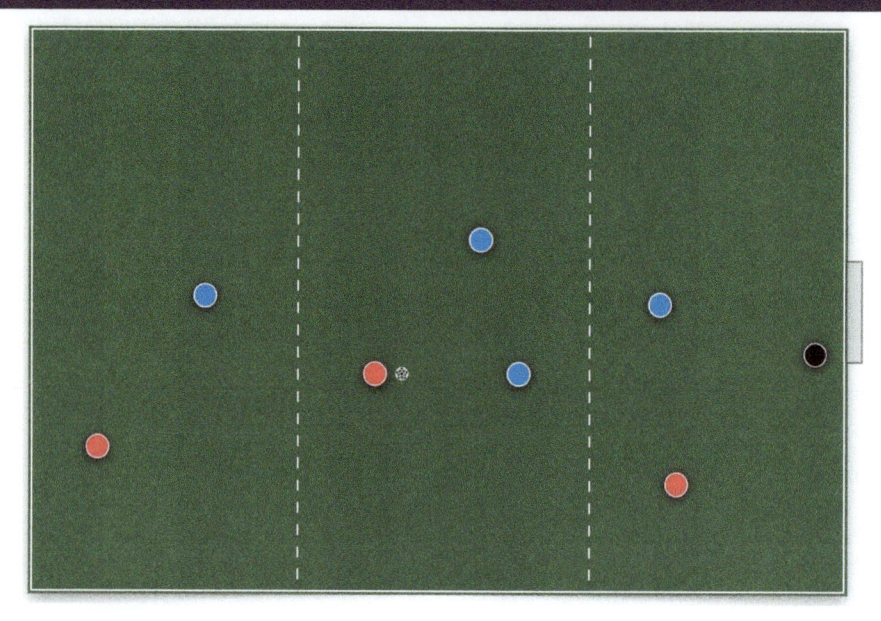

SESSION DETAIL

This is a uniquely designed task, to try and create situations where players are challenged to deal with their emotions when playing (defending). In the task, there are five players. Two situated behind the goal, who compete in a 1v1 battle. Two at the other end, who will look to attack the goalkeeper who is in the centre of the practice.

The setup is very simple; on the right hand side the red and the blue battle to try and stay in possession, this is an aggressive and physical 1v1 battle where one player looks to fight of the opponent from the ball. This 1v1 will challenge players who struggle to deal with the physical and emotional side of the game, as they will begin to struggle to deal with the emotional strain of the opponent being aggressive and picking at them, attempting to win the ball. As soon as the player in possession loses the ball, the coach will blow the whistle and they will need to run out and defend 1v1, in a realistic situation, in front of the goalkeeper, against the opposite colour bib.

This is looking to replicate a difficult moment of the game, within a controlled environment. The player will experience the emotion in the area behind the goal, and then be forced to control that emotion, and put it to one side to instantly defend 1v1 in a critical situation. Those who are able to control that emotion, are more likely to be successful with competing against the opponent.

Defending With Emotion

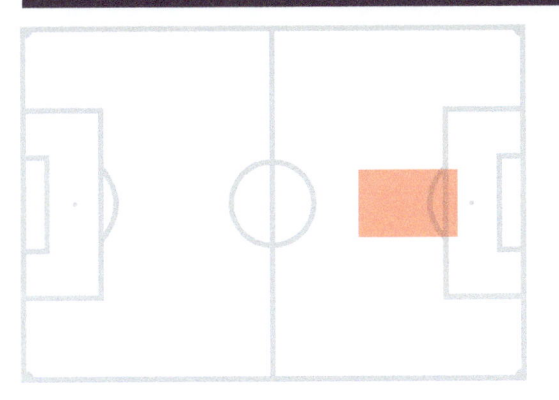

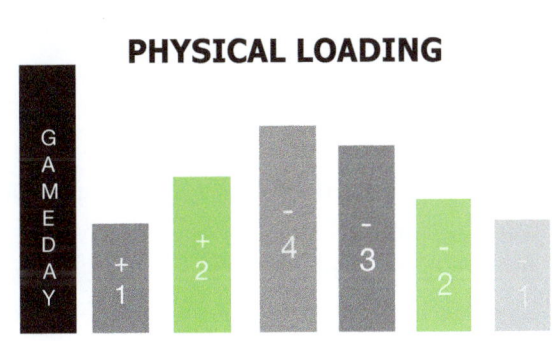

THE FOOTBALL COACH

PHYSICAL LOADING

| GAMEDAY | +1 | +2 | -4 | -3 | -2 | -1 |

WORKING	RECOVERY	BLOCKS	TOTAL
3 MINS	2 MINS	4 BLOCKS	20 MINS

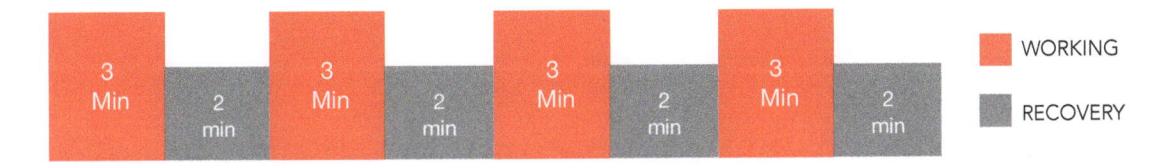

3 Min / 2 min / 3 Min / 2 min / 3 Min / 2 min / 3 Min / 2 min

- WORKING
- RECOVERY

PITCH SIZE:

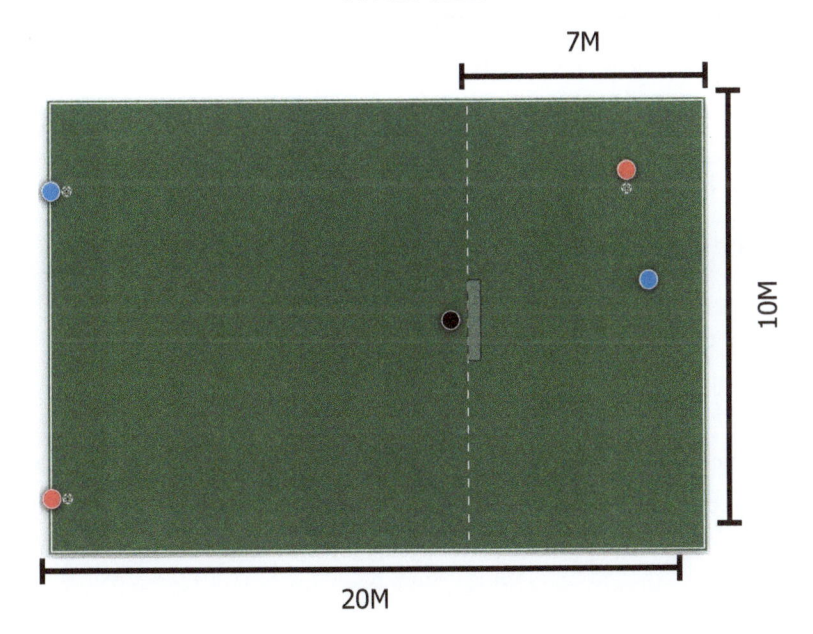

7M × 10M, 20M

Defending With Emotion

EMOTIONAL CONTROL

The ability to control our emotions is evidently important in all aspects of life however, it is as important in sport and specifically football. We have all seen the negative effect of a failure to control emotion; from the catastrophe theory, where athletes see a significant drop off in cognitive and physical performance to the loss of control and the consequence of punishment from match officials. However important emotional control is, it gets little grass based training opportunity with the modern training program. The period of adolescence offers great opportunities to develop emotional control in players.

In this practice, not all individuals will 'react' with a negative response to losing or competing in the 1v1 battle, some will relish the opportunity and look to compete. Some will become overly aggressive and look to dominate the 'fight' and consequently forget about the process and the outcome; the process being the technical information around defending 1v1, the outcome being the idea of keeping the ball out of the net in a 1v1 moment.

Others will react differently; some will be negatively influenced by the competitive and at times physical battle, and retreat in to a 'defeated' like state and lose task-engagement and motivation. At this point, we now know that the athlete is unable to perform at his or her highest level of performance. It is the responsibility of the coach, where possible, to frame the situation as a positive challenge rather than a negative threat for the player, where all setbacks are opportunities to learn and redirect negative toward positive emotions (energies).

COACHING IMPLICATIONS

For a coach training these moments can be difficult and requires consistency to frame and reframe moments to try and make players 'self-aware', if players are more aware of their emotions and the effect they have on personality, life and performance, they are more likely to try and control them. This is not our only responsibility as a coach; those players with more self-confidence are more likely to not lose task-engagement and application to the task. For these individuals it is important, as coaches, that we reframe performance and try to encourage and reward, creating a level of self-confidence.

Defending With Emotion

COACHING IMPLICATIONS

For others, they will require self-control and emotional-control and we as the coaches are able to influence and support the development of this. We know from research that we cannot always achieve full consistency in this area as; one, our players are human and, two, our players are still seeing huge amounts of neuron development. We are still able to scaffold the development, when players look close to losing control and your player-coach relationship allows, you should challenge the individuals to try and remain in control. These moments of aroused emotion allow teaching and learning opportunities where players can strengthen connectivity between frontal control and emotion circuits in their brain. Using tasks such as the 'red' and the 'blue' will help create a self-aware and self-controlling individual.

PLAYER IMPLICATIONS

For players, sessions like this can be very effective for creating the above mentioned 'self-awareness', but won't create lasting change; this is because players require consistency in how they are coached. Players who play in this session and are then punished for losing control of their emotions, will likely suffer more with their emotions. This is because those players will develop a fear of losing control however what we actually want is to develop their confidence in controlling their emotions. This means our players will require a consistent and open-minded approach at all times.

Players will struggle with emotions on different ends of the scale, some with aggression and at times perhaps violent approaches when they lose control of their emotions; becoming over aggressive in the defending 1v1. You may then find some players fail to remain engaged with the task and bring an almost 'defeated' approach. It is your job, as the coach, to recognise the type of personalities your players possess and use your player-coach relationship to manage and influence the person not the player.

THE FOOTBALL COACH

SESSION PLAN

One Step Ahead of the Game

One Step Ahead of the Game

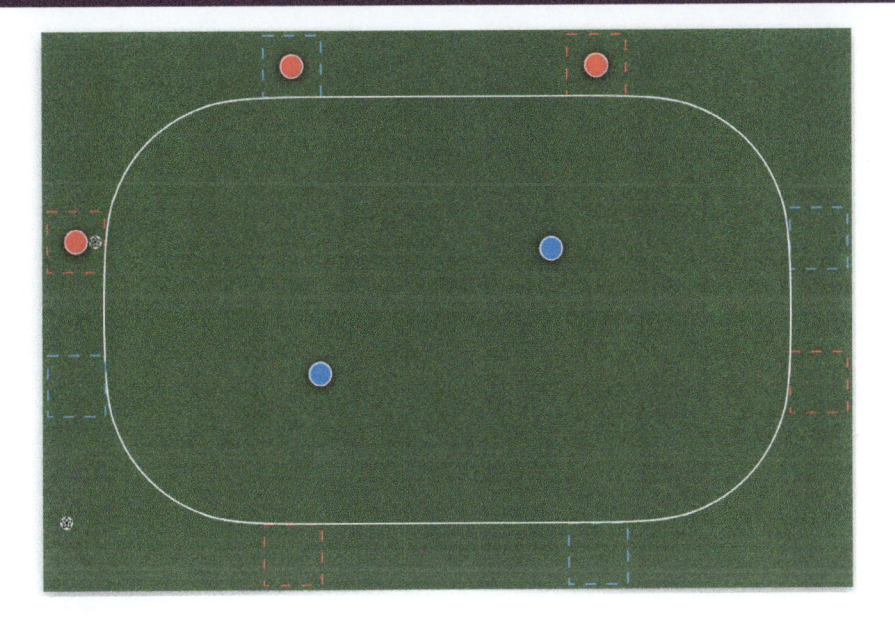

THE FOOTBALL COACH

SESSION DETAIL

This unique rondo-like session is a great way to develop decision making and engagement in a simple task. The task only requires five players and a small amount of space. The cognitive challenge is very simple, we want to challenge the decision making process players take. For example, when does a player start thinking about their decision, not what is the decision? In this task we are valuing the timing of the thought; the players who are able to think earlier and find the open space might be able to have a greater influence in the task.

The task itself is very simple to deliver to players; the space is 18m long and 12m wide. The inside two (in blue) look to win possession from the three outside players (Red). The task complexity comes in as players can only pass the ball from different coloured zones. For example, the ball can only go from a red square to a blue square and not from a red square to a red square. If this happens, then the practice changes over and the two blues come out of the centre of the practice and onto the outside.

This is now training the task complexity we want to achieve, the players must now have a high level cognitive engagement for people to recognise space, find gaps in the opponent shape, find team mate movement and recognise the colour of the space they have made their movement into.

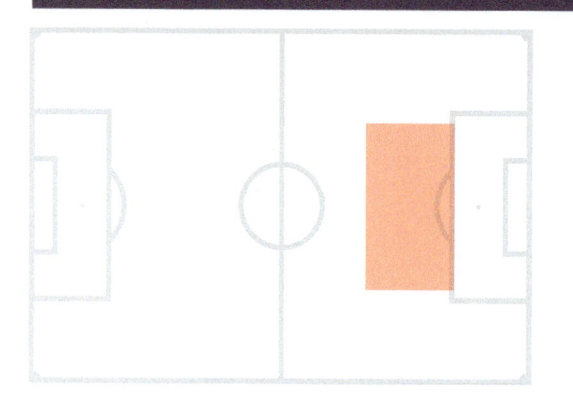

One Step Ahead of the Game

PHYSICAL LOADING

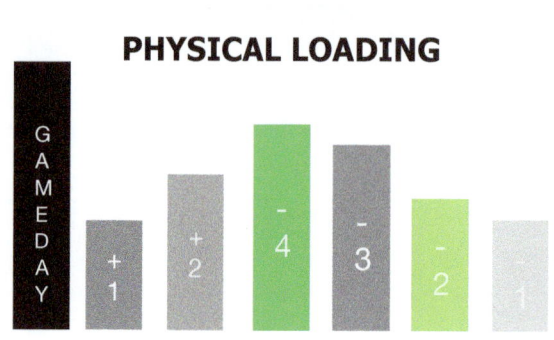

GAMEDAY | +1 | +2 | -4 | -3 | -2 | -1

WORKING	RECOVERY	BLOCKS	TOTAL
4 MINS	1 MINS	4 BLOCKS	20 MINS

- WORKING: 4 Min
- RECOVERY: 1 min

PITCH SIZE: 18M x 12M

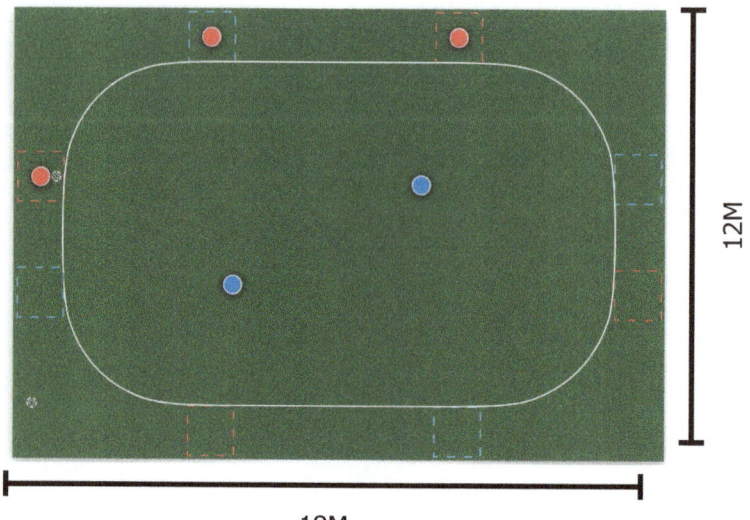

One Step Ahead of the Game

DECISION MAKING

Decision making plays a huge part in football, it is often said that the wrong decision with the right technique is still a negative outcome. This just shows that however important technique and tactics are within the game, our ability to make effective decisions under pressure, still outline our effectiveness. The decisions created within this practice are realistic to the challenge players will see in games, and create the kind of task complexity required. The complexity in this task is directed at every player involved.

Out of possession - those out of possession will need to make decisions that try and force the opponent to play passes to and from the same colour areas. This will offer them opportunity to win possession

Passing Player - will need to take in a raft of information when playing a pass, area, distances, opponent grid colour etc

Receiving Player - where is my next pass going, who can pass me the ball, where can I receive?

COACHING IMPLICATIONS

For coaches, creating decision makers can effectively be trained and improved by the use of intelligent task design, along with an environment and approach to coaching that is consistent and deliberate. What that means is, allowing players to make decisions, and following up with them when they have made a poor decision, along with recognising when to step in and speak with the player properly if it has become a habit, and the player needs support. It is also important to recognise that making a mistake is normal, and not every mistake requires coach intervention. Sometimes, we must be self-aware; players know when they've given the ball away, they know the consequences and they didn't mean to do it; it might not be the decision that was poor, it might have been the application of technique. We know at this phase of development that learning through instrumental or 'trial and error' feedback (dopamine delight and dopamine disappointment) is at its most efficient, where learning signals peak relative to other stages for growth.

One Step Ahead of the Game

With this in mind, we still need to communicate with our players when decisions are made in this practice in order to understand their thought process, and challenge their way of thinking. We do not necessarily want to change it, but we want to help them understand why they are making the decisions they are. Feedback and the bandwidth of feedback will not directly transfer to those who are more successful in these tasks, we know from evidence that some players/people are much more able to discuss their thought than others.

PLAYER IMPLICATIONS

For players, these tasks are a fantastic way of creating deeper thinking when competing within a task; the players are challenged to think with a level of complexity that will be similar to those game moments they experience. Players who aren't aware of their surroundings and are not thinking about the decision ahead, will struggle to be successful in this practice because of the constant cognitive challenge that exists.

With the use of tasks like this on a consistent basis, we will see players adapt to try and deal with the failure they are experiencing; they will begin to lift their head, take their eyes off the ball and begin to see the bigger picture of space and movement around them.

They will improve their decision-making by immersing themselves in the environment in an embodied process. Once they are able to use this space around them, we will naturally see an increase in the success of players in this practice, and practices like it.

We must also remember that learning is not linear and as players begin to develop the confidence to scan and make braver decisions, so will we see an increase in transitions because of the risk taken. We as coaches must be brave enough as individuals to accept this and praise the process over the outcome.

SESSION PLAN

Warzone – FOOTBALLROYALE

Warzone - FOOTBALLROYALE

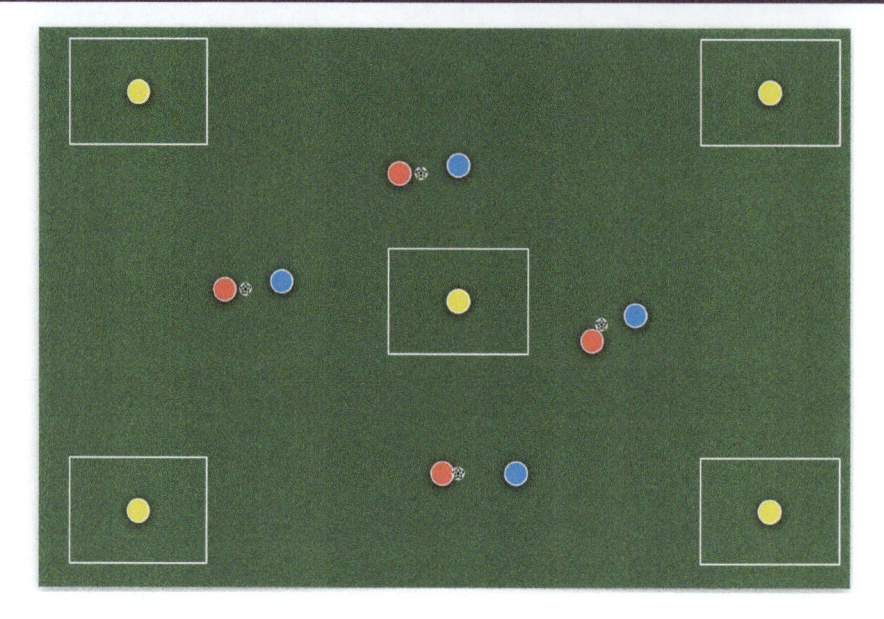

SESSION DETAIL

Warzone provides players with a chaotic session, packed with decision making and creativity. The players in this session will work hard physically and will make decisions throughout the practice, both simple and complex. They will need to be creative to dominate 1v1 situations and unlock space to hurt the opponent.

The session has three teams, Red, Blue and Yellow. The yellows act as bounce players and sit inside small boxes in the five detailed areas (these can be in different areas to challenge a game model). The reds then have possession of the ball, in this example; the blues are defending. The idea of the game is for the reds to play a bounce pass with every yellow (or a specific amount of bounce passes e.g. 10 bounce passes) in order to win. The blues look to steal possession and achieve the same task themselves, whilst the yellows just have to bounce pass.

Every time the task ends, the yellows switch with the reds, and the reds switch with the blues, going around in a circle, meaning every player has a different job to do every time the session restarts. Within this practice, although players are only competing 1v1, they will need to make constant cognitive decisions as well as find space within. A great chaotic and complicated task.

Warzone - FOOTBALLROYALE

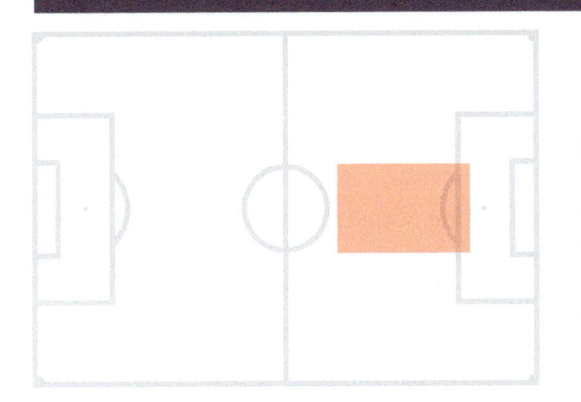

PHYSICAL LOADING

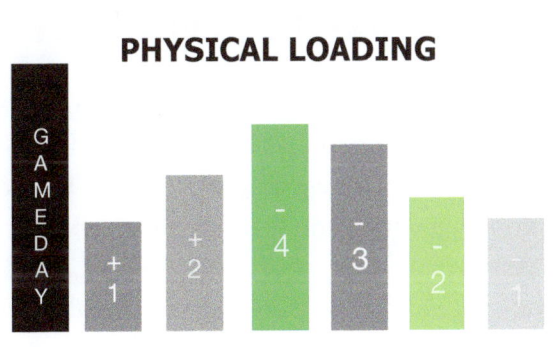

GAMEDAY | +1 | +2 | -4 | -3 | -2 | -1

WORKING	RECOVERY	BLOCKS	TOTAL
4 MINS	1 MIN	4 BLOCKS	20 MINS

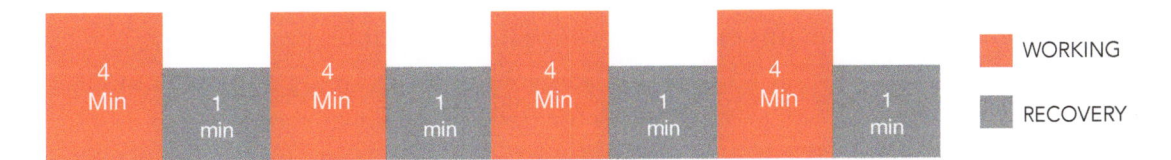

- WORKING
- RECOVERY

PITCH SIZE: 20M × 15M

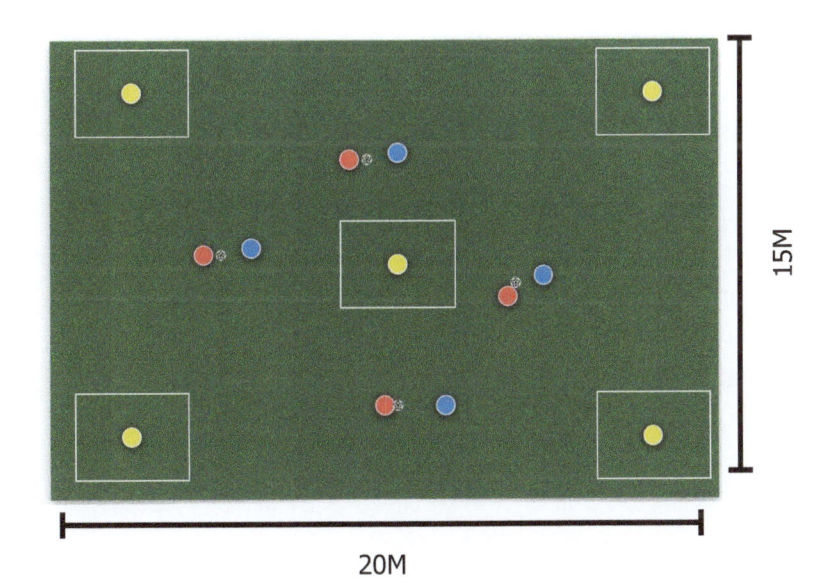

Warzone - FOOTBALLROYALE

DECISION MAKING / CREATIVITY

Decision making and creativity are two psychological traits challenged in this practice. Players will need to make decisions under pressure from different stimuli. They will need to be innovative and resourceful. The session will be compact with 10 players competing within the space at a high intensity, covering lots of distance and constantly changing direction, speed and point of attack. This will make it difficult for players to find space and recognise when to pass the ball and when to run with the ball. This is one of the key decisions in football, when to release the ball. The task is even more complex as the decision will also require a greater level of thinking and you are now aware that you're not the only player in possession. The pass you might be about to play, might be the same pass a teammate is about to play, so at the last minute you might need to stay in possession.

Once you have to stay in possession, you might find yourself being pressed and under pressure from the opponent, this means that you will need to either be very strong in possession or find a moment of creativity to beat your opponent and get away from the opposition. This creativity will be mixed with the decision making, when will you use the creativity? Will being effectively timed and deployed allow you to find a successful response to the pressure being applied by the opponent?

COACHING IMPLICATIONS

When delivering this session there isn't a huge amount of coaching that is required, this is because of the task design. What is required, in all instances where coaches aim to foster creativity, is a secure, non judgemental environment. Where 'interesting mistakes' are made that can be learnt from. This session is of a high intensity and creates a non-stop design in its setup. The natural flowing session will provide repetition in either the success or failure (or a mixture of). During the recovery (60 seconds), it might be poignant to just share one consistent problem that players are experiencing just to challenge the thought process and response from players. For example, if the players are all passing the ball into the same end player and losing possession.

Warzone - FOOTBALLROYALE

Question Boys/Girls, how many times have we seen balls role out of the practice because two players make the same pass? How can this be avoided? Answer: Communication and eye contact with the person receiving possession to make sure that the receiver is aware of the action and you're not passing to a player who is distracted or not comfortable receiving possession. It will also be an important moment for coaches to praise positive intent in 1v1 situations in these practices as this can be a challenging environment to find success from a creative point of view in 1v1 situations. However this doesn't mean that some players with better technical ability, won't find success.

PLAYER IMPLICATIONS

For players this is a fantastic opportunity to be creative within a low risk environment which will offer compact space and little decision making time. This challenge will be one that is realistic to the challenge they encounter in match day situations and will provide an opportunity to players, both with and without the ball. In order to challenge the decision making, players might need opportunity to discuss their options and plan with teammates.

This might mean bringing the reds together for example and challenging them to find a way in which they are able to find more success (what is success? Making more passes in the yellow areas). Creativity is a mixture of generative and analytical thinking. Players can generate creative play in secure, nurturing context and then analyse the usefulness of these outcomes in discussions with peers and coaches.

Players might become frustrated and disheartened by a lack of success and too great of a challenge. If this is the case, frame the positive moments they have but also rotate the players to ensure we don't come across a situation where a player is put into a physical challenge they can't gain success from.

SESSION PLAN

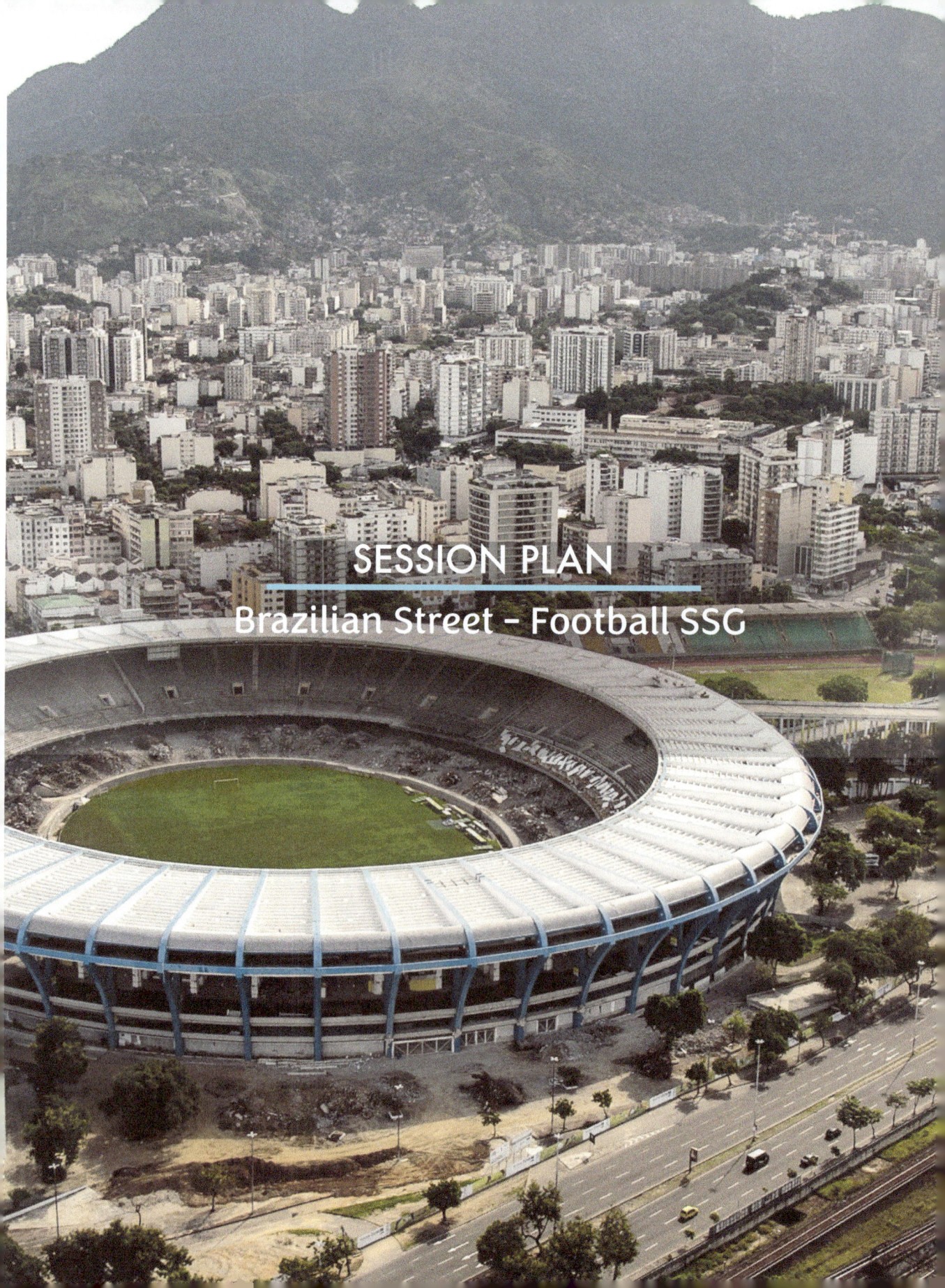

Brazilian Street – Football SSG

Brazilian Street Football SSG

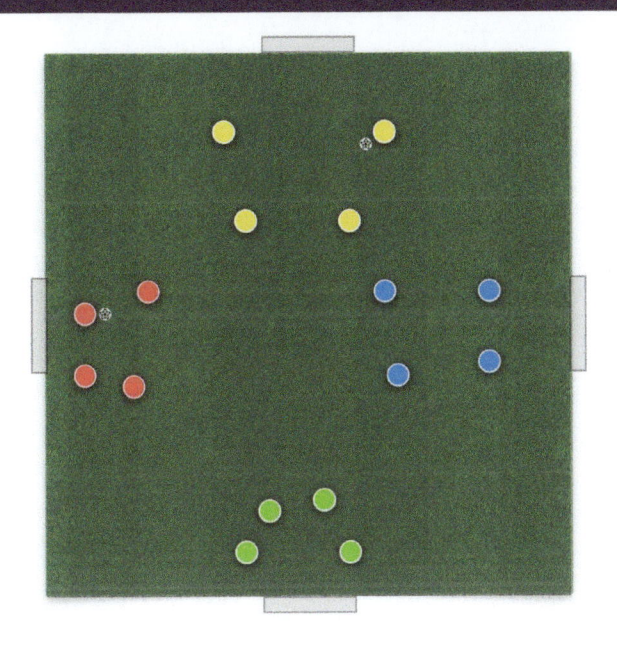

SESSION DETAIL

Brazilian Street Football Chaos is a 16 player, small sided game that involves four different teams. To set this practice up, all you need is four mini goals, four sets of bibs, and 16 players (or a group of players divided by four). You then very simply play 4v4 across the width of the pitch, with 4v4 being played from top to bottom. This is a very simple practice, that creates chaos for the players as they are playing against four players, but the complexity of 16 players within the space makes life difficult for players.

The players' decision making process is challenged by the design of the practice, there is not multiple challenges and stimuli, the complexity of the practice is created by the design of the session and the lack of space players have to deal with. Players will constantly need to scan and move to find space in a compact and chaotic playing area. If players are to be successful in this playing area, they will need to be dominant and dynamic in 1v1 situations and must be able to make movements away from pressure in tight space, that allow them to get in possession and stay in possession of the ball.

The difficulty in this session will be finding the right playing size dependent on the age and ability of the players involved. For example we recommend a 20x20m area but this will vary dependent on the age, size and ability of the group involved.

Brazilian Street Football SSG

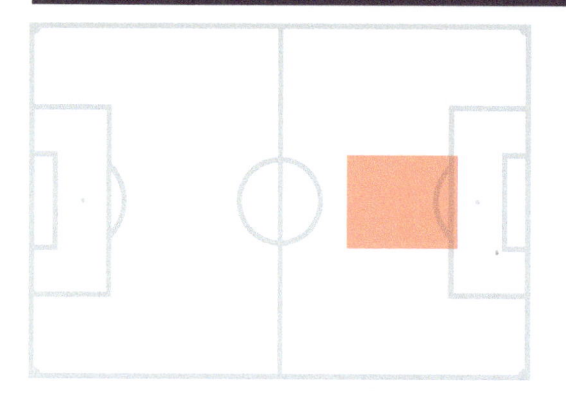

PHYSICAL LOADING

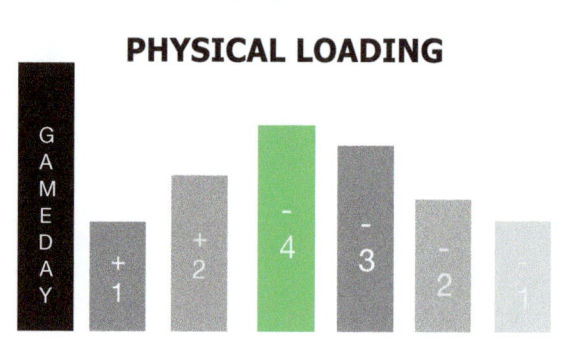

GAMEDAY | +1 | +2 | -4 | -3 | -2 | -1

WORKING	RECOVERY	BLOCKS	TOTAL
WORKING	RECOVERY	BLOCKS	BLOCKS

6 Min — 1 min — 6 Min — 2 min — 6 Min — 1 min

- WORKING
- RECOVERY

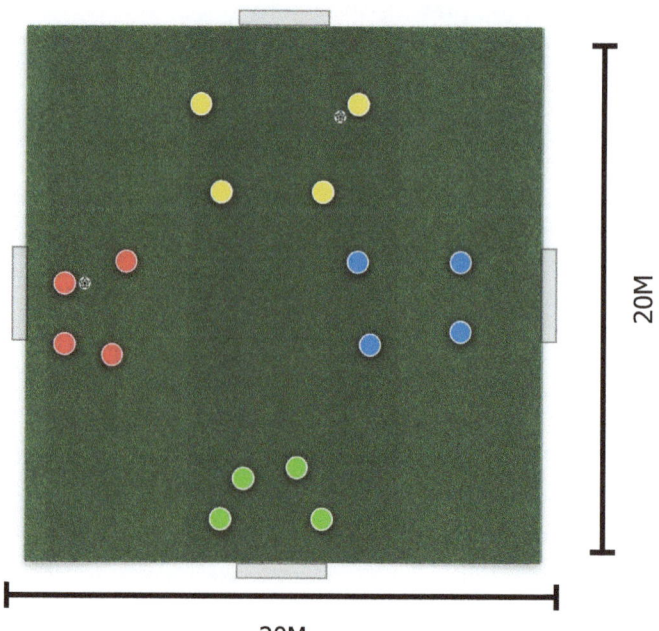

20M × 20M

Brazilian Street Football SSG

DECISION MAKING / CREATIVITY

This chaotic small sided game, provides players with a challenge to their decision making process. They will be used to make decisions with space around them in a single directional game. This multidirectional game, will make them aware of the space around them, the chaos around them and the challenge in manoeuvring around these problems. The element of direction (the multi direction) will challenge players thought process when seeing players. Who are the players? Can they engage me? Which game are they playing in? Where are they likely to move?

All the above questions are thoughts that players in possession of the ball will be thinking at all times (either consciously or intrinsically) in order to exploit the opponent and have some sort of dominance over them. Decision making is not the only element trained within here. Creativity will be very important within this small sided game, this is because the small space and large numbers outs of possession 4v12, will mean players become detached and isolated very quickly. Once this happens, can players be creative in the 1v1 moments in order to exploit the opponent and create goal scoring opportunities? Finishing will also need to be creative, as using small goals can require a one touch finish to create realism; being creative with that one touch will lead to more goals being scored in the practice.

COACHING IMPLICATIONS

With a small sided game, we must accept that the game is the teacher to an extent. The players will experience the decision making and creative moments regularly because of the fluidity of the task. The constant opportunity to train these moments will ensure opportunity for success and failure.

The learning happens at the mind, body and brain level, through dynamic engagement with the environment rather than instruction from the coach. To build this understanding during the adolescent years is important as we've mentioned before, it is a good period to strengthen brain connectivity.

Brazilian Street Football SSG

There are implications for coaches in many different ways during this practice. Coaches may watch this session and notice individuals who struggle to make decisions under pressure, this can have future implications for modifying practice design for individual development.

When we notice these moments, we don't always need to react instantly, as advice or modification might not provide instant success to the player. The reality is, we will need to take in the information and use the other sessions we have detailed, in this book, over a long period of time, to help the player discover the decision making and spacial awareness traits that are required to be successful.

PLAYER IMPLICATIONS

The players will relish the opportunity to compete within a small sided game that provides a technical challenge, because of the chaos caused by the lack of space. Players will do a few different things within the practice, some will hide from the chaos and find space towards the outside of the practice.

We might try and challenge those players to play within the practice, in a more central space. This will challenge the individual to be more aware of the space from all 360 degrees. We also need to challenge those players who start internally and look to dominate 1v1's constantly. Are they doing this because they see the opportunity or because they just want to attack? Let's frame the session as a challenge to find space and see if this has an impact on how they play within the practice.

SESSION PLAN
Complex Positional Rondo

Complex Positional Rondo

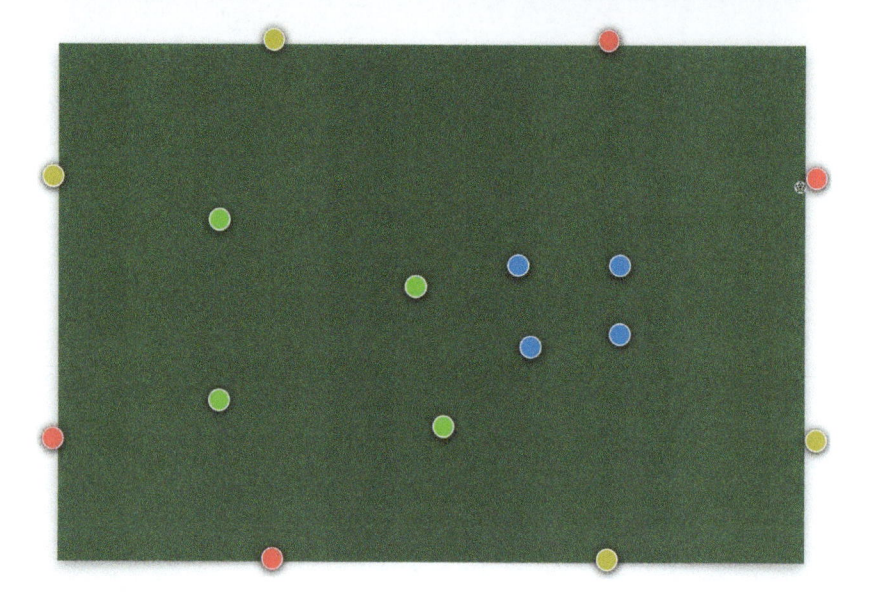

SESSION DETAIL

The session name 'Complex Positional Rondo', explains exactly what this session is. It is a simple rondo task, modified to ensure that it drives cognitive engagement and deliberate decision making tasks. These decisions vary from transitional moments, to decisions to pass or to stay on the ball etc. The size of the pitch will also mean that a variety of technical skills are required. This could be running with the ball, dribbling, passing or 1v1 skills. This variety increases the decision making spectrum and makes the practice more realistic and more transferable to skills that are required in the large sided game.

The task itself is very simple; remember it is a rondo within a 18x25m shape. The players are split into four teams, reds, blues, greens and yellows for this example. Two teams pair up to make the practice 8v8. For example, in this practice the reds are playing with the blues. The yellows are situated on the outside and cant receive possession from blue or red. The reds are combining to keep possession with the blues, and the yellows are pressing. If the blues give away possession they must transition out, and the reds come in. Now the yellows have the ball inside the rondo combining with the other yellows. They will keep the ball until it is given away; once they give possession away, they will transition outside and the yellows will come inside. This game has a constant transitional element that challenges decision making, focus and concentration.

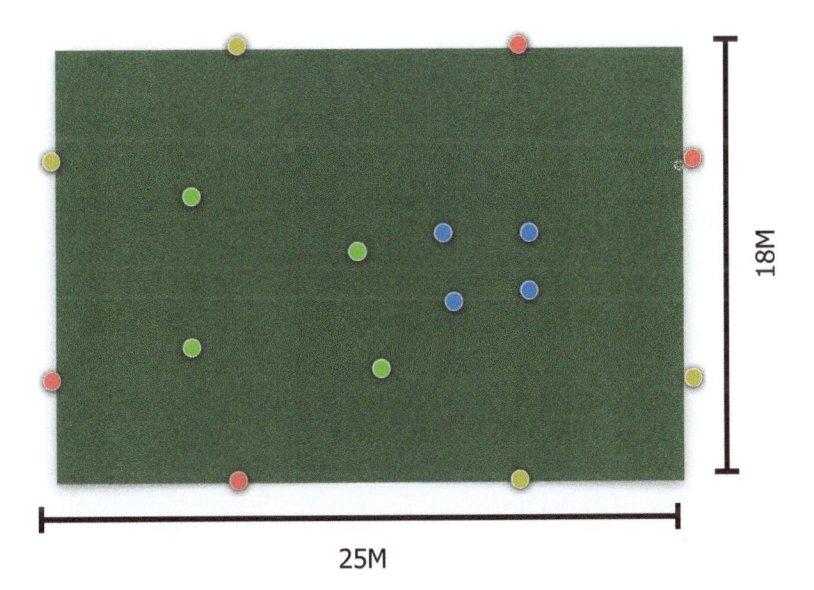

Complex Positional Rondo

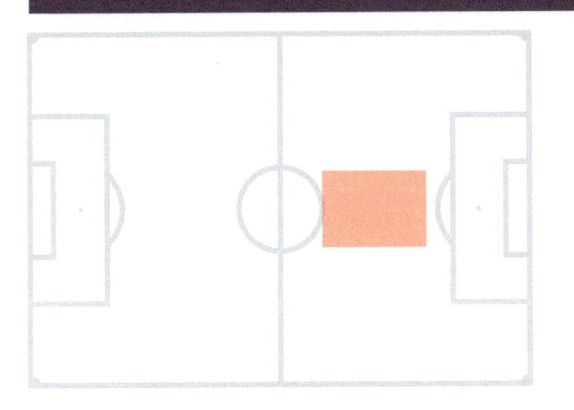

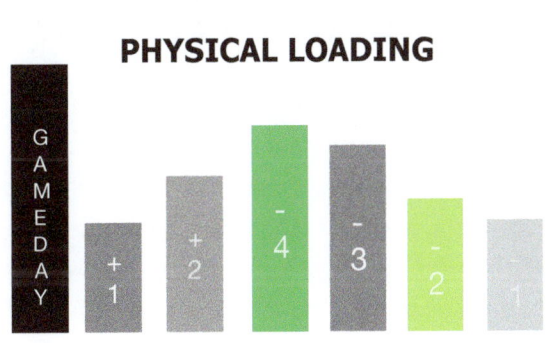

PHYSICAL LOADING

GAMEDAY | +1 | +2 | -4 | -3 | -2 | -1

WORKING	RECOVERY	BLOCKS	TOTAL
5 MINS	1 MIN	4 BLOCKS	24 MINS

- WORKING: 5 Min × 4
- RECOVERY: 1 min × 4

PITCH SIZE: 25M × 18M

Complex Positional Rondo

DECISION MAKING / CREATIVITY

The idea of a complex positional rondo, is a really effective way of challenging the decision making process players will experience within a context that is manageable but realistic and tangible to the game. We will see players who naturally turn to play passes to the outside of the practice because it is a rondo, with out taking in to account the information and detail that is required to be successful and efficient. These players will be caught out because of the complexity to the task. The complexity comes from the outside players being both team mates and opponents, players now need to raise their head find the right player, take in to account the space and position of other team mates and the opponent, then make a decision. This complexity is more game like.

However, these are not the only psychological tasks that occur within the game, because of how transitional the task is, players will need to recognise the offensive and defensive transition instantly and then make the movement that is required. This is not a 'decision' like other moments of the game, because of how the outcome is already decided e.g. lose ball = get to the outside of practice. This trains the reactive and proactive elements of performance, with players needing to react quickly and recognise the game moment. Once they recognise the game moment, they must move quickly to ensure they are able to have an influence on the practice.

COACHING IMPLICATIONS

For us as coaches, we must know how to influence the practice, and what we are looking for within the practice. The decisions that are most coachable within here, are the decisions where the outcome is black and white, these are the moments where the ball is lost; this is more of a requirement than a decision. When you lose the ball, you must make your way to the outside of the practice, this is directly transferable to the game and directly coachable and can be a more instructional manor coaching.

On other occasions, the complex nature of the task enables players to make decisions in an embodied way. This occurs in frantic 'at action' moments, where there is 'no time to think'. Here, players' learn in a 'non-conscious' manner by engaging with the environment in a trial and error fashion. The coaches' role in these instances is one of a facilitator, offering guidance on occasion and concentrating on 'getting the game right'.

Complex Positional Rondo

Other decisions within the practice will need a more open minded and chorused approach to coaching, when players are making rational decisions in the central area. They might be flustered or confused by the tightness and complexity of the task, this is OK and support can be provided to players to help them deal with this problem. It is important for coaches to recognise who the individual is and why they are struggling, if it is a player who doesn't usually struggle, is there a specific part of the task that is providing them with a problem? If it is the majority of the group struggling, is it that the space itself is either too narrow or too short, and consequently players are struggling to be able to control possession?

PLAYER IMPLICATIONS

Players who are more cognitively engaged in these tasks, will likely be those who are more cognitively engaged in games. Encouraging engagement with the complexity of the task will hopefully help engage those who drop in and out of engagement. We have all worked with those individuals who struggle to remain focused, although not all of those individuals will be ones we can influence.

Encouraging engagement within an engaging task will help influence a portion of those individuals. Some players will show a lack of understanding from a technical and tactical point of view during these sessions, and that lack of understanding or skill set will have an influence on their ability to find effectiveness with good decision making.

This is why it is so important, as coaches, that we reward the process and not the outcome. By rewarding the process not the outcome, the player becomes engaged and understands that its not only important to get the the correct outcome, but it is even more important to find the outcome the right way

SESSION PLAN

1v1 Attacking Small Sided Games

1v1 Attacking Small Sided Games

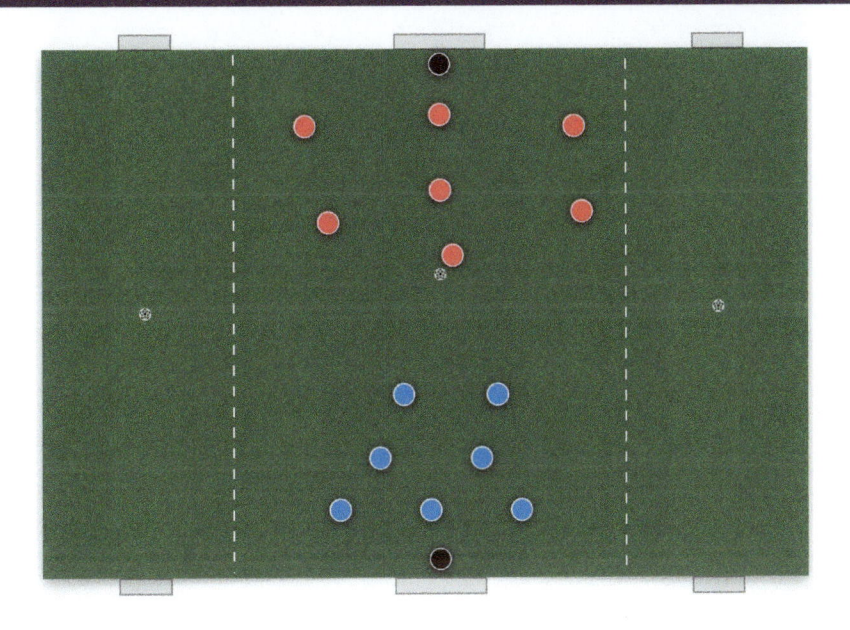

SESSION DETAIL

1v1 attacking small sided games, is a really insightful decision making session, that requires players to have a deep understanding of the task and the implications their decisions can have on the game. The practice exists as a 7v7 in the central pitch, this can be a 5v5 or a 6v6, or as you see fit. The game is very simple, the players play a standard game of football in the central space. Once a goal is scored, the players must make a decision, they can use either or both of the wide areas to try and double or triple their goal. However, there is a catch, the opponent can defend in the 1v1 situation, and if they win possession back, they can go and score at the opposite end. This means the reds can score and end up 2-1 down from that goal. This will challenge the risk and reward element of decision making and force players to give consideration to the way and approach of their attack.

Decision making paves a huge part of the game young players play, they must recognise the risk, the reward and the situation. In this moment we are asking players to be aware of the bigger picture, the game environment and the consequence of their decision. This type of accountability and self-awareness will hopefully drive a more conscious and aware individual, who is able to make decisions that are not only important for themselves, but their collective team as well.

1v1 Attacking Small Sided Games

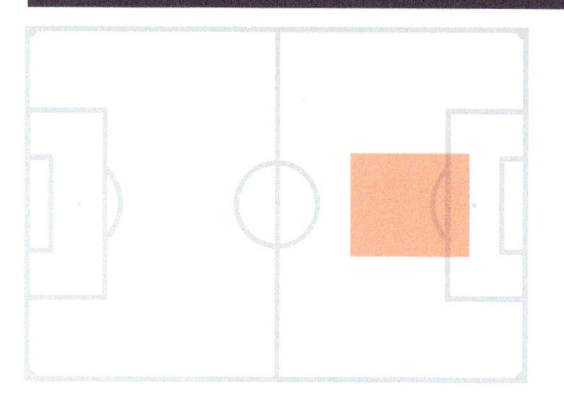

PHYSICAL LOADING

| GAMEDAY | +1 | +2 | -4 | -3 | -2 | -1 |

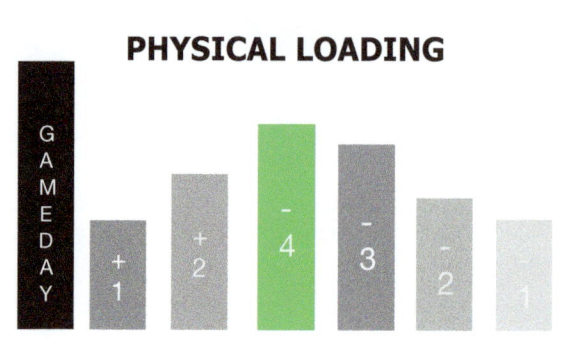

WORKING	RECOVERY	BLOCKS	TOTAL
5 MINS	1 MINS	4 BLOCKS	24 MINS

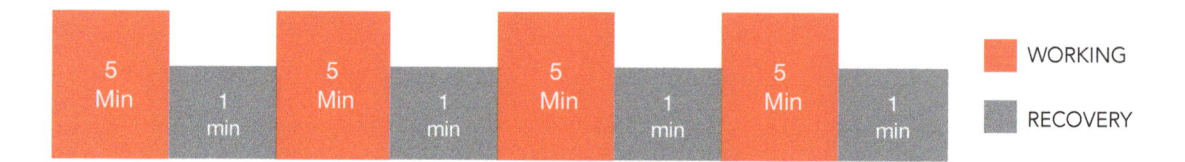

- WORKING: 5 Min × 4
- RECOVERY: 1 min × 4

PITCH SIZE: 35M × 20M

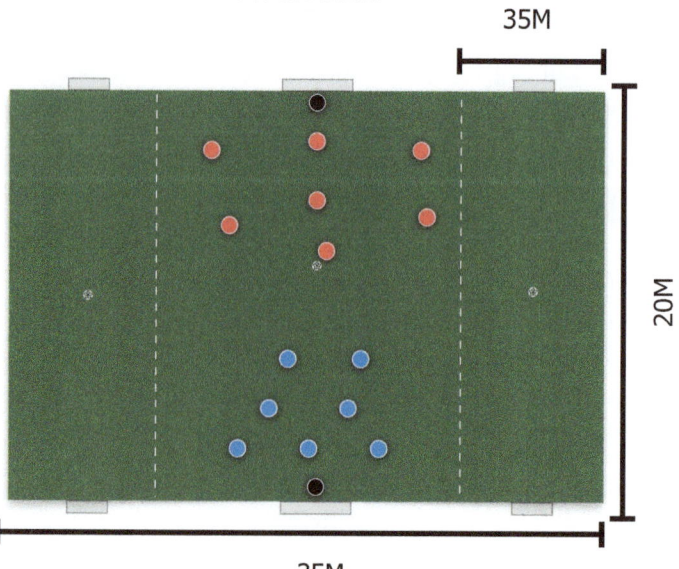

1v1 Attacking Small Sided Games

DECISION MAKING / CREATIVITY

1v1 Attacking Small Sided Games really does give a good opportunity for coaches to challenge players' decision making processes, help understand the thought process and try and build stronger processes to those decisions. We will naturally see individuals make different decisions during this practice. We may see younger players with less of a developed pre-frontal cortex, make much riskier decisions because they are unable to effectively see the risk. That imbalance between the value of reward and the consequence of risk can provide highly risky individuals, and individuals we should take caution with managing. If we are to instruct these individuals that they are 'wrong', they won't naturally experience the failure and begin to see the implications of the risk as the front of their brain develops. It is much easier to instruct, and much more important to allow mistakes to occur, speak with players, ask questions that involve deep level thinking and challenge the player to give an in-depth understanding of what they saw and why they made the decision they made.

It might be poignant for us as coaches to try and drip feed information about the consequence of the risk, but with young adolescents the neurological damage of instructing, could lead to players becoming to fearful of the coaches' consequence and consequently turning down positive moments for the desire of pleasing the coach.

COACHING IMPLICATIONS

Deep level learning is something we want to achieve as coaches; we want our players to have an understanding and level of thought that is much deeper than just what they see. The only way we will be able to achieve this, is to challenge individuals in sessions like this, that have a complexity across many different components. Sessions that involve physical and cognitive stress as well as coaching methods that really look to dig into the thought process of young players and attempt to see the game, and the world through their eyes. Once we have this depth to our design, we can begin to drip feed information and play principles into the training, as we have done here. To encourage risk-taking and creativity the coach must construct a psychologically safe environment. This occurs where the 'fear of failure' is minimised and 'mistakes' are seen as inevitable, even potentially useful. This is especially the case for adolescents.

1v1 Attacking Small Sided Games

In this practice, we will likely be able to really drive positive behaviours, leading to players who want to go and attack players in 1v1 situations, but we must also be consciously aware of the impact our 'driving' and 'influence' can have on the players' decision. Not only can we make players make negative decisions because of our forceful coaching, we can at times over emphasise the importance of being positive and take the decision away from the player. In these situations, the coach has forced the player to make the decision they 'think' they want the coach to see, and not a decision based on the technical, tactical, physical and psychological information they have experienced in the moment.

COACHING IMPLICATIONS

For players in the adolescent years, these sessions can give such a high level of task enjoyment, and repetition that they begin to see the risks and understand the situation because of the repetition and the engagement from those who might be more engaged through further development and understanding. They are learning in a trial and error capacity, something that the adolescent brain is primed for. Either way, these high engaging sessions will have a vast amount of returns for the player, from technical and tactical, to physical and psychological. The individual's decision making ability can be trained through a complex task that trains the coaches' game model.

Some individuals might struggle to cope with the consequence of costing the team in an individually responsible session design like this. It is important as coaches that we recognise the individuals who we believe might suffer in this way and encourage them and try to reframe the moment as an opportunity to be successful, rather than a moment of high consequence. Although this might be difficult, the use of highly influential members of the group to support you might encourage a more positive approach from others.

1v1 Attacking Small Sided Games

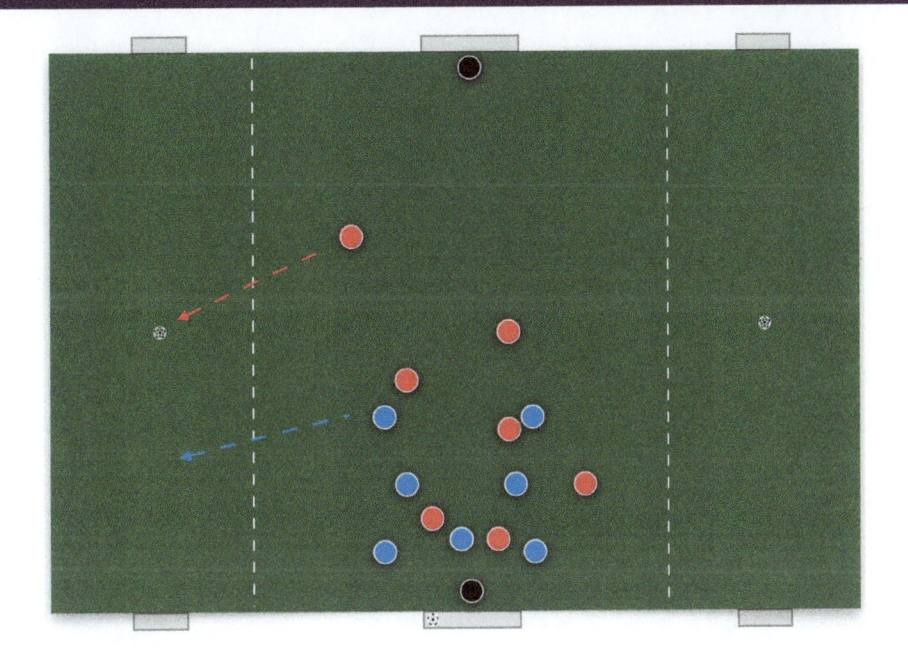

The second and third image here show how the practice might look when players enter the wide area. In this image the reds have scored and have decided to take on one 1v1 opportunity to double their goal. In the third image at the bottom, the reds have got beyond the blue defender and have scored to make it 2-0.

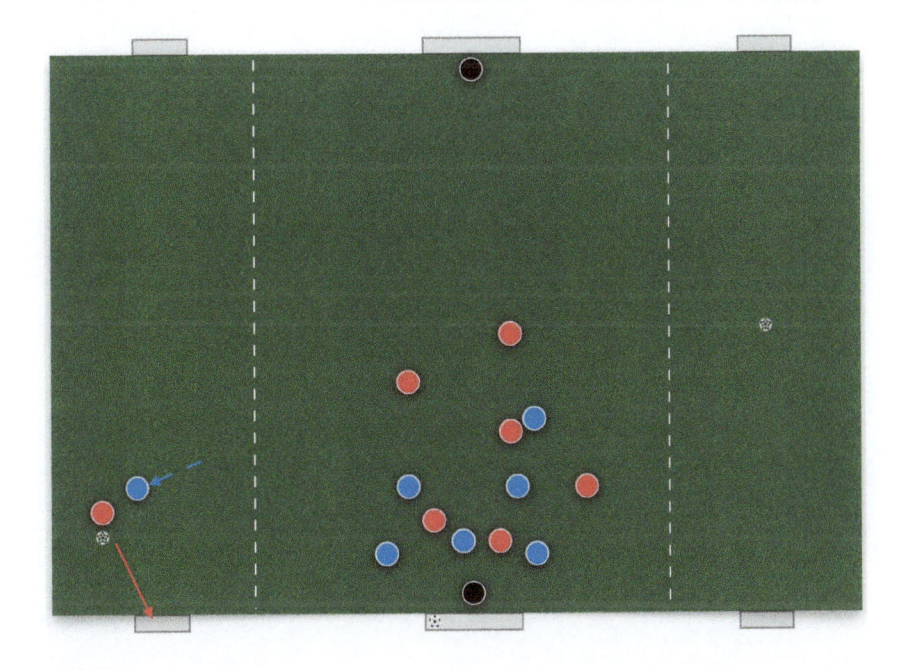

SESSION PLAN

Small Sided Games – Question Game

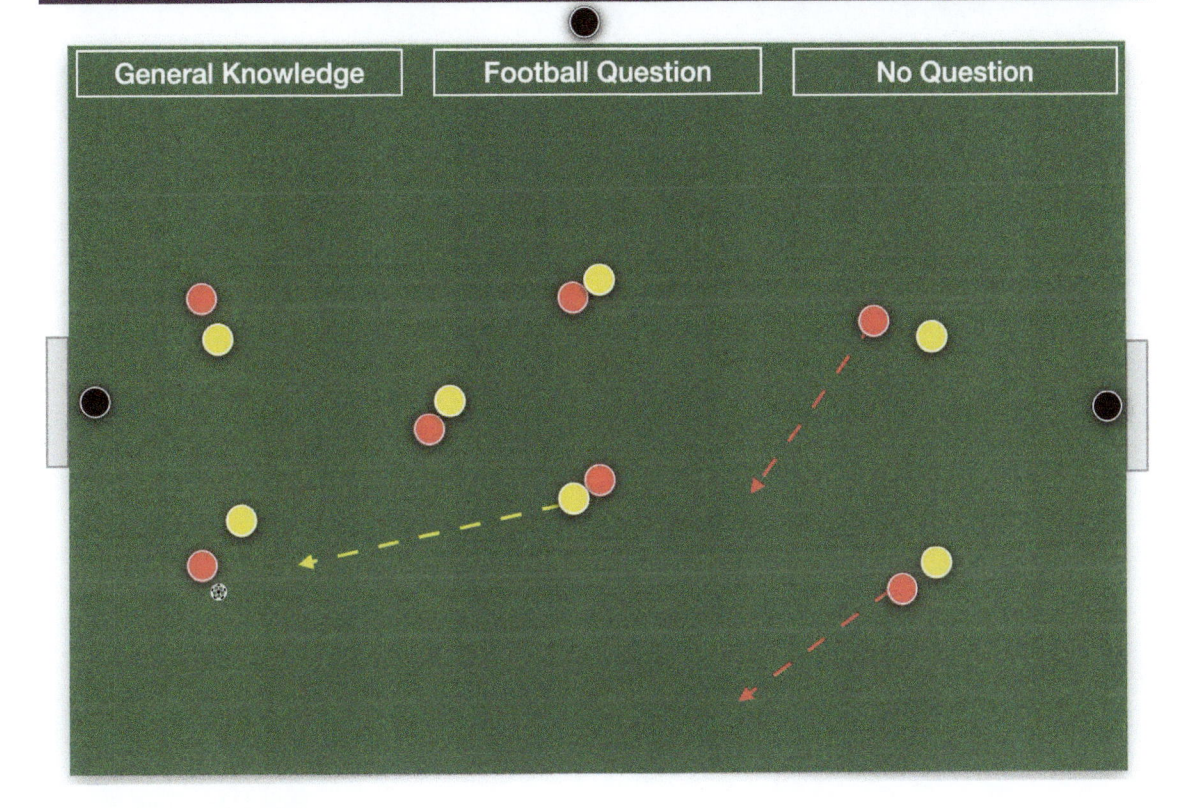

Small Sided Games - Question Game

THE FOOTBALL COACH

| General Knowledge | Football Question | No Question |

SESSION DETAIL

The question game is a fun and enjoyable game that drives engagement through a task complexity involving each goal scored. Within this small sided game, each time a team scores, the player who scores has a to make a decision from one of three options. Option one, is they run to the 'no question box' and this means they receive their one goal and can rejoin the practice.

The second option is to take a 'football question', for professional clubs this might be a historical question based on the club they are at. This drives a deeper understanding of the club and it's history. This question is a double or quits question, if the players get it correct, they get to go to 2-0 up, however if they get it wrong, the goals are awarded to the other team, meaning they go 2-0 down.

Small Sided Games – Question Game

| General Knowledge | Football Question | No Question |

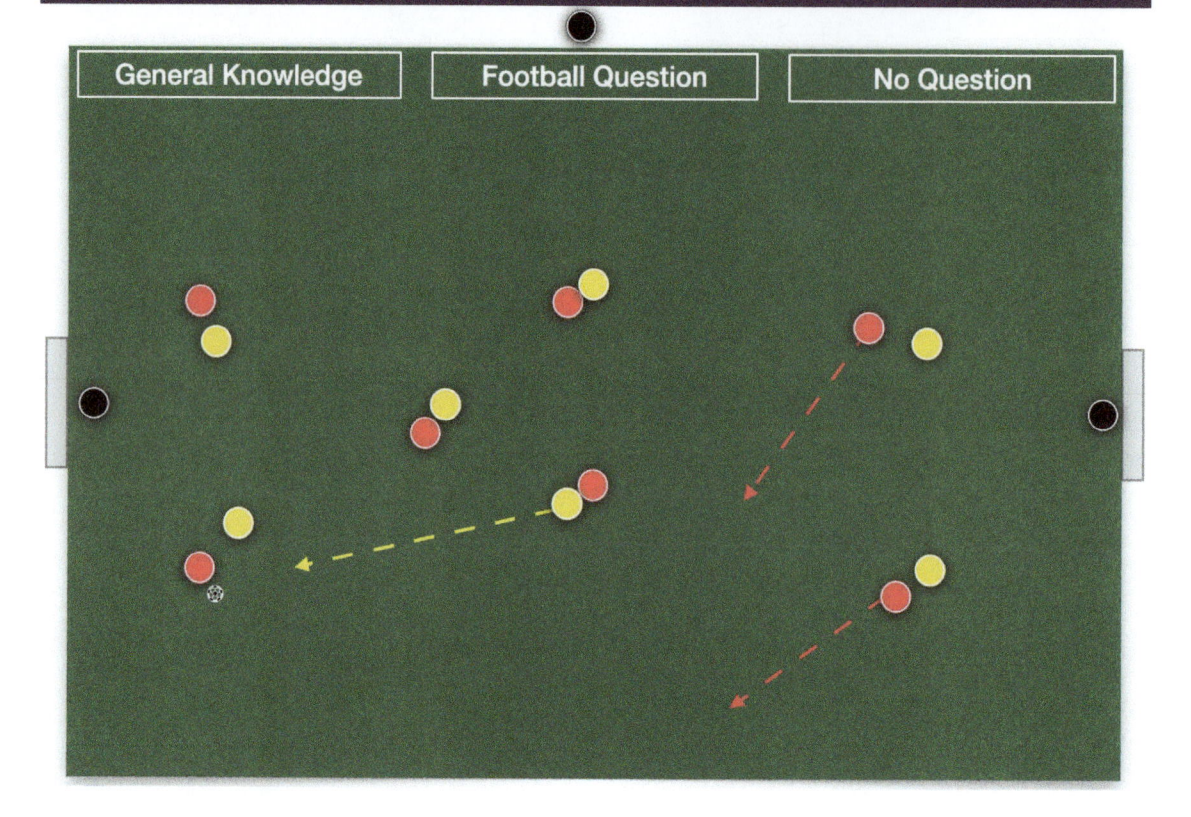

SESSION DETAIL

The third option is to take a general knowledge question, this general knowledge question is worth triple goals but again, is a double or quits question. This means it would make the opponent lead 3-0 if the question is correct.

This type of practice challenges players to make decisions involving the outcome of the game, whilst developing life skills and understanding of the world and cultures around them. The questions can be intelligently designed to drive a deeper understanding of the world whilst the tactical outcomes mean that whilst a player is answering a question, the team that have conceded have the opportunity to attack with an overload. The coach should try and make the goal question last around 30 seconds, this way the team out of possession will have to start attacking with an overload for a short period.

Small Sided Games – Question Game

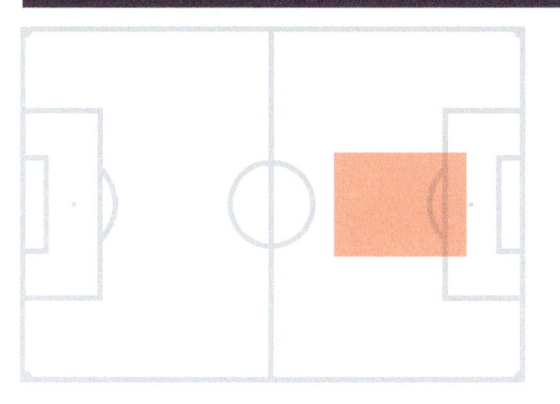

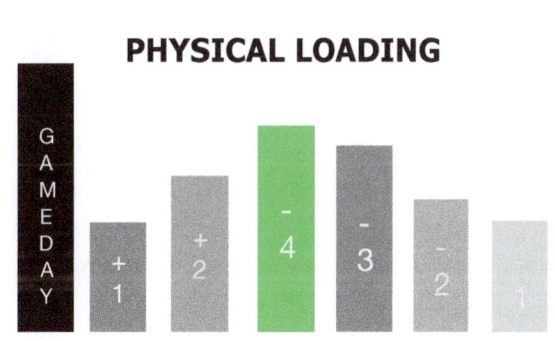

THE FOOTBALL COACH

PHYSICAL LOADING

GAMEDAY | +1 | +2 | -4 | -3 | -2 | -1

WORKING	RECOVERY	BLOCKS	TOTAL
8 MINS	1 MIN	4 BLOCK	36 MINUTES

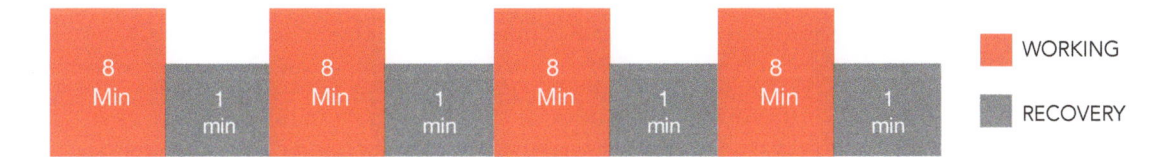

8 Min / 1 min / 8 Min / 1 min / 8 Min / 1 min / 8 Min / 1 min

- WORKING
- RECOVERY

PITCH SIZE:

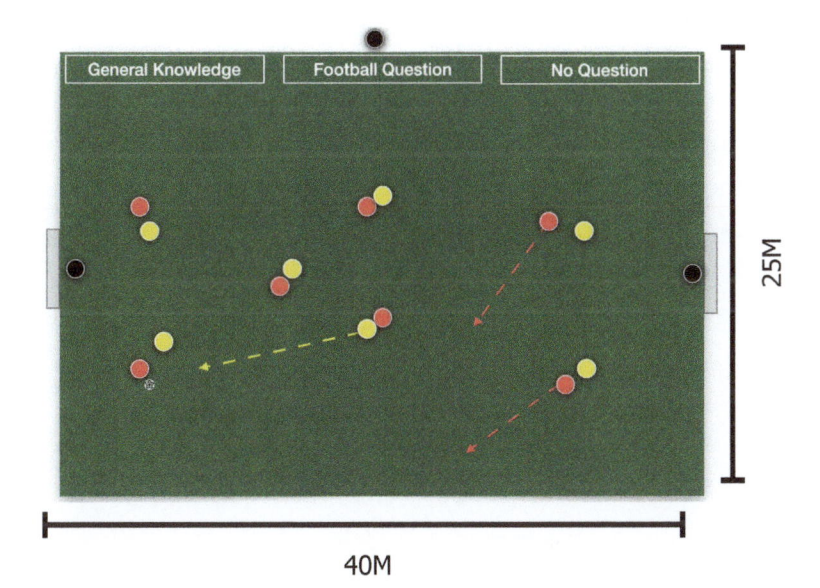

General Knowledge | Football Question | No Question

25M × 40M

Small Sided Games - Question Game

DECISION MAKING / CREATIVITY

In order to find players who are confident and empowered to make their own decisions based on the game they see, players must have an environment that is challenging but also forgiving, relaxed and balanced. The forgiving element of the environment allows for players to make the wrong decision, and not feel a punishment of consequence for their mistake. A good coach might recognise the mistake being repeated and offer support to understand the thought process, but won't punish or condemn that mistake. The coach can make this explicit at they start, by reinforcing that mistakes are essential for learning and 'how we respond to them' is the most important factor.

The relaxed environment is also very important, it allows players to become settled and comfortable and begin to have the confidence to believe in their decisions and make brave decisions based on what they see. Relaxed, non-judgemental environments are associated with more creative thinking. The relaxed environment should also mean that players are able to enjoy the practices. Enjoyment is a very important component for young people, not only does it help players long term engagement with the sport, but it also has been proven in research that enjoyment leads to increased physical work, higher cognitive engagement and long term health benefits.

The balanced environment is also very important, coaches need to be able to take their own personal mood, feelings or happiness away from the coaching environment, consistency provides balance to the coaching environment and this makes players feel more at home, more open and more relaxed in the environment they are working. Over emotional coaches can create over protective and withdrawn adolescents.

Small Sided Games – Question Game

COACHING IMPLICATIONS

Whenever performing a session of this type there is an unusual element that can have an influence on the practice, such as the asking of questions to have an impact on the awarding of goals. However unusual and chaotic this can make the session, the technical and tactical detail must still be there to provide relevance and accountability to the game model at all times. For example, this session naturally creates a lot of overload and underloading actions, and also drives really deep level thinking about how actions can have implications on the result of a game. These are all moments that can be directly linked to counter-attacking sessions.

This means a coach can deliver a session like this within a counter-attacking game model, and know that the core principles and sub-principles of the coaches' game model can be trained with the cognitive and physical challenge that a small sided game like this requires. This high level thinking from a coach means that a session can have a much varied set of learning outcomes for a player, they will be able to be exposed to in-depth detail in every area of performance from the technical and tactical, to the physical and psychological.

Small Sided Games - Question Game

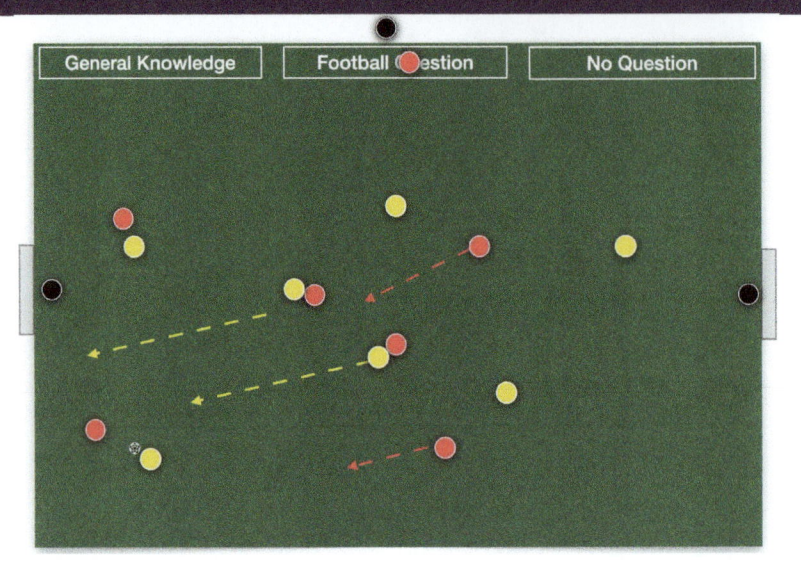

The small sided-game here just shows the impact of a team scoring and the effect it can have on a game; whilst the red is speaking with the coach to receive a football question, to double the goal. The yellows have played forward quickly and are looking to use their overload to score. Although they aren't potentially maximising their numerical advantage, they do have the opportunity to double their points with the red answering incorrectly and scoring whilst the opponent has them overloaded.

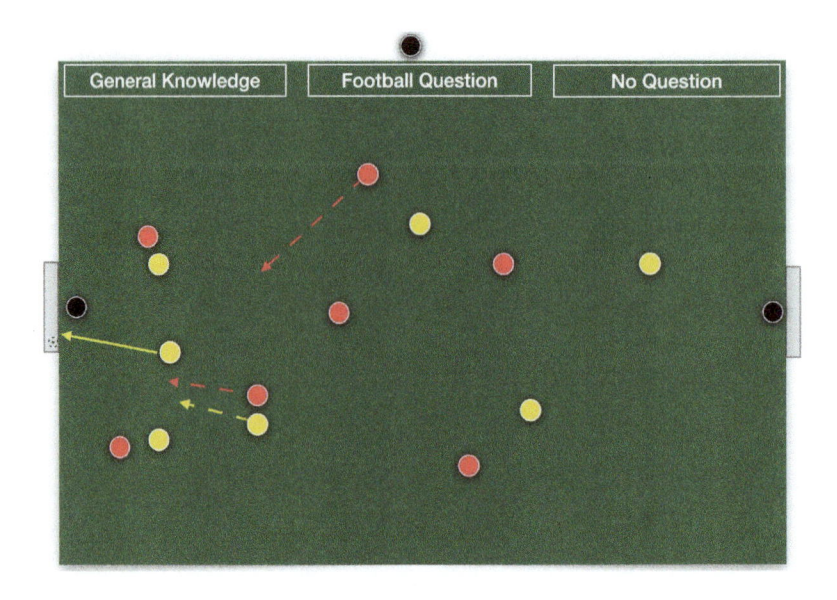

THE FOOTBALL COACH

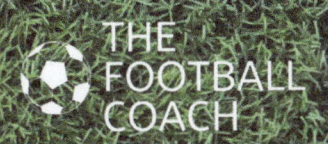

SESSION PLAN

Small Sided Games - Everyones Goal Game

Small Sided Games - Everyone's Goal Game

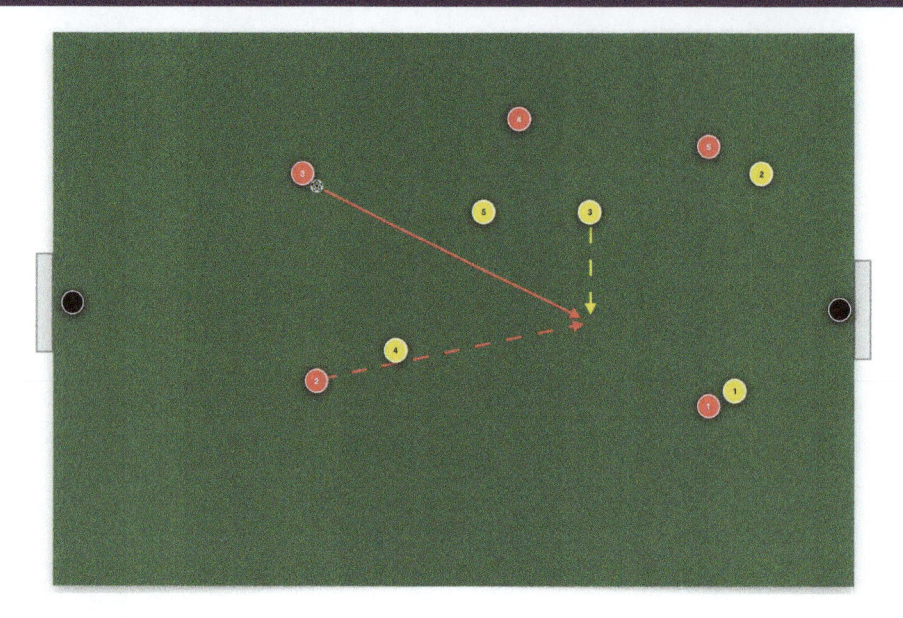

SESSION DETAIL

This small-sided game really does challenge individuals to think deeper about the game they are playing. The players are playing a 6v6 (5v5+Gk's) where every player is numbered 1 to 5, they aren't numbered in any particular order. The order is completely random. The number they have been assigned, is the value of the goals they score. So for example if yellow 3 scores, the yellows lead 3-0 but if Red 4 scores, the reds lead 4-3. However there is a catch, a player can only score once, until the other four numbered members of his or her team, have scored.

This forces teams to work as a group, and collectively manipulate the playing system, the personnel and the structure to make sure that the most valuable players are placed in the correct position, before moving them away from goal once they have scored. It also provides tactical outcomes out of possession; if the opponent number 5 has not scored, what can our team do to keep this player away from goal and limit the scoring opportunities? By doing this, we might be able to prevent the opponent having success.

This is a session with high cognitive engagement and high levels of enjoyment as well. The challenge can be manipulated by providing the players with numbered bibs to make it easy to see which player has a greater numerical value in the session.

Small Sided Games – Everyone's Goal Game

THE FOOTBALL COACH

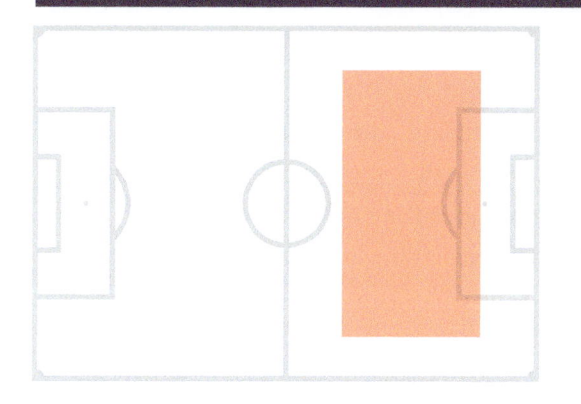

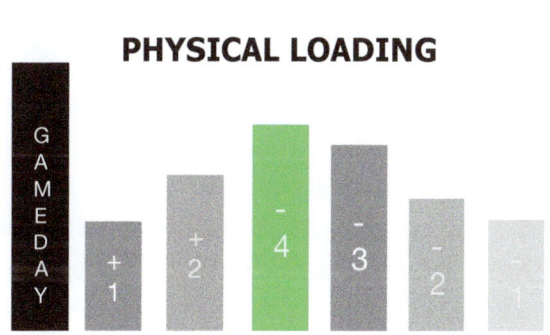

PHYSICAL LOADING

WORKING	RECOVERY	BLOCKS	TOTAL
8 MINS	1 MIN	4 BLOCKS	36 MINS

- WORKING
- RECOVERY

PITCH SIZE:

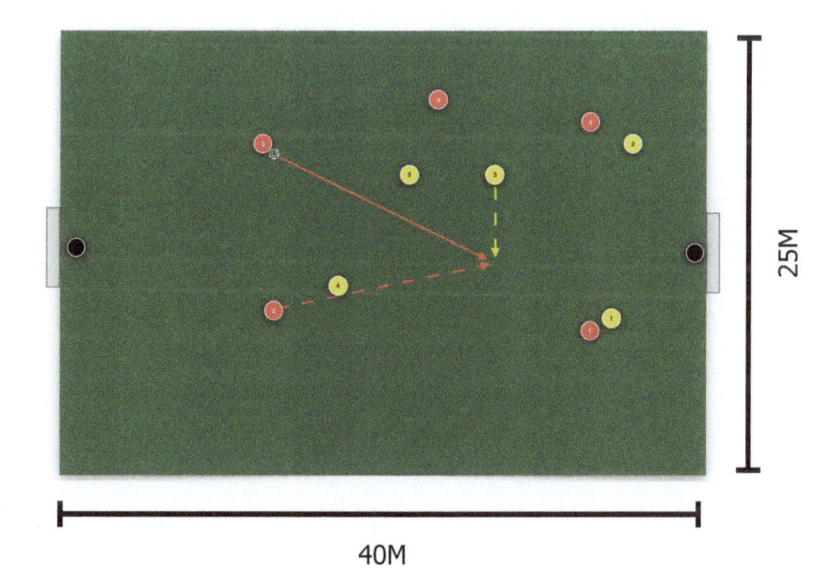

25M × 40M

Small Sided Games - Everyone's Goal Game

PLAYING CHALLENGE

These small-sided games have often been considered 'brain games' or practices that focus on training the brain, and not the game. However this is really not the case, and training the 'football brain' in isolation is nothing without the engagement of the technical, tactical and physical elements of performance. The structure of this session drives a cognitive engagement, a level of self-awareness, decision making and team work; all very important skills for adolescents and footballers. It also drives technical skills as small sided games naturally have quite high demands on technical performance. It will also force players to multi-task in possession of the ball.

They are now being forced to scan in possession of the ball, looking in more detail than before, for to when to play a pass. Not only are they looking to find team mates, but they are now assessing which team mate they are looking for and why. Should I pass to the left side or the right side? The right side has a player worth five who hasn't scored, let's switch the play that side.

This deep level of thinking can only transfer into making more comfortable decision makers; players who are confident and equipped to make split second decisions in game situations, where we the coach aren't able to influence or affect the outcome. This is built further by our delivery of autonomy supportive behaviours, allowing players to learn through their own doing and support that behaviour as discussed throughout the academic part of this book.

SESSION DETAIL

There are some things to be aware of when delivering this session, it is important to ensure that the players understand the value of the number on the shirt, the shirt does not grade them or define them, it is a random approach and there is no meaning behind the number. It can be dangerous when sorting players in this manner, that the individuals who struggle within the group are handed the number 1, and feel this is because they are not good enough or valued enough to be higher in the group.

Small Sided Games - Everyone's Goal Game

There is also an alternative way of thinking here, where it can be counter productive to the individual who does struggle with confidence and self-belief, to hand them the number five jersey in an attempt to boost their confidence. This can actually be an increased pressure on the individual as they fear the responsibility of being the most important player on the pitch. Then the player struggles from increased anxiety from the pressures applied to them because of the bib number.

If you are confident in knowing the individuals within the group, and think it is manageable within the group (especially older players), you might decide to let them number themselves from 1 to 5, with older players and especially good quality players, they might not fear the numbering but understand it. This will further challenge their decision making skills. They will now be setting up a team, trying to find attacking space for the individuals who are most likely to score. At this point, they will recognise who is the most likely to score, e.g. the teams striker along with which player is least likely to score.

It might also drive a further level of thinking from players, as they might have an alternative plan to put defenders as the most valuable players, allowing them to score first as an element of surprise, before the attackers go forward and score for a much lower amount of points.

Small Sided Games - Everyone's Goal Game

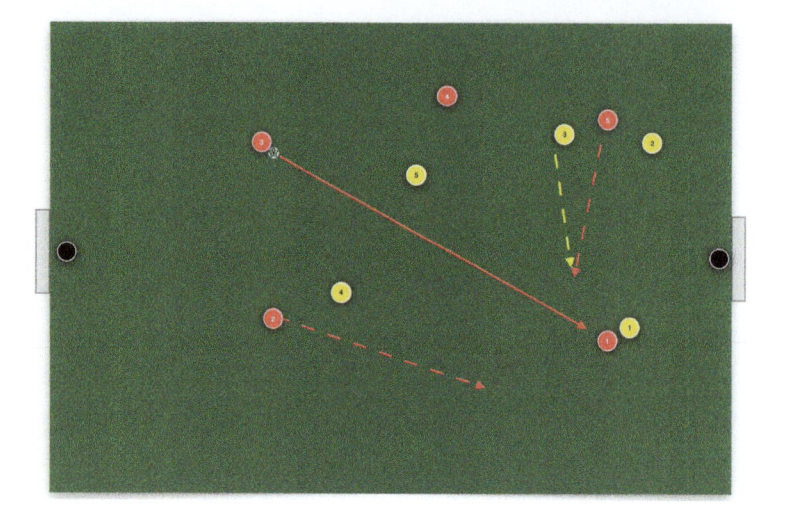

The first image shows how the yellows might defend against the red 5 to ensure he or she does not have success against them. In this image, they have left the two number 1s together because of their low value. Whilst they have squeezed the red 5 out of the game with a 2 v 1 marking situation.

In the below image, we can see how a side might approach this differently, in this image they have put the lowest value players forward first, in order to get the most difficult goals out of the way first, whilst the game is in it's highest element of control.

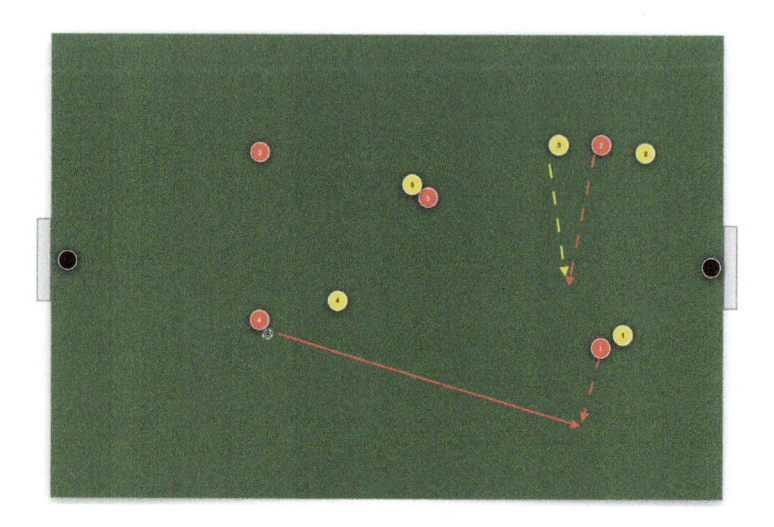

SESSION PLAN

Small Sided Game – Dice Roulette

Small Sided Games - Dice Roulette

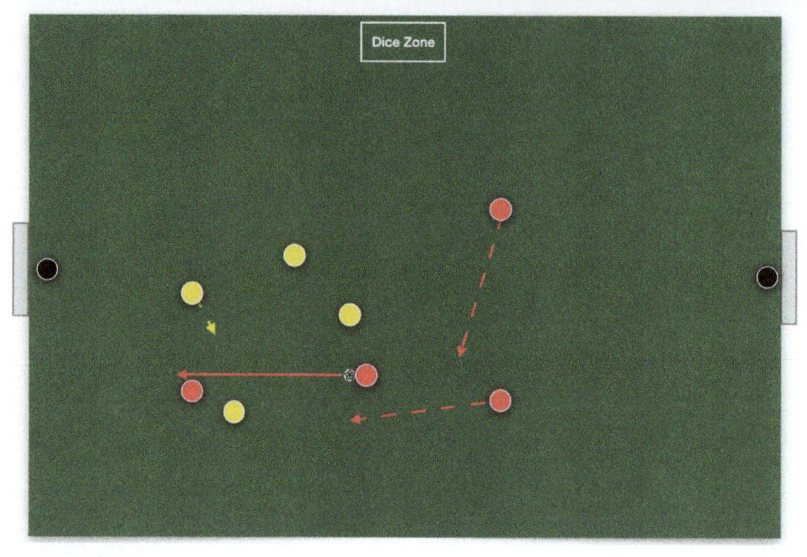

SESSION DETAIL

It is very simple to organise and easy to run a small-sided game. We set the players up in a format that suits our physiological model, e.g. we might use a 6v6 practice. The players then get a decision when they score. Take the goal or roll the dice, if they roll the dice, then the outcome is not controlled by them, it is controlled by the luck of the dice. The game can be played a few different ways to ensure that the challenge is constantly different for the players.

Game 1 - Once a goal is scored, a player can choose to roll a dice, the number on the dice is the amount of goals they receive. This will create a time where every player should roll the dice as every number is either the same as their goal or more

Game 2 - Each number on the dice has a different consequence. e.g. 2 = 2 goals, 3 = 0 goals, 4 = one touch football and no goal, 5= opponent gets two goals and 6 = one touch finish. This setup will really give the players more to think about and challenge where and when they decide to roll the dice.

Game 3 - The team roll two dice after scoring, the format is they receive the total on the first dice, minus the amount on the second dice, meaning they could gain 5 goals or lose 5 goals in the worst scenario.

Small Sided Games - Dice Roulette

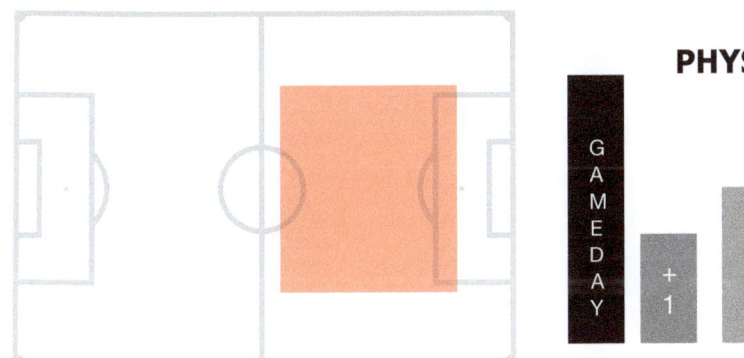

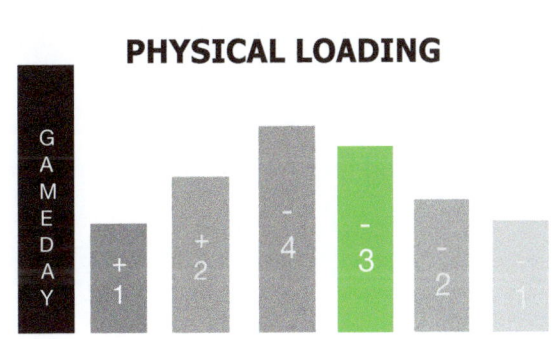

THE FOOTBALL COACH

PHYSICAL LOADING

GAMEDAY | +1 | +2 | -4 | -3 | -2 | -1

WORKING	RECOVERY	BLOCKS	TOTAL
10 MINS	2 MINS	3 BLOCKS	36 MINS

10 Min | 2 min | 10 Min | 2 min | 10 Min | 2 min

- WORKING
- RECOVERY

PITCH SIZE:

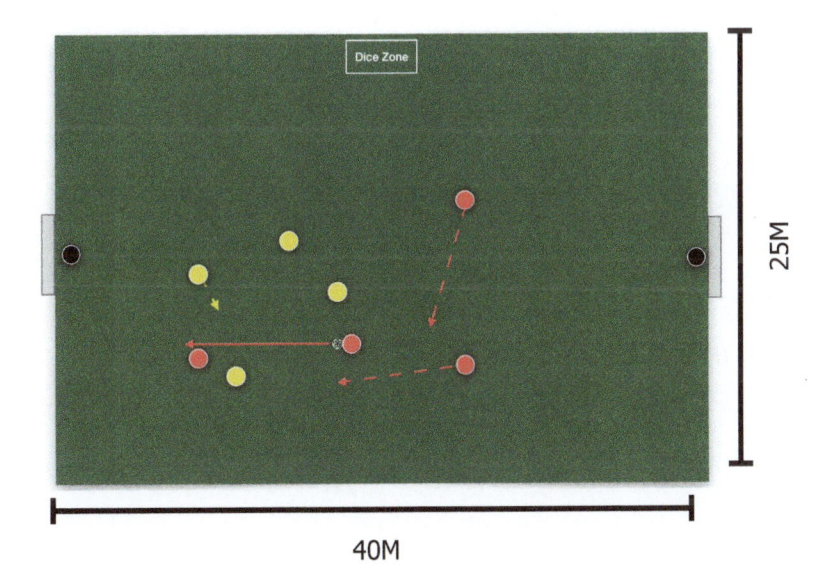

Dice Zone

25M × 40M

Small Sided Games - Dice Roulette

COGNITIVE CHALLENGE

Sessions like these are important, not only do they drive task enjoyment, which we know has great links to improved participation, psychological benefits and physical benefits; it also drives task engagement, which allows us to train tactical principles, with cognitive consequences. This means we are training the body and the brain in tandem with each other.

Many coaches spend the majority of their time working hard to encourage players to engage in tasks and think deeper about the game they play. Engaging the mind is not something you can just ask a player to do, a player must be trained to engage, think and communicate in the same way a player learns to improve technically and tactically. Performing tasks such as this drives awareness of the task along with awareness of the situation and will create players who think instinctively.

The decision making element of the session will be consistent and also provide tactical opportunities to be trained within the game model. For example, when a team rolls the dice and scores 5 goals, to take them from 2-0 down to 5-2 up, it will force both teams to be able to change the way they play and adapt their approach to playing. This means that the challenge that is outlined to players can be changing dramatically. It will be important for us as the coaches to ensure that the teams are fairly even and the competitive element is maintained. This is because in practices where one team is able to run away with the game, we could see quite one side quickly start to take a dominance, and the consequence could be the engagement of players.

The recovery time in-between sessions will also pave an important learning moment for players; during this adolescent age, social interaction and peer interaction is an important tool for development. Allowing the players to discuss the task will help increase understanding, motivation and help those in the group who have less ability to stay engaged, to see the value and importance of being engaged and think about the task and game that you are playing.

Small Sided Games – Dice Roulette

COACHES INFORMATION

For us as coaches or practitioners, these small-sided games are an effective way to train a game model and challenge and develop the adolescent brain. A simple and easy to manage task like this, will drive deep thinking and task engagement. We must be prepared to step in with individuals or manage the practice if it doesn't work for whatever reason. For example, at times, if the spaces are too large, the practice will become chaotic and unmanageable because players can't find the realism in the environment. At this point, we as the coaches need to step in and make sure that the spaces are reduced and the challenge is made realistic.

In order to effectively manage individuals, we must also be prepared not to stop the session during the working period, and remove the players from the practice to speak to individually. Providing individual feedback and challenge within a small sided game can be a more effective way of dealing with players and getting a response and a reaction to the information shared.

Stopping the session during the small-sided game really should be a last resort, as this can affect the physical returns of the session but can also limit the psychological returns as players are forced to concentrate in smaller periods with less challenge.

Small Sided Games - Dice Roulette

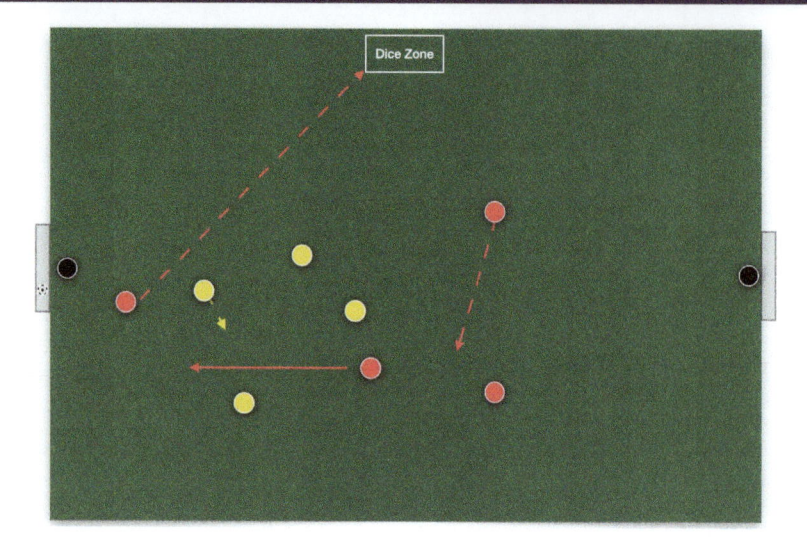

The next two images show the two most poignant moments of the session. In the top image we can see that the red through ball has been finished, and now the red is making a recovery run out towards the dice zone to make a decision whether to roll the dice or not. The below image shows the consequence of the player making that movement. The player is now out of the practice, it has become a 3v4 in the central area, meaning the yellows are able to counter attack and try to expose the space behind the opponent. This risk-reward will have to play into the mind of the team both in and out of possession of the ball.

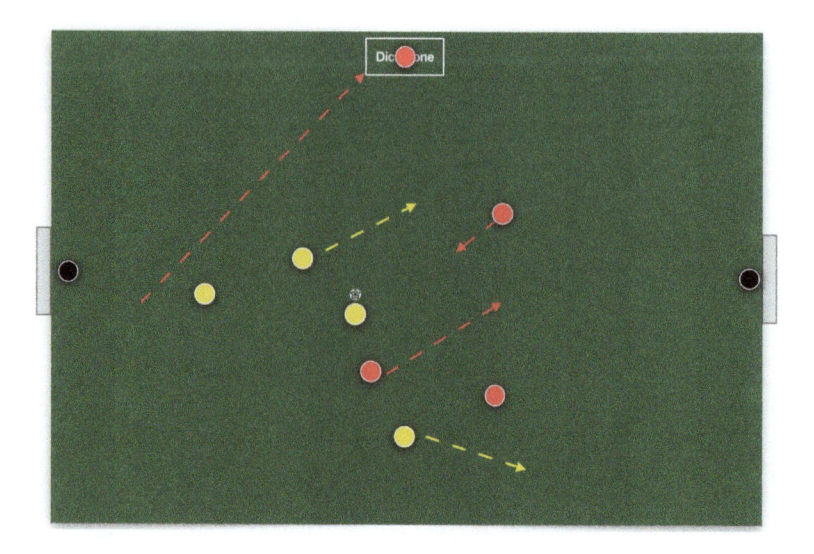

SESSION PLAN

1v1 Emotional Control

1v1 Emotional Control

THE FOOTBALL COACH

SESSION DETAIL

This is simple to design for any coach, and can be adapted to many different numbers, shapes and requirements. The players split into 3 groups, as you can see here we have Red, Blue and Yellow. The blues start with possession of the ball and they are going to look to play a 1-2 pass with every outside player and complete as many of those passes as possible within a specific amount of time. The player with the most 1-2 passes wins at the end of the time limit.

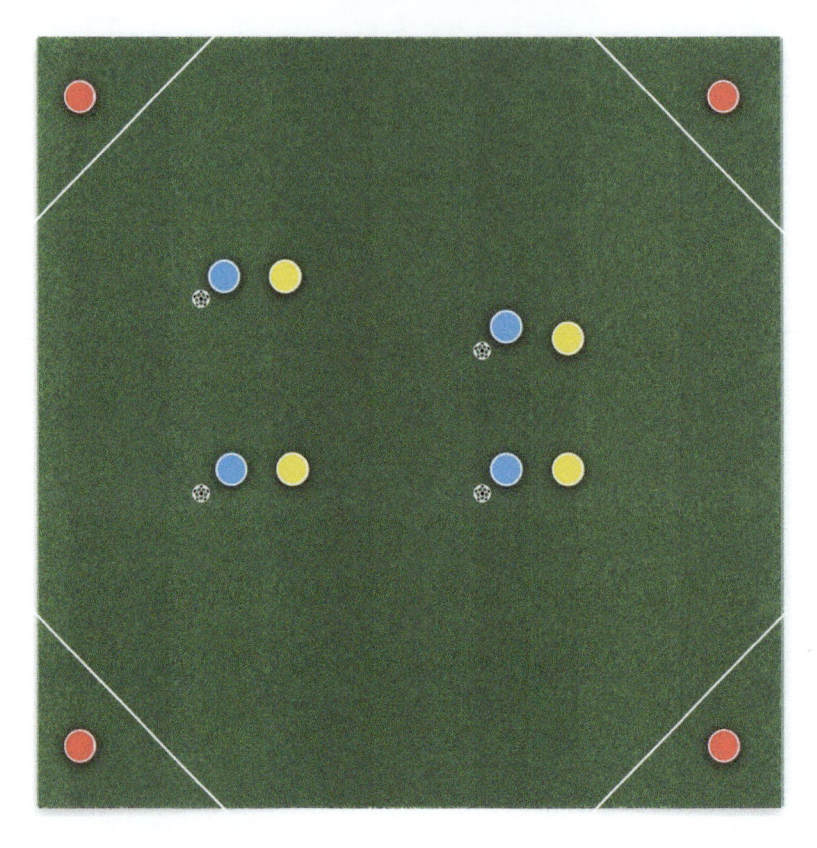

The challenge in the session will come from the additional yellow players who pair up 1v1 against the blues and look to steal possession from them. If the player wins possession, they then need to work hard to complete as many 1 to 1 passes with an outride player, whilst the red they have stolen possession from, will work extremely hard to win possession back in order to try and win.

This challenges players to be competitive and deal with constant and dynamic pressure from one player. This can create a rivalry and level of aggression, failure and emotion that can challenge the control of the player and this exposure is perfect for our session design.

1v1 Emotional Control

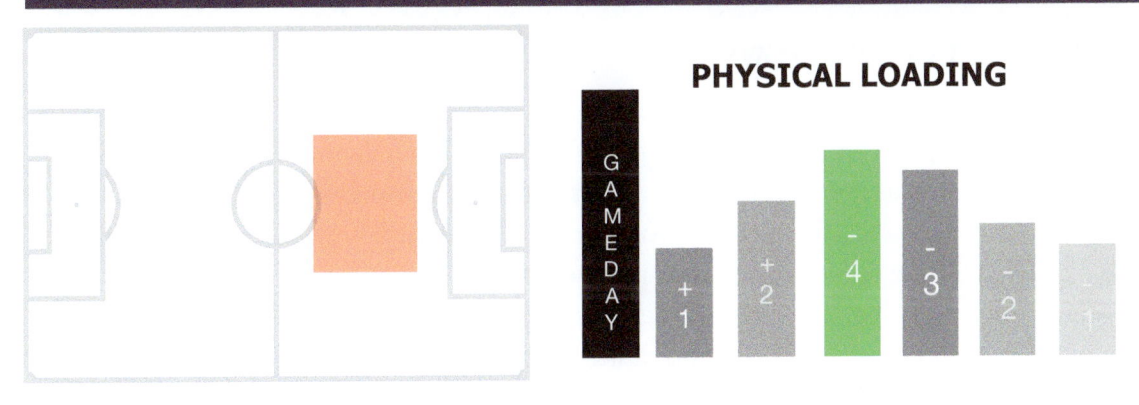

PHYSICAL LOADING

| GAMEDAY | +1 | +2 | -4 | -3 | -2 | -1 |

WORKING	RECOVERY	BLOCKS	TOTAL
WORKING	RECOVERY	BLOCKS	BLOCKS

2 Min — RECOVERY
2 Min — WORKING

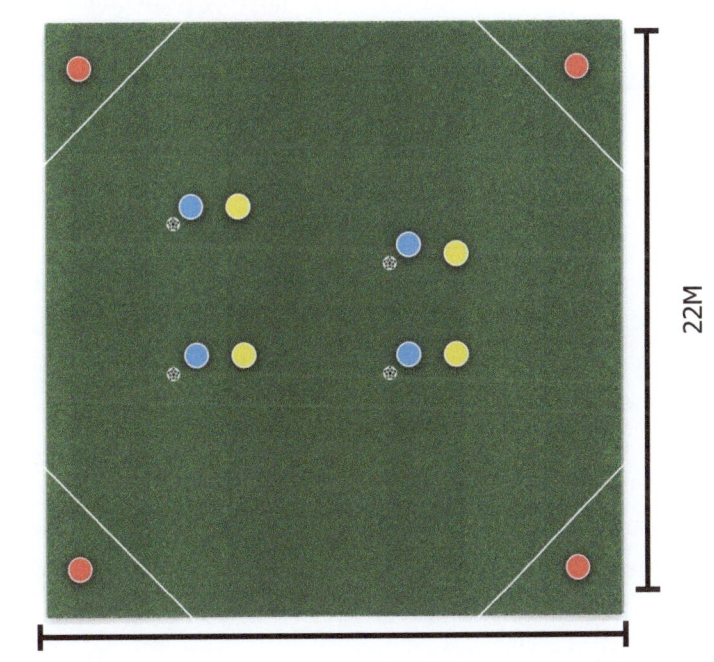

PITCH SIZE: 22M

1v1 Emotional Control

CONTROLLING EMOTIONS

Having control plays a huge part in being successful in football and the wider sporting world. It allows us as individuals to have control over our impulses, emotions and desires. Within football, we need control over all of these areas especially as they might be amplified during adolescence. Training them is also an important part of the training program. The above session places our players into situations where they might be exposed to emotions, impulses and desires. These look very different within a footballing context to the wider world, but the principles still exist.

Players desire control of the ball, and will be exposed to moments where it isn't the correct time to try and win the ball; in these situations players might experience failure and a lack of control of their emotions because they have been unable to complete their intentions. Other situations will also challenge a player's emotional control within the practice. Some players will be over engaged with the task and experience increases in dopamine which have an instant influence on the prefrontal cortex of the brain. As this is happening, players' attention, motivation and engagement might be effected. As dopamine increase continues, combined with relatively under-developed frontal controls, we might start to see players who evaluate decisions 'poorly' linked to their propensity to perceive more reward and less risk in situations or where their decision making is 'hijacked' by strong, unchecked, emotions.

As the above happens, we might see players become emotional, frustrated and lose an element of self-control. If this happens we might see players who kick out, or even lose engagement with the task. Once this has happened it is important that we as coaches are able to recognise what has happened, why it has happened and how we can influence these moments. It is not here that we will look to punish the players, but actually help reframe the situation for them. Taking the player out of this situation, providing calmness, followed by a reframing of the situation. Making the player aware of the need for control, allowing them to see for themselves where control has been lost, putting them back into the environment for the same moments to be recreated, challenging them instantly to recognise the issue and deal with it in their own way. This

1v1 Emotional Control

COACHES INFORMATION

For coaches, helping players control their emotions can provide some of the more challenging situations for us to coach but also offers great opportunities for young players to learn to self-regulate. It provides some of the more challenging situations for us to understand. The most important thing to remember when working with young players and cognitive information, is how every player behaves and reacts in different ways. The heightened emotions experienced during adolescence provides coaches with a great opportunity to foster self-control. Our relationships with different players will allow us to work in different ways with different players to provide strategies to help manage emotions. There can't be a time where we look to treat every player the same, because none of them are the same, they all have different backgrounds, different home lives, and different pressures and challenges.

Recognising when an individual is close to losing control might be the best time to remove them from the session temporarily, challenge their thinking and help them understand that losing control is not the end of the road, just a challenge along the way. Reframe their thinking and allow them to go back and compete. This experience will allow them to be aware of when they are close to losing control, and begin to self govern and understand their own body and mind.

We also must be aware that losing control is not the end of the world, some players need to play closer to the line than others. In order to be successful, we should not look to take this away from them, just help them recognise when they're close to the limit.

1v1 Emotional Control

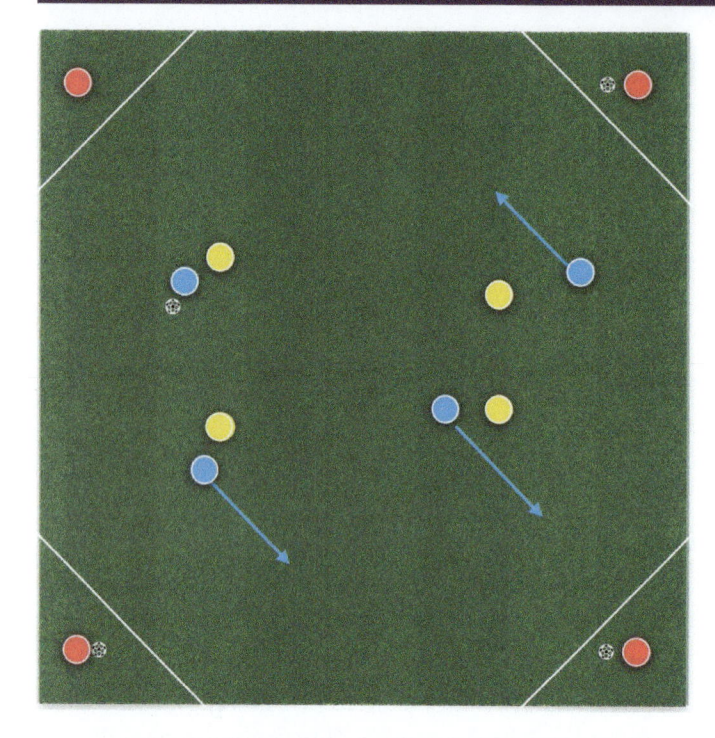

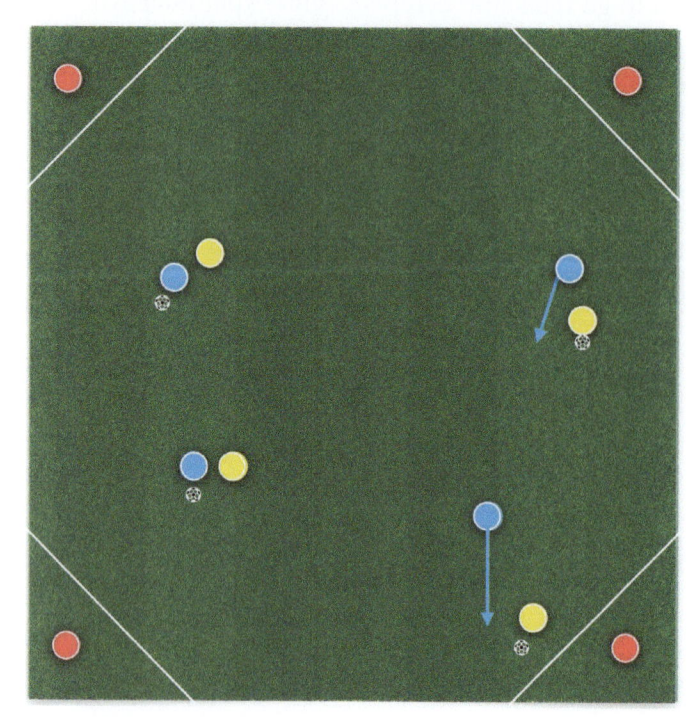

For coaches, emotional control can provide some of the more challenging situations for us to coach. It also provides some of the more challenging situations for us to understand.

The most important thing to remember when working with young players and cognitive information is how every player behaves and reacts in different ways.

We must look at how our relationships with different players will allow us to work with varied techniques to support them and their individual needs.

There can't be a time where we look to treat every player the same, because none of them are the same. They all have different backgrounds, different home lives, and different pressures and challenges.

SESSION PLAN

Creative Combinations

Creative Combinations

THE FOOTBALL COACH

SESSION DETAIL

This is a really simple session for any coach to setup or implement. It is important to recognise that this creativity session is a progression from unstructured creativity sessions; this session is more relevant to age groups that play 9v9 and above because of the tactical detail that can be included by the players, as their understanding increases.

The session itself is very easy for us as coaches to setup and deliver. The players play within a relevant sized space outside the penalty area. Here we have used PA Width with 13m length, this is enough room for players to create space within the opponent's three with both width and depth. The challenge now is for the coach to play into the central, into the reds who have a 4v3 then allow the reds to attack the yellows with no rules or coaching from the coaching staff.

Here, we are looking to create players who aren't bound by repetition, but creative within the vast frame work set out by the coach. This doesn't mean we will get unrealistic and reactionary creativity, but we will get players constantly finding themselves in realistic situations, with the freedom and confidence to perform actions to beat the opponent. Here, we are challenging the players belief, confidence and creativity to perform unexpected actions with, what at times can be, a predictable area of the pitch.

Creative Combinations

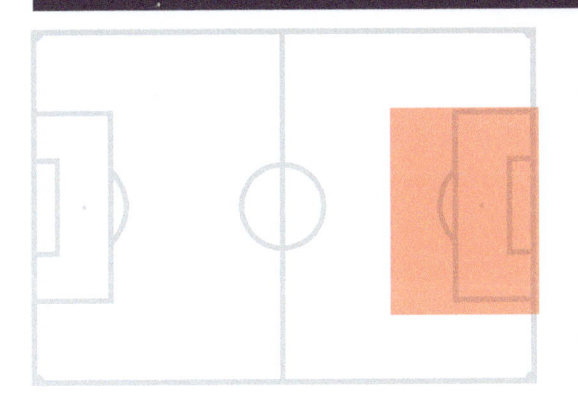

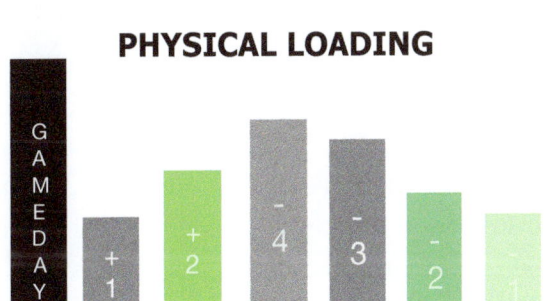

THE FOOTBALL COACH

PHYSICAL LOADING

GAMEDAY | +1 | +2 | -4 | -3 | -2 | -1

WORKING	RECOVERY	BLOCKS	TOTAL
5 MINS	1 MIN	4 BLOCKS	24 MINS

5 Min — 1 min — 5 Min — 1 min — 5 Min — 1 min — 5 Min — 1 min

- WORKING
- RECOVERY

PITCH SIZE:

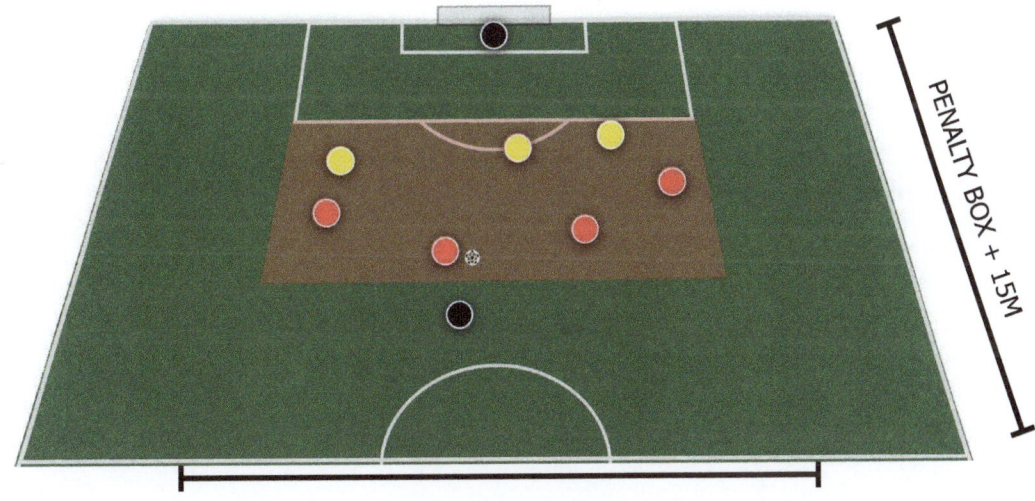

PENALTY BOX + 15M

PENALTY BOX WIDTH

Creative Combinations

CREATIVITY

When we look at creativity in football, it often seen is straight lines. Creative players are those who are able to do step overs or combinations of step overs in attacking areas to beat opponents. We don't tend to see much creativity in any other moment of the game however we must accept that creativity can be found in many different elements. We can combine in creative ways, like in the above session, we can encourage players to be risky and creative with their movements to unlock the space behind the opponent. We are all aware of how 'freedom' in the attacking third can unlock defence lines.

This creativity in movements can be the key to unlocking the opponent. We also see creativity in our passing, how do our players disguise their passes, hide their intentions and create spin on the ball? All of these moments require creativity and require us, as coaches, to allow it happen and train it. In the session above, we must encourage players to play what they see, try to find different ways to attack and penetrate the opponent without fearing a consequence or failure.

Consequence plays a huge role in creativity; if we as the coach want to create, creative players we must be willing to allow us to do things that don't sit within our game model. We must be willing to allow the goalkeeper to try and chip the centre forward and we must allow the centre back making a Rabona pass, because in order to find the right area, they must experience failure. If we are to provide them with a consequence and show them failure, we will limit their willingness to perform actions out of the ordinary.

Within this environment, players are going to need encouragement to be creative. Some will naturally have the confidence and the mindset to keep at it, others will wilt away at the fear of losing the ball; with our support they will become less conscious of the outcome and more conscious of the opportunity.

Creative Combinations

COACHES INFORMATION

For the coach, the other sessions on creativity share a message, the environment and the consistency of the environment is so important for creativity. It is not a part of the brain that can be trained once a week, and then transfer into great things in games. It is something that needs encouraging, supporting and nurturing in every moment of life. As soon as players prefrontal cortex starts to rapidly develop and consequences become increased, we are naturally losing that window of opportunity for players to develop creativity and want to become more creative! As we become older, creativity becomes difficult as we become more rigid and safe in our actions. In order to keep the right environment we need to:

- Celebrate effort
- Encourage team work
- Encourage thinking outside the box
- Encourage feedback
- Care for each other
- Celebrate innovation and experimentation
- Notice intention as well as outcome

Creative Combinations

In the first image here, we can see how the red has decided to go alone in penetrating the space left by the movement of team mates; this is a great example of a creative run, and a creative moment to create space - both should be celebrated. In the second image, we can see two very 'off the cuff' creative movements; one is a wide player running across a full back to tie them inside, the second is to run around the wide player and create space down the outside.

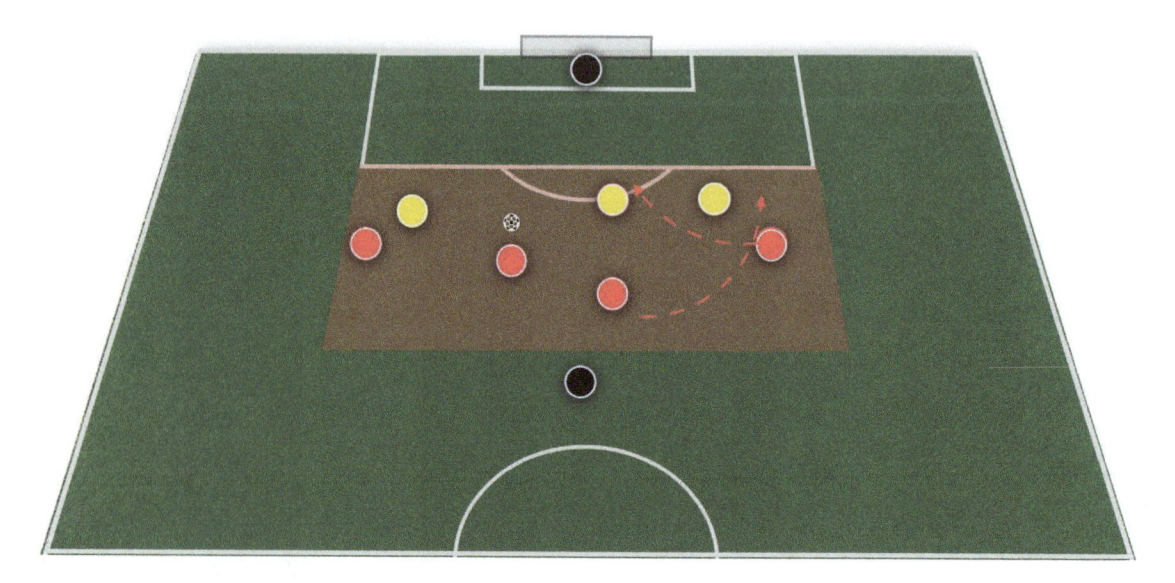